BAPTISM RECONCILIATION AND UNITY

KEVIN ROY

FOREWORD BY GEORGE BEASLEY-MURRAY

BAPTISM RECONCILIATION AND UNITY

KEVIN ROY

paternoster
press

Copyright © Kevin Roy 1997

First published in the UK 1997 by Paternoster Press

03 02 01 00 99 98 97   7 6 5 4 3 2 1

Paternoster Press is an imprint of Paternoster Publishing,
P.O. box 300, Carlisle, Cumbria CA3 0QS

The right of Kevin Roy to be identified as the Author of this Work has been asserted by him in accordance with the Copyright, Designs and Patents Act 1988.

Material from *Baptism, Eucharist and Ministry* (1982) © The World Council of Churches. Used by permission.

British Library Cataloguing in Publication Data

A catalogue record for this book is available from the British Library.

ISBN 0-854364-815-8

This book is printed using Suffolk Book paper which is 100% acid free.

Typeset by WestKey Ltd, Falmouth, Cornwall
Printed in Great Britain by Clays Ltd., St. Ives plc

Contents

Foreword to Baptism, Reconciliation and Unity by Kevin Roy

George R. Beasley-Murray

Baptism is an issue that has been to the forefront of the Church's proclamation and practice from the beginning of its existence. Its meaning and importance will have been contemplated by Jesus, for his submission to it at the hands of John the Baptist initiated his own ministry. It should surprise no one that a rite that has marked the entrance of individuals into the family of God for two thousand years should be interpreted in a variety of ways, not least in the light of differences of culture and religious traditions of the multitudes who have received it. As the generations have come and gone the theologians of the churches have paid close attention to what the scriptures say about baptism, and their writings have frequently been emphatic in setting out their own understanding of baptism. The result of this has been increasing divisions between the churches as to what actually takes place in the rite of entrance into the Church, how it should be prepared for and what should follow from it. Two millennia are long enough to produce a bewildering variety of answers to such questions, and for the answers to have hardened the attitudes of Christians who accept them to members of churches which reject them. Needless to say the literature on the subject has become enormous, and has led to great confusion among the churches' leaders and still more among lay members who depend on their instruction.

In the providence of God there has arisen in the century now approaching its end an unprecedented concern among the churches about the divisions that have taken place, especially relating to the rite which has traditionally been viewed as the entrance into the Church, i.e. baptism. If, for example, a particular mode of entrance of Christians is challenged as invalid, it is tempting to conclude that those who have received such a baptism are not members of the true Church. That is not an uncommon conviction among some groups who believe that baptism is intended to be a seal of the faith of the baptised, and therefore that infant baptism is no baptism. The World Council of Churches has made strenuous endeavours to bring together representatives of the various denominations to examine the grounds for the theological differences of the churches, notably those relating to baptism, since recognition of the validity of the rite which forms the entry into the Church of God would form the greatest step to the acknowledgement of the unity of the churches throughout the world.

No little suspicion, not to say scepticism, has greeted this attempt, especially among the ever increasing number of evangelical Christians who form a formidable part of the Church today. Not so the author of this book. He has had an unusual pilgrimage of faith: born and reared in a Roman Catholic home, school and church; enabled to make a personal commitment to Christ through a largely Protestant Christian Union in a University, but without forsaking his Catholic upbringing; baptised later in a Plymouth Brethren community, then serving as an evangelist in various countries of South Africa; pastor of various Baptist churches in South Africa; lecturer in Church History in the Faculty of Theology at the University of South Africa; representative of Koinonia South Africa and the National Initiative for Reconciliation; currently lecturer in Church History, Systematic Theology and Missions in the Baptist Theological College Cape Town. He has reached the conviction that the various forms of baptism practised by the main line churches, which he divides into Roman Catholic, Reformed, and what he terms as "Credobaptist", i.e. believer-baptist, have strengths and weaknesses, and so are partly right and partly wrong. These elements of "right" and "wrong" he carefully expounds and illustrates in the light of the Old Testament and New Testament and the history of the Church. He argues that the "rights" and "wrongs" are insufficient to justify the divisions of the Church. Dr. Roy rightly observes that most works on baptism have concentrated on the meaning of baptism, analyses of the various interpretations and practices of baptism, expositions of single approaches to it or attempts to find a consensus. In this work the author is "concerned to develop a theological basis for the coexistence of different baptist practices and understandings within the unity of the one Christian fellowship". Accordingly the goal of the book is to make a contribution to the reconciliation and reunion of Christians alienated from one another over the question of baptism.

As one who has spent much time in producing literature that concentrates on the rights and wrongs of the Church's interpretations of baptism I find myself in agreement with Dr. Roy, and commend this book to the careful study of the reader, such as the author himself has put into its production.

Chapter 1

Introduction

A broken world and a healing God

In the closing years of the 1980s and the opening years of the 1990s there was a remarkable mood of hope in the world. The collapse of communism in the former Soviet Union and Eastern Europe signalled the end of the cold war. The release of Nelson Mandela and the demise of apartheid ushered in a new democracy in South Africa. Military dictatorships in South America were replaced by democratic governments. Such events led to a certain euphoria in many circles, the expectation of a new world order in which the nations and peoples would be willing to work together for the good of all. Such hopes, however, were quickly dissipated by the grim realities of the new patterns of conflict that emerged in the post cold war era: ethnic and religious conflict in the former Yugoslavia and other former communist countries, ongoing violence and bloodshed in various parts of Africa and other regions of the world. All these serve as a reminder of the brokenness of the world, its terrible divisions and hostilities along the lines of race, ethnicity, language, culture and religion.

For the Christian believer this brokenness, hatred and violent conflict is a manifestation of the deep and terrible alienation with which sin has cursed the world. People have become alienated from their God and thus also alienated from one another, hostile to God and hostile to one another. Christians also believe, however, that this same God, the one true God who made all things and all peoples, is actively and savingly involved in the world to overcome these alienations so that human beings might be reconciled to God as their Father and to one another as brothers and sisters. The Holy Scriptures, venerated as such by Christians, contain powerful images depicting a reconciled and united world, united and reconstituted around the healing and saving Word of God. The prophet saw the mountain of Yahweh's temple becoming pre-eminent in the last days. All the nations will stream to it saying: 'Come, let us go up to the mountain of the L ORD, to the house of the God of Jacob. He will teach us his ways, so that we may walk in his paths' (Is.2:3). The beneficial consequences of the divine law spreading from Jerusalem to the ends of the earth will be peace and prosperity among the nations; they will 'beat their swords into ploughshares and their spears into pruning hooks. Nation will not take up sword against nation, nor will they train for war any more' (Is.2:4). In another place Isaiah also speaks of the coming of the Anointed One, a descendant of David, who will rule the earth with righteousness, justice and power. The fruit of his just and beneficent rule will be a state of unprecedented peace, reconciliation and harmony in which

> the wolf will live with the lamb, the leopard will lie down with the goat, the calf and the lion and the yearling together; and a little child will lead them. The cow will feed with the bear, their young will lie down together, and the lion will eat straw like the ox. The infant will play near the hole of the cobra, and the young child put his hand into the viper's nest. They will neither harm nor destroy on all my holy mountain, for the earth will be full of the knowledge of the LORD as the waters cover the sea (Is.11:6,9).

This prophetic vision of a reconciled, healed and united world is focused in a unique way in the coming of Jesus, the Anointed One, the Word of God incarnate who by his atoning death destroys the dividing wall of hostility and alienation that he might reconcile to God all things, whether on earth or in heaven (Eph.2:14, Col.1:20). Through him, the divine Word, anointed with the Spirit and power to bring salvation and healing to the world, it is the Father's purpose to accomplish his grand recapitulation, bringing together under one head all things in heaven and on earth (Eph.1:10). It is significant that the book traditionally placed at the end of the New Testament, the Revelation or Apocalypse, which draws so heavily on the apocalyptic and eschatological imagery of the Old Testament prophets, also contains some of the most moving pictures of a reconciled humanity and a healed world. John glimpses 'a great multitude that no one could count, from every nation, tribe, people and language, standing before the throne and in front of the Lamb. They were wearing white robes and were holding palm branches in their hands. And they cried out in a loud voice: "Salvation belongs to our God, who sits on the throne, and to the Lamb" ' (Rev. 7:9–10). Precisely the differences that have always given rise to so much hostility and conflict – national, tribal, ethnic, linguistic – are seen in a reconciled unity around God and his Christ. The final chapter of Revelation, reworking a vision of the prophet Ezekiel, here freely combined with other biblical themes, portrays a healed, redeemed and fruitful world:

Then the angel showed me the river of the water of life, as clear as a crystal, flowing from the throne of God and of the Lamb down the middle of the great street of the city. On each side of the river stood the tree of life, bearing twelve crops of fruit, yielding its fruit every month. And the leaves of the tree are for the healing of the nations. No longer will there be any curse. The throne of God and of the Lamb will be in the city, and his servants will serve him. They will see his face, and his name will be on their foreheads. There will be no more night. They will not need the light of a lamp or the light of the sun, for the Lord God will give them light. And they will reign for ever and ever (Rev. 22:1–5).

The firstfruits of this redeemed, renewed, reconciled and saved community, born from above by the power of the Holy Spirit, found concrete and visible reality in the community of people who believed the good news of the kingdom and were baptised by one Spirit into the fellowship of Christ, in which 'there is neither Jew nor Greek, slave nor free, male nor female, for you are all one in Christ Jesus' (Gal. 3:28). To the church, as the beginning of God's new creation on earth, is given also the ministry of reconciliation, to act as God's ambassadors on earth urging all people everywhere to be reconciled to God in Christ (2 Cor. 5:16–21).

However the process is not quite as simple as might appear from a superficial reading of the New Testament. From the very beginning the church itself stands in need of healing. Christian believers struggle to realize their unity and to shake off the old patterns of hostility. Jews find themselves instinctively repulsed by 'unclean' Gentiles. Masters find it difficult to regard their slaves as brothers in Christ. Men do not readily grant equal status to women. The spirit of the world and the Spirit of Christ strive for supremacy within the church and within every believer. The alienations, hostilities and prejudices of the world are too easily and too often imported into the church, straining its unity, sometimes to breaking point. Again and again the church is divided along exactly the same fracture lines which divide the rest of society, and differences between Christians in certain points of doctrine and practice give rise to even further divisions within the body of Christ. For all these reasons the church in history has struggled to maintain (or to achieve) unity. Christian divisions have sometimes resulted in terrible violence and bloodshed, as for example in the religious wars of the sixteenth and seventeenth centuries in Europe.

While the bloody violence and hatred between different Christian communities witnessed in previous centuries have, mercifully, for the most part, passed away, yet patterns of intolerance, division and hostility still persist to a large extent. Indeed, the extraordinary and rapid proliferation of new Christian denominations in the present time, each with its own particular doctrinal and liturgical distinctives, would seem to point to a growing disunity rather than unity among Christians today. Nevertheless, whatever the visible appearance of things might be and however we might interpret them, Christians remain committed by their very faith to be always making efforts to promote unity and reconciliation between believers – as well, of course, as reconciliation and peace in a broader sense among all peoples. This book represents one such effort. The causes of division between Christians are legion: doctrinal, cultural, historical, political – in fact all these factors are invariably involved in any particular division. This book focuses on one particular issue that has been and still is the source of much division between Christians and churches, the question of baptism. What is the nature and function of baptism? What happens when a person is baptised? Ought baptism to be restricted to those able to confess their faith in Christ or may the children of believers also be baptised?

A historical survey of baptismal differences and discussions

The early church

The early church experienced surprisingly little strife over baptism, despite the development of a wide variety of baptismal practices. Although scholars differ in their interpretation of the evidences of baptismal practices in the early centuries, there is one matter in which a broad and general consensus of scholarly opinion is agreed: that for a period of at least two hundred years there existed in the church considerable flexibility in baptismal practice. There is evidence of infant baptism, child baptism, adult baptism (also of those born in Christian homes), immediate baptism, delayed baptism and various modes of baptism. All that can be said with certainty is that within the one catholic church there was both development and variety in baptismal practices until at least AD 400. Even when there was some contention and strife over baptism, the particular issues were strange to modern ears – not the question of whether or not infants could be baptised, or whether sprinkling was as legitimate as immersion but whether baptisms performed by heretics were valid or whether there could be any forgiveness for sins committed after baptism.

The establishment of Christianity as the official religion of the Roman empire by the end of the fourth century and the growing body of legislation making any form of heresy or dissent punishable by law bode ill for the continuance of a broad and flexible policy concerning baptism. The baptism of infants born to Christian parents now (if not earlier) became established as the norm and factions opposed to infant baptism became marginalized and were increasingly forced into dissident groups outside the church. Rebaptism, in particular, was viewed in a most serious light. The heretics against whom Theodosius II (408–450) issued no fewer than sixty laws included rebaptisers. A law of the Emperors Honorius and Theodosius II of the year 413 provides that

> If any person is convicted of having undertaken the rebaptism of a member of the Catholic Church, the one who has committed this shameful crime, together with the one – provided he is of accountable age – who has allowed himself to be persuaded thereto, shall be punished with death without mercy.[1]

The Middle Ages

Justinian (527–565) renewed and made more severe the laws against heretics. Part three of his *Corpus juris civilis* elevated the resolutions of the great church synods into statutes, concerning which all further discussion was legally forbidden. An entire section dealt with rebaptism. As Roman law was adopted in nearly all European states the laws against heretics found general application.

Notwithstanding the harshness of these penalties inflicted on nonconformists, there is evidence of dissident groups of Christians, of varying degrees of orthodoxy, throughout the Middle Ages, many of them displaying credobaptist tendencies (i.e. refusing to baptise infants). The Paulicians, a highly independent Christian sect which arose in the heart of the Eastern church about AD 750, believed 'the Lord has taught us not to confer baptism on a person until he has reached the age of maturity' (according to their manual, *The Key of Truth*, translated by F. C. Conybeare in 1898). In France, Peter of Bruys, who was burnt in St. Gilles in the year 1130, strongly emphasized personal faith as the sole means of salvation, and made such faith a condition of baptism. He also repudiated the charge of rebaptism. Arnold of Brescia, burnt in 1155, also rejected infant baptism.

The Reformation

When, in the sixteenth century, the western church broke up into various national Protestant churches, largely in the Teutonic north of Europe, and the Roman Catholic church loyal to the Pope, largely in the Latin-speaking south of Europe, it is not surprising that groups of credobaptist or 'anabaptist' Christians also flourished, especially in German-speaking areas. No love was lost between any of these contending parties, Catholic, Reformed or Anabaptist. Luther, for example, considered the Anabaptists to be 'fanatics and scoundrels who abominated the Word of God'.[2] Naturally he felt nothing would be gained by entering into discussion with such. Not that the Anabaptists themselves were very much inclined to engage in discussion with those who held to infant baptism, 'the highest and chief abomination of the pope', as the Schleitheim Confession described it.[3]

The modern period

The restoration of the monarchy and the Church of England resulted in renewed difficulties for Baptist and other Nonconformist groups in England, leading many of them to settle in the newly-founded colonies in America. Despite initial difficulties encountered even there, it was in America that Baptists for the first time enjoyed full liberty of conscience, and during the eighteenth and nineteenth centuries experienced extraordinary numerical expansion, so much so that by the twentieth century they constituted the largest Protestant ecclesiastical tradition in the country. This was a new and unusual experience for Baptists, who in previous times and other places had always been regarded as a small and insignificant sect. Indeed, the very successes achieved by Baptists in America, resulting in their becoming an established, main line church, have given rise to serious discussions and considerable debate over the question of a Baptist theology of the child and how Baptists should view their own children.[4] Baptists have increasingly acknowledged that in their historical struggle against infant baptism and their struggle for freedom to maintain their witness they have failed to develop an adequate, coherent theology of the child. The trend towards the baptism of ever younger children in the Southern Baptist Convention, the largest Baptist body in the world, has led to the charge that 'you Baptists have come the full circle – right back to infant baptism'. Some Baptist theologians (admittedly very few) have even suggested that in certain circumstances infant baptism is valid and desirable.[6]

If the success of the Baptist movement has led to Baptists asking some critical questions concerning their own practice, the twentieth century has seen unprecedented critical discussion by paedobaptist scholars on the subject of baptism. It was Bishop Westcott who at the beginning of this century prophesied that the next great theological controversy would be centred upon baptism, and so it has been (along with other issues). Mention can be made in passing of the debate between Joachim Jeremias and Kurt Aland in a series of books during the 1950s and 1960s on the question 'Did the early church baptise infants?'

The sheer theological stature and influence of Karl Barth meant that his repudiation of infant baptism provoked an intense and scholarly debate.

Barth's own colleague at Basel, Oscar Cullmann, wrote defending infant baptism as a primitive practice. Many other leading theologians and scholars contributed to this debate. The document *Baptism, Eucharist and Ministry* produced by the World Council of Churches is widely regarded as the most significant theological product of the ecumenical movement to date. The greater freedom enjoyed by Roman Catholic theologians after Vatican II has resulted in many valuable contributions from that quarter as well, such as the collection of papers on baptism published by the Murphy Centre for Liturgical Research (1976) under the title *Made, Not Born*. Indeed, amongst all the confusion and growing complexity of the contemporary ecclesiastical scene one positive gain can be registered: the twentieth century has witnessed a greatly improved tone in baptismal discussions.

The positive note on which the last paragraph ended needs to be tempered by a few realistic observations. Most of the contributions to the baptismal debate on a scholarly level from the credobaptist perspective have come from ecumenically-minded Baptists. To what degree these scholars represent the rank and file of Baptists and Baptist Associations around the world is questionable. Furthermore, Baptists represent only a minority of those Christians and churches in the world today holding to a credobaptist position. The twentieth century has seen the phenomenal growth of the Pentecostal movement, from small beginnings in Azusa Street in 1906 to more than fifty million adherents in the 1980s. For the most part Pentecostal churches strongly reject infant baptism. Closely linked to the Pentecostal movement has been the Charismatic renewal movement which really began to take off within the main line churches from about the 1950s. Those influenced by the Charismatic renewal have been estimated at about one hundred million. The late David du Plessis claimed there were close on 50 million Roman Catholic Charismatics alone.[7] More recent estimates of Catholic Charismatics have been 80 million.[8] Now while these 'main line' Charismatics have shown every indication, by and large, of staying in their denominations, the indications are that they will be accentuating the baptismal debate within those same denominations. Prof. Walter Hollenweger of Birmingham once forecast that by the turn of the century the Pentecostal-Charismatic component will comprise more than 50 percent of Christianity. All of this points to one certainty, that discussion around the subject of baptism will continue to be lively for the foreseeable future, both in scholarly and academic circles as well as in the arena of popular debate. It points also to the urgent necessity of finding ways to ensure that this discussion can be fruitful and constructive, for the edification, enrichment and empowerment of the whole church in its primary task of working for the salvation, reconciliation and healing of the world and all its peoples.

Getting started

The writer's viewpoint

It is impossible to divorce a book of this kind from the perspective and context of the writer. The writer's own experience and convictions play an important role in the development and creation of such a work. Anyone taking up such a book will inevitably ask not only 'What does it say?' but also 'Who is saying it, and why? From what church does he come, and what theological framework?' The answers to all these questions contribute to the understanding of the work. The following brief sketch of the writer's spiritual and theological pilgrimage will answer some of these questions.

Raised as a Roman Catholic, my early faith was shaped by the disciplined and ordered life of the Roman Catholic boarding schools in Zambia and Zimbabwe which I attended from the age of five. Daily mass, regular catechism classes, periodic special retreats and the pervasive religious environment of a Catholic school all contributed to a faith which was accepted and appreciated as an important part of life. This faith, however, did not long survive the harsher environment of a brief spell of employment at the lead and zinc mine in Kabwe, Zambia, my birthplace. By the time I went up to study engineering at the University of Bristol in England I was a lapsed, or non-practising, Catholic. The sudden conversion of a close friend (a Presbyterian) brought me into immediate contact, for the first time in my life, with evangelical Protestantism and its understanding of the gospel. After a period of resistance, debate and reflection, I experienced a renewal of Christian faith and took up again the practice of Catholicism, attending mass regularly and using the sacraments. In the zeal of this renewal of faith, accompanied now by a regular study of the Bible, I found myself especially attracted to the enthusiasm, faith and Bible knowledge of a group of Christians associated with the Christian Union, an evangelical interdenominational Christian organization on the university campus. By degrees, without ever making a conscious decision to leave the Catholic church, my worship and fellowship came to be entirely in Protestant evangelical circles, and the subsequent development of my faith and spirituality were strongly influenced by that tradition.

But Protestantism, I soon discovered, had its own perplexing varieties: Calvinism, Pentecostalism, Paedobaptism, Credobaptism and many other ecclesio-theological systems claimed 'highest truth' status. Return to Zambia and fellowship with a Brethren assembly there led to my being baptised as a believer. A vocation to full-time Christian ministry brought me to South Africa to work in the townships under the auspices of the Dorothea Mission.

Exposure there to the multiple groups of Christian churches and organizations, orthodox and unorthodox, foreign and indigenous, brought home to me the devastation wrought by the fragmentation of the Christian community into countless divided and often antagonistic groups. Convinced that I should at least identify myself with a particular church (up to then I had been satisfied to be a Christian 'belonging to no particular sect'), I became a member of Central Baptist church in Pretoria. Some years later I entered the Baptist ministry.

Further experiences and studies led me to another conversion, a very gradual conversion over a long period of time, an ecumenical conversion. This in no way nullified my previous evangelical conversion, but rather complemented it, putting it into perspective. Together with conservative evangelicals, I remain convinced of the supremacy of Christ, the authority of the Scriptures and the urgency of world evangelization. With ecumenicals, I share the pain of the scandal of Christian divisions and the burden to promote reconciliation and unity between Christians, all Christians, 'until we all reach unity in the faith and in the knowledge of the Son of God' (Eph.4:13). The conviction that the various Christian traditions, whatever the legitimacy of their historical origins, can and ought to engage in dialogue with each other for mutual enrichment, the strengthening of common bonds and the advancement of the gospel in the world is the inspiration behind this book. Only as Christians walk in the way of reconciliation and unity can they be witnesses to a divided and broken world and instruments for its healing.

The structure of the book

The very wide variety of baptismal practices in the world today can be classified into three broad categories: Catholic, Reformed and Baptist. Chapter 2 of this book summarizes these three approaches. By 'Catholic' is meant the teaching not only of the Roman Catholic church but of all churches which hold a 'high' sacramental view of baptism, stressing its efficacy in conveying that which it represents, regeneration by the Holy Spirit. The Reformed understanding of baptism is also sacramental, but one in which special emphasis is laid on the divine covenant of grace, particularly in the case of the children of believers who are baptised as children of the covenant. The Baptist understanding is one which restricts the administration of baptism to those able to make a personal confession of faith. I am convinced that there are theologically powerful and compelling cases to be made for each of the above approaches and that it is important to realize this as a basis for any further considerations of reconciliation and unity. That is why this book begins with a brief exposition of these three approaches.

In Chapter 3 the writer enters into a limited dialogue with these three perspectives, not in order to judge who is right or wrong but rather with a view to probing and discerning particular strengths and weaknesses present in all three perspectives. A few pages are also devoted to pointing out some neglected areas not usually dealt with in most books on baptism, particularly the issue of lay baptism.

Chapter 4 is devoted to the historical question. The debate between Joachim Jeremias and Kurt Aland – 'Did the early church baptise infants?' – is examined and the writer suggests an alternative hypothesis to those proposed by Jeremias and Aland as an explanation of baptismal developments in the early church. This chapter closes with the conclusion that *all* contemporary baptismal practices are developments of those of the early church.

Chapter 5 could be seen as the 'heart' of this book. It seeks to show that there can be no effective pursuit of truth apart from a deep concern for unity. With application to the controverted question of baptism, this means that all attempts to discover 'the truth' about baptism are in vain if they are pursued in loveless separation from other Christians. A deeper understanding of baptism will be achieved only in an atmosphere of respect for other views and love for those who hold to them, together with a desire to be reconciled to them.

Chapter 6 asks what steps the various separated Christian traditions could take to promote a greater sympathy with and understanding of each other, with a view to facilitating a process of growing together. Just as divorce and schism are invariably preceded by a period of growing apart of two parties that were united, so a period of growing together is needed to prepare the way towards unity and reconciliation between estranged parties.

Chapter 7 explores the concept of a hierarchy of truths, seeking to distinguish between primary and secondary aspects of the Christian faith, and to make the point that obedience to the truth of the gospel sometimes requires a certain flexibility in secondary issues.

Chapter 8 examines a number of congregations and churches which have attempted to bridge 'the waters that divide', and attempts to gauge what measure of success has attended these efforts at reconciliation. The Faith and Order paper *Baptism, Eucharist and Ministry* is also examined as an attempt to produce a consensus document on baptism.

Chapter 9 begins with a summary of Appendix C (an analysis of the responses received from 182 theological students in five theological institutions to a questionnaire on the practice of baptism and its relation to Christian unity.) It then offers some concrete proposals for reconciliation and unity.

Final conclusions are drawn in Chapter 10.

A question of terminology

Symptomatic, perhaps, of the misunderstandings, tensions and conflict over baptism is the difficulty of finding a mutually acceptable terminology. One term, in particular, is problematic: 'believers' baptism'. This has acquired general acceptance in the literature on baptism, being used to indicate the position of those who insist that personal faith is an essential requirement for baptism, and who therefore do not baptise infants on the grounds that they cannot (yet) believe. The objection, however, has been raised that paedobaptist churches also practise believers' baptism, baptising as believers all those coming to faith in Christ from a non-Christian background and those who have never been baptised for whatever reason. It is also argued that even infant baptism is just as much believers' baptism as the baptism of adults, since the importance of faith is equally emphasized in both cases, being required from all parties, including the infants being baptised – as soon as they are able to believe. Those who argue thus would further urge that the real distinctive of so-called 'believers' baptism' is not the insistence on faith but the rejection of infant baptism; that position might better be described as 'antipaedobaptist'. Technically speaking, there is some force to this argument. Practically, though, it is no solution, since the term is unacceptable to those holding this position. Just as the sixteenth century Anabaptists never accepted that term for themselves as they did not see themselves as 'rebaptising' anyone, so contemporary adherents of 'believers' baptism' find it unacceptable to be defined in a negative way, seeing themselves simply as insisting on the necessity of faith as a condition for baptism. In an ecumenical context it is undesirable to indicate a group by using a term to that is offensive to them. The problem remains, however, that paedobaptists also practise believers' baptism alongside the baptism of infants and do not like the restrictive use of the term 'believers' baptism' as if it were practised only by those rejecting infant baptism.

There is no completely satisfying solution to this problem, and I have attempted to show sensitivity towards those who are unhappy about restricting the term 'believers' baptism' to churches which reject infant baptism, by avoiding it where possible, sometimes putting it in inverted commas, and more often using the term 'credobaptism'. This latter term was first encountered in a Lutheran journal[9] and seems to go some way towards solving the problem by creating two technical terms, paedobaptism and credobaptism, to describe the two different traditions. However even this solution is open to some objections. Let the reader note that the author is aware of and sympathetic to the problems associated with these terms. Furthermore, it must be noted that where the term 'believers' baptism' or 'credobaptism' is used, it is used as a technical term to identify a particular tradition. This is also how the term 'infant baptism' or 'paedobaptism' is used. Paedobaptists, of course, do not only baptise infants, but the term is used as a technical term denoting the whole 'package' of that particular tradition.

The goal

The goal of this book can be simply stated: to make a specific contribution towards the reconciliation and reunion of Christians traditionally alienated and separated from one another over the question of baptism. It is true, of course, that in no case is baptism the single and only issue separating Christians. There are always other issues. But this book focuses on this one issue in the conviction that principles and methods emerging from this study can be applied to other issues as well.

It is a very specific contribution. To begin with it is a Baptist contribution, from one who is deeply involved in and committed to the work and ministry of the Baptist Union in South Africa. It is also a conservative contribution, since the author is convinced of and committed to a conservative and traditional understanding of the historic Christian faith and to the beliefs associated with such an understanding: a high view of the authority and inspiration of the Holy Scriptures; an orthodox understanding of the traditional christological and trinitarian symbols of faith, such as Nicaea and Chalcedon; and a strong desire to see all people everywhere confessing Jesus Christ as Lord to the glory of God the Father. Such a perspective would be branded by many today as fundamentalist. But the spirit of fundamentalism, as that word is commonly understood today, is not conciliatory but separatist and anti-ecumenical. The purpose of this book is to promote understanding, reconciliation and growing unity. The ecumenical note sounded in this book is not the result of a weakening of evangelical and biblical convictions but rather the logical fruit of such convictions; the belief that central to the work of Christ witnessed to by the Holy Scriptures is the reconciliation of all people in one body through the blood of the cross (Eph.2:14–18).

The revival of scholarly interest in the subject of baptism has led to much important work being done in this area. Consultations, dialogues and discussions, formal and informal, official and unofficial, have been carried out in an atmosphere of mutual respect unprecedented in more than a thousand years of Christian history. Valuable and fruitful work has been done in trying to resolve differences and to come to an agreement on a single consensus statement on baptism – such as the work of the Commission on Faith and Order in producing the BEM document. And such work must continue. This book is concerned to show that reconciliation and unity cannot wait until such agreement is achieved, but can and must be implemented while the discussion is still in process. There are pressing theological and psychological reasons for such action, and, indeed, the fruitful progress of the ongoing baptismal discussion is dependent upon it. The goal of this book is to show that immediate, concrete steps towards reconciliation and unity are both possible and necessary, theologically and practically. Most work being done in the area of baptism tends to concentrate on the meaning and implications of baptism, the careful analysis of different understandings and practices of baptism, the exposition of one particular approach or the attempt to find consensus. This work is concerned to develop a theological basis for the coexistence of different baptismal practices and understandings within the unity of one Christian fellowship.

Notes

1 J. Warns, *Baptism* (London, Paternoster, 1962), p.119.
2 J. Dillenberger, *Martin Luther: Selections from his writings* (New York, Doubleday, 1961), p.229.
3 J.H. Leith, *Creeds of the Churches* (Richmond, John Knox, 1973), p.284.
4 G.G. Miller, *A Baptist Theology of the Child* (Pretoria, UNISA D.Th thesis, 1992), p.58.
5 W.E. Ward, 'The Conflict over Baptism,' *Christianity Today* 14 (1966):12.
6 V.E. Hayward, 'Can our controversy with the Paedobaptists be resolved?' *Baptist Quarterly* 22 (1967):60.
7 H.I. Lederle, *Study Guide STH 408-Y: Charismatic Theology* (Pretoria, UNISA, 1986), p.5.
8 P.J. Pierson, Interview with K.B. Roy, Cape Town, 1993.
9 J.D. Kingsbury, Editorial *Interpretation 3* (1993):228.

Chapter 2

Three Perspectives

Even within one denomination there will inevitably be found quite a wide diversity of views concerning the nature of baptism, its function and meaning, and its proper administration. For simplicity's sake, however, we will speak of three major perspectives concerning the doctrine and practice of baptism, a Catholic perspective, a Baptist (or credobaptist) perspective, and a Reformed perspective.

In reality it is extremely difficult for anyone accurately and sympathetically to convey a perspective that he or she does not fully share. This puts the present writer (a Baptist) at a disadvantage in attempting to convey a Catholic or Reformed perspective. This shortcoming will be borne in mind by the reader. The writer does, however, have a genuinely sympathetic appreciation of these traditions, which qualifies him, in some small measure, to attempt a description of these perspectives.

A Catholic perspective

At the heart of a Catholic understanding of baptism is the belief that baptism is more than just a symbol of God's saving grace, being also an effectual vehicle of that grace. Anyone who is properly baptised with the right intention is truly born again by divine grace into the kingdom of God. By means of this sacrament, sinners are cleansed from their sins, renewed by the Holy Spirit and united to Christ and the church.

Catholics point out that all the biblical passages containing references to baptism are characterized by a strong realism. Baptism is never spoken of as merely symbolizing something but as actually conveying something. On the day of Pentecost, Peter exhorted his hearers to 'Repent and be baptised . . . for the forgiveness of your sins. And you will receive the gift of the Holy Spirit. The promise is for you and your children and for all who are far off – for all whom the Lord our God will call' (Acts 2:38,39). Here the forgiveness of sins and the gift of the Holy Spirit are assured to those who receive baptism in repentance and faith. Paul reminds the Christians in Rome: 'Don't you know that all of us who were baptised into Christ Jesus were baptised into his death? We were . . . buried with him through baptism into death in order that, just as Christ was raised from the dead through the glory of the Father, we too may live a new life' (Rom. 6:3,4). Paul's words point to baptism being the occasion of the Christian's union with Christ in his death, burial and resurrection, and not just a symbol of it. So we can continue through the New Testament. To Titus Paul writes: 'He saved us through the washing of rebirth and renewal by the Holy Spirit' (Tit. 3:5). To the Galatians he writes: 'All of you who were baptised into Christ have clothed yourselves with Christ' (Gal. 3:27). In these and in all other New Testament passages baptism is consistently spoken of as the means whereby the grace of God and the saving benefits of Christ's redemption are conveyed to human beings.

Perhaps the most dramatic example of baptism as a real encounter with God in the power of the Holy Spirit is the baptism of Jesus himself. On that occasion the heavens were opened, the Holy Spirit descended on Jesus and a voice from heaven was heard. This was no merely symbolic rite, but an event packed with the reality of a powerful encounter with God the Father and the Holy Spirit. While unique because of the uniqueness of the one being baptised, this baptism also relates to Christian baptism in general, both being occasions of real encounter with God: Father, Son and Holy Spirit.

When Catholics insist on the efficacy of baptism in not only signifying but also conveying the blessing signified, they do not thereby mean that baptism has nothing to do with faith. On the contrary, baptism is a sacrament of faith, and the blessings it conveys do not occur apart from faith. It is faith that brings the candidate, desiring union with Christ and the church, to baptism, in order that that desire might be realized. It is faith that motivates the church, the community of faith, to administer baptism, believing this to be the means which God has ordained for those desiring the grace of life to receive it. At every point faith is involved. Without faith there could be no baptism. And when we are speaking about faith in connection with baptism, it is primarily the faith of the church which calls people to baptism and gives baptism to those desiring it, in the belief that this is the way which God has ordained that sinners be cleansed from their sins, united to Christ and the church, and receive newness of life through the power of the Holy Spirit.

This is why the church baptises infants. Infants are brought to the church by believing sponsors and parents who desire for those infants the gift of life and who request that they might be incorporated into Christ and the church through the sacrament of baptism so that they might be brought up as Christian children, sharing in the redemption which Christ has wrought for his people. If it be objected that baptism cannot possibly benefit little infants who are completely passive in their reception of the rite and do not even know what is going on, Catholics will reply that there are many instances in the New Testament where the power of God was savingly exercised towards people who themselves were completely passive, on account of the faith of others. The centurion's servant was healed by Jesus through the request and faith of the centurion (Mt. 8:13). The dead daughter of Jairus was raised up through the request and faith of Jairus (Lk. 8:50). The demon-possessed daughter of the Syrophoenician woman was delivered by Jesus on account of the faith and request of the mother (Mk. 7:29). Lazarus was raised from the dead after Jesus had said to his concerned sisters: 'Did I not tell you that if you believed, you would see the glory of God?' (Jn. 11:40). We can see that there were many instances when the saving benefits of God's grace were given to those who themselves were incapable of exercising faith, at the intercession and believing prayers of others on their behalf. So it is with infants. Born in sin and corruption, they are brought to God and the church in the desire and prayer that they might be cleansed, renewed and incorporated into the church through baptism. In the faith of the church they are baptised that they may be brought up, not as heathen who do not know God, but as Christian children, learning to pray to God as their heavenly Father and to believe that they are his children through faith and baptism. This is how Liam Walsh describes the role of faith in baptism, even in the case of infants:

> For this reason [baptism] has within it not just the ministry of the Church that gives grace but also the Church's response of faith and love that receives grace. The response of the individual to the grace of Baptism is always cultivated and carried within this response of the community. . . . In identifying with the care and responsibility felt by the parents, the Christian community shows that it wants the gift of God for the child in Baptism. It is in this wanting of the Church (its faith in God's will to save this child) that the gift of God is actually given.[1]

In the rite of infant baptism the faith is being professed by parents, sponsors and other church members who ask, in faith, for the baptismal grace that leads to faith in the one for whom they are responsible and who is dependent on them for his or her very being.

Such children are baptised into Christ in order that they might believe in him and follow him. And believe in him they must, according to their capacity, as they grow up. Should they ever cease to believe in Christ, rejecting the faith of their fathers and the church into which they were baptised, repudiating the vows taken on their behalf by their sponsors and turning their back on God and Christ and the church, then they will surely bring down upon themselves the wrath of God and his judgment, just as was so often the case with the children of Israel of old. But even such a tragic outcome would not imply they had never received any benefit from their baptism as infants. Rather they would be like those sick people who were healed by Jesus but who never showed any gratitude for their healing and never followed him. Their healing was real, but served only to aggravate their judgment on account of their unbelief and disobedience.

So for Catholics baptism is much more than a symbol or a witness to the grace of God in the gospel. It is nothing less than the divinely appointed instrument whereby men, women and children are born again to life eternal in Christ Jesus. Walsh summarizes the Catholic understanding of baptism as follows:

> Baptism is a work of God, in which he realizes his intention of giving salvation and the forgiveness of sin to all humankind, by incorporating into Christ, through regeneration in the grace of the Holy Spirit, and adoption to divine sonship those who believe in the Gospel and are converted from sin; this work is realized in and through the Church which is the community of those who proclaim Christ's death and resurrection and re-enact it in a water-rite that, as a sacrament, signifies and effects regeneration, incorporation and adoption by Father, Son and Holy Spirit.[2]

With such a 'high' doctrine of baptism, do Catholics therefore exclude from the possibility of salvation those who have never been baptised? Not necessarily. While God has ordained baptism to be the normative way whereby sinners are reconciled to himself through Christ, yet he is not bound by the sacraments which he himself has instituted for the salvation of humankind. God remains free to extend his salvation by other means to those who have not been or cannot be baptised. We can cite a few instances of how the church has worked out this understanding in practice, particularly in the concepts of the baptism of desire and the baptism of blood.

Very early in the church's history, those desiring to be baptised into Christ were first enrolled into the catechumenate where they received instruction for up to three years before being baptised. It would sometimes happen that a catechumen would suddenly die before receiving baptism. In such cases the catechumen was said to have received a baptism of desire, having desired baptism, but having passed away before actually receiving it. The church has also made use of this concept in the case of those who have never heard the gospel. For those who sincerely sought after God according to the light they had, desiring to be united to him, there is the hope of salvation through the baptism of desire. This concept of a baptism of desire should never be abused,

Catholics believe, to neglect the importance and urgency of water baptism. There can only be grave consequences for those who neglect to receive baptism when it is within their reach.

In the early church there were also those who became convinced of the truth of the gospel but suffered martyrdom before having an opportunity to be baptised. These were said to have received a baptism of blood, which was regarded as a better baptism, ensuring the martyr's crown. The concept of a baptism of blood has also been extended to embrace those who in seeking after good and truth have given their lives in the cause of justice, truth and love though they were never acquainted with the gospel of Christ and never had an opportunity to be baptised.

What of children dying in infancy without baptism? Led by the rigour of his own logic in his polemic against Pelagianism, Augustine could see no way of salvation for children who die without baptism. In practice, however, the church has tended to modify the strict Augustinian position by holding that infants dying without baptism would at least not suffer the pains of hell, although they would be deprived of the vision of God because they had never been reborn in grace. But even this is not fully satisfactory to many Catholic theologians, who are still prepared to search for an alternative to the theological postulate of Limbo and to look for a way of affirming the salvation of unbaptised infants that will not contradict the tradition on the universal necessity of baptism, and the correlative universality of original sin. It can be reasoned from the universal saving will of God that unbaptised infants are saved in a way we know nothing about because God has not revealed it. Walsh has mentioned the thesis of V. Wilkin[3] who argues that infants are saved by the very fact of the resurrection of Christ, without exercising any choice, just as they were afflicted by original sin by the very fact of being born.

A Baptist perspective

Just as the Catholic perspective, dealt with above, covers a group wider than the Roman Catholic Church, so the Baptist perspective dealt with here covers a group much wider than those Christians and churches called 'Baptist'. Those holding to a Catholic sacramental view of baptism would include the Eastern Orthodox Church, many Anglicans, Lutherans and quite a few Reformed and Congregational Christians. Those holding to a Baptist understanding of baptism would include most pentecostal and charismatic churches together with other denominations such as the Disciples of Christ and many independent congregations throughout the world. In fact Baptists are a minority among those holding to what could be called Baptist views on baptism. For this reason the term credobaptist has been adopted in this book to describe all those who do not baptise infants, as opposed to paedobaptist, which describes all those who do. In this chapter the terms Baptist and credobaptist will be used more or less interchangeably.

The one distinctive element in a credobaptist perspective on baptism is that baptism is a confession of faith on the part of the candidate receiving baptism. Like other Christians, Baptists make use of water and the triune name of God in baptism. Most credobaptists today would insist on full immersion in water, although historically that has not always been the case. The Anabaptists of the sixteenth century baptised by pouring or sprinkling, and the early Baptist congregations in England in the seventeenth century did not baptise by full immersion. The mode of baptism is not the most central distinctive of the Baptist way, but rather the claim that baptism is a confession of faith made by the one being baptised. Baptism is an ordinance for believers only, so it is necessary that those who wish to be baptised should already have come to Christ in faith and repentance. No one can be brought to baptism. People must come to baptism, freely as responsible persons, so that their baptism is a personal response to the word of God.

Credobaptists build their case firmly on the New Testament and the claim that every recorded case of baptism in that document is the baptism of believers. Indeed credobaptists normally refer to their understanding and practice of baptism as 'believers' baptism'. The dominical commission recorded in Mt. 28:19 was: 'Go and make disciples of all nations, baptising them in the name of the Father and of the Son and of the Holy Spirit.' People must therefore become disciples, Baptists conclude, before they are baptised. The same emphasis is distinguished in the promise recorded in Mk. 16:16, 'Whoever believes and is baptised will be saved.' Again, credobaptists point out, baptism is for those who believe. On the day of Pentecost the apostolic command was, 'Repent and be baptised', indicating the proper order to be observed: first repentance, then baptism. Continuing through the book of Acts, the Ethiopian eunuch was baptised after confessing his faith that Jesus Christ is the Son of God (Acts 8:36). Saul of Tarsus was baptised after his conversion experience on the Damascus road and after being filled with the Holy Spirit when Ananias laid his hands on him and prayed for him (Acts 9:17,18). Cornelius and those with him were baptised after they heard the gospel, believed and were filled with the Holy Spirit (Acts 10:44–48). Lydia and the members of her household were baptised after responding in faith to the message of Paul (Acts 16:14,15). The Philippian jailer and his household were baptised after hearing and believing the word of the Lord spoken by Paul (Acts 16:31–33). In all these cases, Baptists hold, it is believers who are baptised, establishing a pattern and a precedent for believers' baptism.

In the letters of Paul and other apostles we find again that the references to baptism are invariably conjoined with references to faith. Paul reminds the Colossian Christians that they had been circumcised with the circumcision done by Christ: '. . . having been buried with him in baptism and raised with him through your faith in the power of God, who raised him from the dead' (Col. 2:12). This spiritual circumcision and union with Christ was accomplished through baptism *and faith*. Peter teaches that the water of the flood in Noah's time 'symbolises baptism that now saves you also – not the removal of dirt from the body but the pledge of a good conscience towards God' (1 Pet. 3:21). He emphasizes that it is not the physical rite that saves but the pledge to God. To the Galatians Paul writes: 'You are all sons of God through faith in Christ Jesus, for all of you who were baptised into Christ have clothed yourselves with Christ' (Gal. 3:26,27). Faith and baptism are juxtaposed here to show that effective baptism is that which is an exercise of faith. Indeed, Baptists would claim, the words baptism and faith are virtually interchangeable in the New Testament. Wherever the word baptism occurs, it could be replaced by *faith* (or *believe*) and the text would make perfect sense.

The importance of faith as a prerequisite for baptism necessarily excludes infant children. Credobaptists are confirmed in this conviction by the fact, that, in their understanding, the New Testament contains no record of any infant baptism. In response to the claim that the household baptisms mentioned in the book of Acts must have included infants, at least sometimes, Baptists reply that in every recorded case of such a household baptism the context makes clear that infants could not have been involved. In the case of Cornelius and the company in his house, those were baptised whose reception of the Holy Spirit had been evidenced by speaking in tongues (Acts 10:47) – hardly possible for an infant. As for the Philippian jailer who was baptised together with all his family – 'He was filled with joy because he had come to believe in God – he and his whole family' (Acts 16:34). So, conclude Baptists, those who were baptised were those who had come to believe.

For credobaptists, infant baptism is irresponsible, since it seeks to make Christians out of those who know nothing of faith and repentance. This, they feel, can only promote a nominal Christianity among those who have been initiated into Christ and the church while knowing nothing.

Most credobaptists understand baptism as having largely symbolic value. It is a visual and dramatic witness to the salvation which God gives to all who repent and believe the gospel. It is also a step of obedience, as believers obey the injunction to be baptised, thus following the example of Jesus who himself was baptised in obedience to his Father's will in order 'to fulfil all righteousness' (Mt. 3:15). On the occasion of their baptism, believers often give testimony to the saving power of Christ in their lives through the gospel.

When it is said that most Baptists tend to see baptism as having symbolic value, it must not be thought that they see the ordinance as an empty symbol, devoid of blessing and grace. On the contrary, they believe there is always a divine blessing on those who submit to God's ordinances in humble obedience. This is the blessing and grace of baptism, the blessing of obedience rather than regeneration, redemption and union with Christ. The latter are the prerequisites for baptism.

While it is probably true that most Baptists tend towards a symbolic understanding of baptism, there are some who would hold to a more sacramental view, granting that baptism is the occasion in which the candidate receives Christ, calling upon his name and submitting to his lordship. George Beasley-Murray, for example, writes:

> He that in baptism 'calls on the name of the Lord' (Acts 22:16) undergoes baptism in a prayerful spirit; it becomes the supreme occasion and even vehicle of his yielding to the Lord Christ. Here is an aspect of baptism to which justice has not been done in the Church since its early days: baptism as a means of prayer for acceptance with God and for full salvation from God, an 'instrument of surrender' of a man formerly at enmity with God but who has learned of the great Reconciliation, lays down his arms in total capitulation and enters into peace . . . Consequently, baptism is regarded in Acts as the occasion and means of receiving the blessings conferred by the Lord of the Kingdom.[4]

Baptists generally have no great anxieties about the fate of unbaptised little children who die in infancy; they believe all infants and little children to be innocent and therefore taken to God if they should die. Only when they reach the age of reason can they be held accountable for their deeds. At that age children brought up in a credobaptist home would be encouraged to make a personal decision for Christ, receiving him by faith into their hearts.

Theoretically, believers can be baptised at any age. Practically, though, while many Baptist children make a personal decision for Christ at an early age, baptism is often postponed to teenage years when it is felt that children can better appreciate and grasp the significance of the ordinance.

The baptismal practice of Baptists is closely linked to their doctrine of the church. For them a church consists of regenerate members who have voluntarily covenanted together to serve the Lord. Only those who belong to Christ, who have been born again by a personal act of repentance and faith, truly belong to the church. Merely nominal adherence to a state church, usually obtained by simply being born into a particular culture and therefore being baptised into the appropriate church of that culture, can never be adequate grounds for membership in Christ's church. The church is the fellowship of believers who have personally received Christ as Lord and Saviour and therefore only such are the proper candidates for baptism.

A Reformed perspective

In some ways the Reformed doctrine of baptism could be seen as a mediating position between Catholic sacramentalism and the credobaptist rejection of infant baptism altogether. Reformed theologians, however, would insist that their views are not the result of an attempted mediation but rather the direct result of reflection on the teaching of Scripture and the tradition of the church from earliest times.

Together with Catholics, Reformed churches hold that the biblical language about baptism is more than merely symbolic. Also, the baptism of the infants of believers is both valid and necessary. Most Reformed teachers, however, are not comfortable with what they perceive to be the excessive sacramentalism of Catholic teaching – its very 'high' views of the efficacy and necessity of baptism. On the other hand, while Reformed teachers would agree with credobaptists in stressing the importance of faith and repentance, they would not agree with what they regard to be the excessive individualism of Baptists – their failure to take into account the corporate nature of the community of faith, the people of God.

Perhaps the most distinctive element of the Reformed approach to baptism is the way in which they relate the sacrament to the biblical concept of covenant. God has called to himself not only individuals but a people who are his own, the people of God. He has sworn to be the God of this people and their descendants after them, according to the promise he made to Abraham: 'I will establish my covenant as an everlasting covenant between me and you and your descendants after you for the generations to come, to be your God and the God of your descendants after you' (Gen. 17:7). The people of God are a community, likened to a flock consisting of sheep and lambs, all cared for by one Shepherd. *All* the members of this community, young and old, share in the covenant blessings of salvation graciously given by God to his people. When God called Abraham, he imparted his saving blessings not only to him, but to all of his household. For this reason they all received the covenant sign of circumcision, the seal of God's saving blessings to his people. When the Philippian jailer inquired what he should do to be saved, he was informed: 'Believe in the Lord Jesus, and you will be saved – you and your household' (Acts 16:31). Not only the jailer but all his household were baptised into Christ, sharing together in the blessings of salvation.

While infants are too young to understand the significance of God's covenant, they are beneficiaries nevertheless of that covenant and its blessings. This has always been a characteristic of God's chosen people, both in the Old and the New Testament. Christian children share in the blessings which God freely pours out so graciously and abundantly on believing parents and their homes. As Adrio König has put it:

> For this reason the children of believers in the Old Testament were circumcised and in the New Testament they were baptised as a confirmation of God's promises to them . . . for whenever God begins to bless believers, their children have a share in these blessings. And because baptism is also an incorporation into the covenant of grace, the children of believers need to be baptised as their incorporation into this body or community of people blessed by God, of which the children obviously form a part.[5]

The children of believers are raised from infancy in the knowledge of the true God and taught to pray to him as '*our* Father'. They are Christian children, not heathen children. Therefore it is only right that from infancy they should share in the new covenant rite of salvation, holy baptism. Credobaptists might object that such infants cannot believe. Yet credobaptists themselves hold that children dying in infancy – especially the children of believers – are saved. So, paedobaptists would answer, if Baptists believe that an infant can be saved without personally believing, why can they not be baptised without personal faith? They are baptised on the grounds of their being the covenant children of God's people and therefore the rightful heirs of God's promises made to the faithful *and their descendants*.

Of course, infant baptism does not eliminate the need for personal faith and repentance. On the contrary, it demands it. Christian children baptised in infancy must personally appropriate the promises of the gospel according to their capacity as they grow up. They must learn to follow Christ daily and make personal decisions with respect to self-denial, commitment to Christ and keeping his commandments. The faith they develop must be a personal faith of which they are fully convinced in their hearts. And if those children who were baptised and raised in the Christian faith should later turn their backs on Christ and abandon the faith they will be counted as covenant-breakers and apostates and would be subject to all the judgments which the Scriptures threaten against such.

Reformed Paedobaptists point out that the baptism practised by most credobaptists is a delayed baptism of witness rather than the baptism found in the New Testament, which is a baptism into Christ. Biblical baptism is incorporation into Christ (Gal. 3:27) and the church, which is the body of Christ (1 Cor. 12:13). It is a washing away of sins (Acts 22:16); burial and resurrection with Christ (Rom. 6:3–7); a bath of regeneration (Tit. 3:5). It is, indeed, salvation (1 Pet. 3:21). But credobaptists require that all of the above named blessings should be received before baptism, and that they should be a requirement for baptism. So their baptism is a rite of witness, in which believers testify to what God has done for them. But this is a man-made ordinance, and not the baptism of the New Testament which is a rite of salvation, a rite of union with Christ through faith and the power of the Holy Spirit.

Reformed theology is sometimes termed covenant theology, stressing the one covenant of grace that runs as a redemptive theme throughout the Scriptures. The promises God made to Abraham and his descendants, that he would be their God and that they would be his people, find their ultimate fulfilment in Christ. Christian believers are children of God and children of Abraham (Gal. 3:7). Throughout the Bible, in the Old and New Testament, God deals with his people as a people, Israel, the church, a flock, a holy nation, a people belonging to God (1 Pet. 2:9,10). This corporate nature of God's people must be reflected in the sacraments, the signs and seals of God's promises and blessings given to all of his people, young and old, those who are gathered together in the community of faith. Those who enter this community from the outside by conversion must enter through baptism and confession of faith. Those born into this community as the children of the faithful enter it also by baptism, as infants, from which time they are taught, according to their capacity, to worship the one true and living God and confess Jesus Christ as Lord.

Notes

1 L.G. Walsh, *The Sacraments of Initiation* (London, Hodder, 1988), p.102.
2 Ibid., p.86.
3 Ibid., p.107.
4 G.R. Beasley-Murray, *Baptism in the New Testament* (London, Macmillan, 1962), p.102.
5 A. König, *Die doop as kinderdoop én grootdoop* (Pretoria, NGKB, 1987), p.122.

Chapter 3

Strengths and Weaknesses

The need for understanding

Chapter 2 contained a brief summary of three different perspectives on baptism. This was deliberately placed at the beginning of this book in order to acquaint the reader afresh with some of the arguments put forward in favour of different points of view. Reading alone, however, is of little value unless it is accompanied by a determined effort to gain a sympathetic understanding of points of view other than our own. It is a fallacy to think that we can come to any text with a completely open mind. Far from being open, our minds are loaded with a whole mass of preconceptions and convictions. Therefore a very special effort is needed to really understand other points of view, as everything within us inclines us against upsetting our mental equilibrium by giving serious consideration to viewpoints that clash with our own. Hence much that goes under the name of reading and research is, in truth, an exercise in fault-finding, designed to bolster our own position rather than seriously search for truth. The comment made by an Anglican scholar, Dr. Jenkins, in the context of a dialogue on baptism, is appropriate here:

> . . . this is a place for patient and humble discussion where it is important that each side puts the best interpretation possible on the views of the other, recognizing the truth of the assertion that we are likely to be right in what we affirm and wrong in what we deny . . . and I am sure that if we are humble and receptive and charitable the Lord will look kindly upon our perplexities and lead us together into deeper truth.[1]

The role played by emotion in effectively blocking meaningful access to other points of view was pointed out by Professor Adrio König in his opening address to a congress on infant baptism hosted by the UNISA department of Systematic Theology:

> Who is going to win – those who advocate infant baptism or those who oppose it? Or is it by any chance Jesus Christ's approach that is going to win – the approach of Christian tolerance in the midst of our differences? . . . . The emotionally charged atmosphere surrounding baptism makes it exceedingly difficult for us all to be influenced by even the best arguments of the other group. Emotion forms a barrier around one's thought and can make one totally inaccessible to other points of view.[2]

One of the first steps needed in order to make meaningful progress in understanding baptismal differences is to move away from the too simplistic categories of right and wrong, especially when applied to whole perspectives such as outlined in chapter 2. That is why this chapter is entitled 'Strengths and Weaknesses'. It is far more helpful to analyse a position to discover its strong and weak points. This approach has been emphasized by the Roman Catholic teacher and author Francis MacNutt:

> Proponents of adult baptism are not wrong; we need to see that. Nor are proponents of infant baptism wrong; others need to see that. We do not want a watering down of truth to bring us together at the lowest common denominator. We need to come to a level higher, where both truths can be joined without compromise to either position.[3]

At first glance MacNutt's approach might seem to be an attempt to avoid the real issues and to achieve some kind of cheap reconciliation by simply declaring everyone correct. Yet he is at pains to point out that he is not interested in any watering down of the truth. On the contrary he is concerned to grasp the truth in greater fullness, and the greatest obstacles in this process are prejudice, preconceptions and dogmatic inflexibility.

Underlying this book is the fundamental conviction that unity and truth are not opposed to one another, as if unity can only be achieved at the expense of truth, or as if adherence to the truth will necessarily bring division. Rather, it is the case that unity and truth are intimately bound up with one another, so that it is only in a commitment to unity that we find true freedom to pursue the truth. As the Irish Jesuit priest Declan Deane has observed:

> Christ through the Holy Spirit guides his followers towards the fullness of truth. In any given instance, disunity among Christ's followers is liable to frustrate and retard the process whereby divine truth is communicated and received . . . it is only insofar as the disciples commit themselves to being one, that they can win the inner freedom of mind and heart to be 'dedicated' to the truth. Without a hard-won unity of hearts and minds, truth can only remain a chimera.[4]

In the remainder of this chapter the attempt will be made to reflect critically on the content of the previous chapter, not to try and ascertain who is right or wrong, but to probe and explore and test the various approaches with a view to discovering areas of strengths and weaknesses. There will also be an attempt to try and understand the basic concerns that underlie the various perspectives, the often unstated psychological motivations that play a powerful, even if unrecognized, role in maintaining and buttressing theological positions. There are, of course, considerable areas of overlap and these will be noted as well as the areas of difference. Each perspective is concerned to preserve something that its proponents consider vital and precious, something so important that it cannot and may not be lost to the Christian world. What is this essence, so important that many have been willing to sacrifice life and limb to preserve it? This is what we are concerned to discover and sympathetically understand.

It cannot be ignored that the writer of these lines is not some completely impartial observer (if, indeed, such a creature exists) but a Baptist. Therefore, as was pointed out in the introduction, no claim to impartiality is made. The eyes of the observer (and the spectacles through which those eyes look) determine to a large extent what is seen. But the recognition of this reality by the observer can lead to certain correctives being deliberately applied. So the Baptist reader of this chapter must not be surprised to find the Baptist perspective the target of some of the sharpest criticisms made.

Strengths

It will be instructive, right at the beginning, to note the very considerable degree of overlap in the three views considered. All three maintain that baptism is more than just an empty symbol so that in baptism a divine blessing is imparted to the recipient of the sacrament. Of course Catholics and Baptists will differ as to the precise nature of this blessing.

Furthermore, each view strongly emphasizes the importance of faith and its connection to baptism, so that the efficacy of baptism and the benefits bestowed in and through baptism cannot be considered in isolation from faith and the central role it plays in God's dealings with human beings.

Finally it can be said that each view clearly affirms the primacy of divine grace in the process of human salvation. It is God who takes the initiative in reaching out to fallen and helpless sinners in graciously granting them his salvation and life, and each tradition agrees that this reality must be manifest in baptism, the sacrament of life and salvation. So we note right at the beginning the very important areas of overlap in the viewpoints under consideration.

Catholic strengths

Biblical language about baptism is strongly realistic. Something happens in baptism. People are born anew, regenerated by the Holy Spirit, cleansed from their sins, incorporated into the body of Christ. It is this 'high' sacramental understanding of baptism that Catholic theology is concerned to maintain and uphold. Any watering down of the meaning of baptism that makes it a mere symbol, ineffectual of itself, or perhaps even dispensable or optional, is strongly resisted by Catholic theology in general. Such would detract from the dignity of the sacrament instituted by Christ himself to be the means of appropriating the grace and salvation he offers to human beings. For this reason Catholics take very seriously the failure to ask for or to administer baptism. Although Catholic theology does not necessarily endorse the stricter Augustinian view of the necessary damnation of the unbaptised, it cannot accept any tendency to treat baptism as optional and not really necessary for salvation. The consequences of deliberately neglecting baptism are serious.

For Catholics, the views of the great church Fathers carry great weight and are taken very seriously. So considerable attention is given to the historical development of baptismal thinking and practice. Catholic theologians put great importance on the maxim of 'thinking with the church'. Christ promised that the Holy Spirit would be given to the church to guide her into all truth. Therefore the whole of the Christian tradition must be taken seriously as summing up the church's reflection, under the guidance of the Spirit, on the truths of the gospel. Of course there will inevitably be distortions in the views of individual teachers, even such great luminaries as an Augustine or an Aquinas. And there is unquestionably a process of development and progress as the church continues its reflection on the faith once received and struggles to understand and apply it more perfectly in the changing context of the society to which it ministers. But this is the strength of Catholic theology – its catholicity, its conviction that vital truth is not imparted to some individual in isolation but rather emerges as the consensus of the faithful striving together for the faith of the gospel, and not only the faithful of the present generation but the faithful of all generations as they constitute together the whole catholic church, militant and triumphant. For this reason Catholics often give more attention than Protestants to the teachings of the Fathers and the councils of the church and are careful that their exposition of the doctrine of baptism should not be seen as a contradiction of those teachings but rather as a legitimate and authentic development of them. For a Catholic theologian it is unthinkable that the church today could come to conclusions in some important area of doctrine that flatly contradict the teaching of the church in the past. That would be to call into question the promises made by Christ to his church concerning the abiding presence of his Spirit in the church. This 'thinking with the church' is surely a strength, in line with the truth that the Holy Spirit, the Spirit of truth, has been given to the whole catholic church, the body of all faithful people, past and present, so that that which has been held *semper, ubique, ab omnibus* (always, everywhere, by all) represents the true Christian doctrine.

It must not be thought, however, that Catholic thinking is simply antiquarian, content merely to repeat the formulations of the past and perhaps to codify them for present use. On the contrary there is a freshness and contemporary ring to much modern Catholic writing that shows a thorough acquaintance with the contemporary discussion around baptism. The second Vatican Council has been a profound watershed event in the recent development of Catholic theology with its aim of reinterpreting and restating the Catholic faith so as to be able to speak to the modern world with new power, vigour and relevance.

For Catholics, the biblical elements of the divine action, the regenerating work of the Spirit, and the human response of faith and repentance are always present in baptism. The baptism of children and infants is grounded, like the baptism of adults, in faith – not only the faith of the individual but also the faith of the church of which the individual is a part. A strongly corporate concept of the family (both ecclesial and social) enables Catholics to envisage the reality of family corporate decisions for Christ which bring the whole family, including infants, into a new relationship with God and secure for the whole family, including infants and small children whose personal understanding of these things is necessarily limited, the blessing of God which is life and salvation. Children born to Christian families within the wider family of the church are part of the community of faith. It is the desire of the church that they should be saved, the faith of the church that God accepts these little ones through Jesus Christ, and the commitment of the church to bring them up in the fear and knowledge of the Lord. On the basis of this faith and commitment they are incorporated into Christ and the church through baptism. As a result they are not strangers and aliens in the bosom of the church but fellow citizens and members of the household of God.

Baptist strengths

Baptist theology ties indissolubly together baptism and the personal believing of the one being baptised and allows of no exception to this rule, so that the essential elements of a valid baptism comprise not only a washing in water in the name of Jesus Christ but also a profession of faith by the one being baptised. On this basis Baptists would be willing to grant the efficacy of baptism in procuring the blessings of redemption – the forgiveness of sins, the gift of the Spirit, incorporation into Christ and the church. Baptism is efficacious because it is in essence an act of faith, and faith is efficacious in procuring all the blessings of God.

There is a certain simplicity to the Baptist view of making baptism a confession of personal faith. But it is precisely this simplicity which is its strength. It requires no theological sophistication to understand, which is perhaps a reason for its powerful appeal to so many ordinary people possessed of a strong desire to follow Christ but having little formal theological training. This tying together of baptism and personal faith establishes a strong foundation for baptism and any benefits ascribed to it, as the whole Bible speaks so powerfully and extensively of the benefits of faith. There are relatively few references in the New Testament to the rite of baptism while the importance of faith stands out on every page, almost every line. There is dispute among theologians concerning the precise effects of baptism, but there can be no dispute concerning the role of repentance and faith in securing the blessing, deliverance and salvation of God. For this reason Baptist theology has always felt that to ascribe anything to baptism where baptism is not an act of repentance towards God and faith in Jesus Christ is likely to detract from the centrality and importance of faith, to which the whole Bible testifies so abundantly and unmistakably.

It is agreed by Christian scholars in general that there are no cases of infant baptism as such explicitly recorded in the New Testament and that all the instances of baptism actually recorded involve people who could exercise faith and repentance. This means that Baptist theologians can point to the various instances of baptism recorded in the Scriptures as models of believers' baptism without having to make various inferences derived from certain theological principles in order to justify any part of their baptismal practice.

Not only in the recorded instances of baptism but also in those parts of the New Testament where there is teaching about it, baptism is always connected to faith. Beasley-Murray's book on baptism, for example, consists largely of the careful exegesis of every text in the New Testament that mentions or even alludes to baptism. It is clearly his conviction that the plain exegesis of the New Testament passages that deal with baptism will establish beyond reasonable doubt that baptism is always believers' baptism and that there can be no exception to this rule.

Reformed strengths

Just as Catholics are concerned to think with the church, seeking to define the doctrine of baptism as it has been taught and practised in the historic Christian church guided by the Holy Spirit down the ages, and just as credobaptists seek carefully to expound all the baptismal texts in the New Testament, so Reformed theologians are concerned to develop an understanding of baptism that is in accord with the whole Bible, the fullness of God's revelation to his people, and its basic teaching of how God relates to human beings and grants his salvation and blessings to them. This is the strength of the Reformed perspective.

'All Scripture is God-breathed and is useful for teaching . . .' (2 Tim. 3:16). The greater part of this Scripture is what we call the Old Testament; doctrines claiming to be biblical ought in most cases to be able to draw on this large corpus of divine revelation covering the history of God's dealings with his people over a long period of time. Indeed the very brevity of the New Testament both in its actual content and in the time span it covers constitutes a limitation of sorts. It is quite impossible to expect such a short document to provide explicit answers to every conceivable doctrinal and practical problem arising in the church at different times and in various places. Indeed, it is a deficient hermeneutical approach to regard the Bible as a handbook out of which can be read the answers to all our theological questions. A much sounder hermeneutic is that which sees the Bible as a record of God's self-revelation to his people and as containing the principles which should guide us in our service of God and our fellow human beings.

One of the primary concepts in God's dealings with human beings, to which the whole Bible bears witness, is the concept of the covenant, the covenant of grace. Reformed theology highlights the significance of the covenant and its implications for baptism. According to this covenant God is making a people for himself. God called Abraham and promised to bless him and to make his descendants into a great nation through whom all the families of the earth would be blessed. 'I will be your God and you will be my people' is the essence of the divine promise and the covenant of grace. The promises made by God to Abraham extend right through to the new Testament so that Paul saw the blessing of salvation coming to the Gentiles through faith in Jesus Christ to be the fulfilment of the Abrahamic covenant.

It is this fundamental unity of the whole Bible, of the Abrahamic covenant and the covenant of grace, which Reformed theology underlines, and which is its strength. The covenant community is and always has been a community of faith. Anyone entering this community from the outside must profess faith and cannot be sacramentally incorporated into the community without faith, whether it be by circumcision, as in the Old Testament, or by baptism, as in the New. But the children born into this community are undeniably in a special position. They are not pagans 'worshipping strange gods' from which they must turn to the living and true God. They are part of a community of faith growing up to believe and follow the truth. Neither in the Old Testament nor in the New are they are seen as 'strangers and aliens to the commonwealth' of the people of God. They are the holy seed of a holy people. So as they were incorporated into the covenant at birth through circumcision in the Old Testament it is natural and proper for them to be incorporated into the covenant community today by baptism. This is in keeping with the unity of God's dealings with his people from the time of Abraham, the father of all believers, up to these last days. Reformed theologians point out that the first Christians (who were almost all Jews) would certainly have been influenced by the covenantal way of thinking so deeply ingrained in the Jewish mentality and formed over a history of two thousand years. It is this integrated theological approach to baptism grounded in the covenant of grace and the unity of the Bible that constitutes the strength of the Reformed perspective.

Weaknesses

The pattern of theological debate is often to focus on the weakness of the opponent's arguments while giving no serious consideration to that of our own. In this way theological debate can continue forever as it becomes a crusade to defend the truth against error, with each protagonist firmly entrenched in his or her citadel of truth periodically firing off broadsides against the opponents in error. But weak points can be found in every position, including our own. Just as we have broadly sketched some of the strengths of the three perspectives under consideration we shall now outline some of their weaknesses, primarily as seen through the eyes of the writer. It must be emphasized that what follows is not an attempt to enumerate *all* the weaknesses of a particular viewpoint but rather an attempt to draw attention to just one or two areas which could be regarded as weak points – perhaps even by proponents of a particular viewpoint.

Catholic weakness

It is agreed by all Christian traditions that the practice of indiscriminate baptism is unacceptable and in fact virtually all the great churches have taken steps to eliminate the practice. Yet a Catholic theologian can also speak of the 'urgency that sometimes borders on the reckless' with which the church administers the sacrament of baptism, and a 'generosity that is always prepared to give the benefit of the doubt. For it is believed to be the gift of a God who wishes all to be saved by it'.[5] Between this generosity in the administration of baptism and the acknowledgment of the evil consequences of indiscriminate baptism, surely Catholics find themselves in a difficult dilemma. How can baptism be withheld from an infant on the grounds that the parents are not practising Catholics? In the light of the high sacramental understanding of baptism maintained by Catholic theology, to withhold baptism is to withhold the sacrament of regeneration and salvation. Would it not be cruel to so penalize a helpless infant on account of the shortcomings of the parents? This, after all, is how such actions are invariably seen by such parents. Would not such an action only serve to anger and further alienate such parents, who will feel offended that the church is willing to deprive their child of an essential sacrament? Such considerations put an unbearable pressure on the church and make it virtually impossible, in practice, to refuse baptism to infants brought by parents who are not practising Christians and who are living in a sinful estrangement from the church and its teaching. This guarantees the perpetuation of the cycle of indiscriminate baptism, with the church regularly initiating infants into a defective Christianity which is contrary to the church's own standards – a Christianity characterized by the norm of non-observance and neglect of the church's teaching and concerned only with the maintenance of a nominal connection with the church through baptism.

The whole situation is aggravated even further by the rivalry which exists between churches and the practice of indiscriminate proselytism in which one church does not hesitate to proselytize members of another church. It is hard for a church to exercise disciplinary steps against an erring member knowing full well that that member can easily transfer to a rival church. Many would consider that it is a weakness of Catholic baptismal doctrine and practice that it appears to virtually guarantee indiscriminate baptism in practice. Many would argue that this is also a consequence of too 'high' a doctrine of baptism, which exalts the dignity of the sacrament and its alleged powers and benefits at the expense of personal, intelligent faith.

Baptist weaknesses

In this closing sentence of an article on Baptist theology the British Baptist scholar Keith Clements admits: 'Baptists have also yet to arrive at an agreed theology of children in the church.'[6] This remark highlights the feeling shared by many, including some Baptists, that the chief weakness in Baptist theology is precisely their theology of the child. Many Baptist treatises on baptism leave a whole host of questions simply unanswered. What is the relationship of the children of believers to God? Are they saved? And if they are saved, on what basis are they saved? Are they without sin, or have they been made children of God by the grace of the Holy Spirit? And if they are saved, as most Baptists indeed believe, why are they then not baptised as members of the saved community? If small infants can be saved without exercising personal faith, why can they also not be baptised without exercising personal faith?

In addition to questions concerning the relationship of small children to God there are also important questions concerning the relation of such children to the church. How do Baptists regard their own children; as Christian children or non-Christian children? How do they relate to them, as to Christians or to non-Christians? Do they teach them that they are 'separate from Christ, excluded from citizenship in Israel and foreigners to the covenants of the promise, without hope and without God in the world' (Eph.2:12), or do they teach them to pray to God as 'our Father', to trust in him, to love him and serve him as children of God? The answer is almost certainly the latter, which shows that Baptists in practice treat their own children as covenant children. But if they are covenant children why are they excluded from the sacrament of the covenant of grace, baptism?

Another aspect of believers' baptism that is perceived by many to be a weakness is that in practice it tends to become delayed baptism. Rather than being administered at the point of turning to God in faith, in practice baptism is given some time after that point. In the case of children born to Christian parents the administration of baptism can be many years after coming to faith. The same is true when converts from other churches are (re)baptised. One consequence of this practice is that baptism is held to be largely of symbolic value, symbolizing those gifts and blessings already previously received by the candidate at the point of coming to Christ in faith.

A final critique of the Baptist position that will merely be mentioned here (to be taken up later) is this: if baptism does not function in reality as the initiatory rite of incorporation into Christ and the church, then other rites must be devised to serve that function. This, in fact, is what has happened. Among Baptists (and among evangelical Protestants in general, who all tend to view baptism symbolically rather than sacramentally) the 'real' way to become a Christian is by an act of faith crystallized in some evangelical rite (saying the sinner's prayer, inviting the Lord to come into your heart, responding to an altar call, etc.). This is, in effect, simply the substitution of a modern rite of salvation for a biblical rite. Whatever may be the contemporary value of such rites, practically and functionally, one unfortunate result is that those who believe they became Christians by baptism are regarded with suspicion or, more likely, as being deceived.

Reformed weaknesses

The criticism has been levelled against Baptists that it is impossible to postpone baptism without changing its meaning. Such a delayed baptism cannot have the full and rich meaning which New Testament baptism has, the latter being administered immediately to those responding in faith to the gospel and desiring salvation through Christ. But surely the same criticism can be brought against infant baptism. In the case of an infant, personal faith is clearly impossible, which means there is necessarily a gap between baptism and coming to faith. Surely that must lead to the conclusion that infant baptism, like delayed baptism, cannot have the full and rich meaning which New Testament baptism has. And if that is an argument against the practice of delayed baptism it must also be an argument against infant baptism. The Anglican theologian G.W. Bromiley has stated this criticism thus:

> It is in repentance and faith that we are identified with Jesus Christ in his death, burial, and resurrection. To infants who cannot hear the word and make the appropriate response, it thus seems to be meaningless and even misleading to speak of baptism into the death and resurrection of Christ. The confessing believer alone knows what this means and can work it out in his life.[7]

If baptism is truly and really union with Christ, incorporation into the covenant of grace and into the church then why is it that baptised children in Reformed churches are not recognized as members of the church, in the full sense, until a later confirmation or confession of faith? Is this not also a new rite, replacing the rite of baptism in the function for which it was originally given? Indeed why is it, as an Orthodox priest once put it, that the Reformed church, having initiated its children into Christ and the church through baptism, promptly excommunicates them by barring them from the sacrament of the eucharist, the sacrament whereby the spiritual life received in baptism is nourished and strengthened? Although some Reformed churches have apparently changed their practices in this regard, it seems unlikely that such changes will become general in the Reformed tradition.

Another weakness, in the eyes of some, is the Reformed position that baptism, as the sacrament of the new covenant, replaces circumcision, the equivalent sacrament of the old covenant. In reality, however, both baptism *and* circumcision were practised alongside each other among the Jewish believers in the early church. If baptism had indeed replaced circumcision, then why did not Paul simply point this out in his anti-circumcision letter to the Galatians? And when the circumcision issue was debated at length at the council at Jerusalem, why was not the same thing pointed out there? These are questions that some feel still await an adequate answer.

Neglected areas

Most books on baptism tend to focus on issues such as: the meaning of baptism; what happens in baptism; who are the proper recipients of baptism. Rarely is attention given to the psychological function of baptism as a rite of salvation.

A deeper study of the function of rites in general could cast further light on the role and function of Christian rites, both those in the Bible and those that have developed in various Christian traditions in post-biblical times. We cannot live without rites, and rites play many different roles in human life. One of the functions of rites is to bring to a concrete realization at a point in time those inward convictions that have developed over a period of time. Rites play an important role in the process of decision-making. Decisions concerning marriage, business, political government, peace and war are all accompanied by rites. The role of baptism as a rite of salvation and its function in providing confirmation and affirmation of the gift of God is a subject to which this book will return. Attention will also be given to the development of extra-biblical rites of initiation, salvation and assurance where baptism has ceased to function in this capacity.

The question of the proper minister of baptism is another issue rarely considered in scholarly works on baptism. By whom should baptism be administered? Another related issue, seemingly trivial at first glance, is the question of the proper venue of baptism. Where should baptisms normally be administered? Perhaps the lack of attention to the above-mentioned questions is due to the general assumption that ordinarily baptism should be administered by an ordained minister of the church in the presence of the congregation gathered together. It is interesting to note the comment made by G. W. Bromiley in an article on lay baptism: 'The NT affords neither precept nor precedent for the administration of baptism except by an ordained minister.'[8] But what grounds does he have for such a statement? Certainly very few in the New Testament. A much stronger case could be made for the following statement: that *baptism in the New Testament was administered by any Christian to any person desiring to become a Christian at any place and at any time.* In the following few pages this statement will be developed somewhat for the purpose of highlighting one of the underlying themes of this book, namely, that there are significant differences between baptismal practices in the New Testament and *all* contemporary baptismal practices, so that no contemporary baptismal practice can justifiably claim to be identical with that of the New Testament.

A brief survey of the Acts of the Apostles reveals some interesting patterns concerning the administration of baptism. Wherever and whenever the gospel was proclaimed those who believed were baptised immediately. Furthermore the agent of proclamation was normally also the agent or minister of baptism. This means that where the apostles preached the gospel they also baptised the converts, as happened on the day of Pentecost and also at the baptism of Cornelius with his relatives and friends. But we must immediately ask whether the 'ordained ministers' (apostles and elders) necessarily performed the baptisms themselves in every case. The sheer numbers involved on the day of Pentecost makes it likely that the apostles had some assistance, at least, in this task. In the case of Cornelius a much smaller group of people were involved, the close friends and relatives of Cornelius gathered in his home. Yet even then we read that Peter 'ordered that they be baptised in the name of Jesus Christ' (Acts 10:48). The language used suggests that Peter delegated the task of baptism to some of his companions rather than necessarily doing it himself. And his companions were not 'ordained ministers' but simply 'some of the brothers from Joppa' (Acts 10:23). The possibility that the apostles sometimes delegated the administration of baptism becomes even more likely in the light of Paul's statement that he very rarely baptised anyone himself but usually delegated the task to someone else (1 Cor. 1:14–17).

Nor were the apostles the only agents of the proclamation of the gospel. Early in the Acts of the Apostles we read of a vigorous ministry of preaching and baptising carried out by some of the Seven. It could be argued, of course, that they were ordained ministers since hands were laid on them with prayer. But the function for which they were chosen was entirely practical, the distribution of food to widows. They were chosen, in fact, precisely to relieve the 'ordained ministers' by enabling them to focus on the ministry of the word without distraction (Acts 6:1–4). The reason why Philip baptised the Ethiopian eunuch was not that he was authorized to do so by some special ordination, but simply that he was the instrument in proclaiming the gospel to the eunuch and leading him to Christ. The eunuch wanted to become a Christian so Philip baptised him.

There is further evidence that ordinary believers, disciples, were engaged in both preaching and baptising. The apostle Paul himself was baptised into Christ and the church by a man who is simply described as a disciple (Acts 9:10) and of whom we hear nothing further in the New Testament. The church in Antioch was founded by ordinary believers, described as men from Cyprus and Cyrene, fleeing from the persecution that had arisen in Jerusalem. As they spontaneously shared the gospel, 'a great number of people believed and turned to the Lord' (Acts 11:21). There can be no doubt that those who turned to the Lord were baptised by the disciples. It was only after the establishment of the church in Antioch that a 'leader' was sent from Jerusalem to investigate what was happening, and he found nothing lacking in the church. It is probable also that the church in Rome was established in much the same way as the church in Antioch. There is certainly no evidence of any apostolic visit to that city before the church had already been established. It is surely significant that the two churches that were destined to play such an important role in the history of the church were founded and established by a ministry of what would later be known as lay preaching and lay baptising.

In the light of the above it is astonishing that Bromiley could state: 'The NT affords neither precept nor precedent for the administration of baptism except by an ordained minister.' The facts seem rather to indicate that the majority of baptisms were carried out by ordinary believers. And this fits in with the immediacy of baptism in the New Testament. Baptism was the way in which people became Christians. It was the way in which people were cleansed from their sins and received the gift of life eternal. Hence the urgency of baptism. If a person was once convinced of the truth of the gospel and desirous of becoming a Christian in order to be saved 'from this corrupt generation' (Acts 2:40), there could be no delay. To remain under the wrath of God one moment longer than necessary would be both foolish and dangerous. So those who believed were baptised immediately, whether in the middle of the night, as with the Philippian jailer; or in the middle of a journey, as with the Ethiopian eunuch; at home like Cornelius; or by the river bank, like Lydia. The one important thing was to be baptised, wherever and by whomever, so that deliverance from darkness to light, from Satan to God, and from sin to salvation could be procured.

In terms of understanding the function of baptism in the New Testament, the closest functional parallel today could well be the various rites that evangelical Christians have developed in 'leading the lost to Christ'. Evangelical theology (and this includes pentecostal and charismatic theology) puts great stress on the importance of the individual's making a personal conscious decision for Christ, a decision which can be looked back to as the reception of salvation and the new birth in Christ. All evangelical Christians are encouraged to witness to others and if their witness is received, to lead them to Christ. This may take place anywhere, in a home, on a journey, or on a street corner. Those convicted of their need for salvation would be urged to receive Christ immediately, without delay, for delay incurs the danger of failing to receive the grace of God. This contemporary practice illustrates, in the writer's view, the function of baptism in the New Testament and helps us to understand why baptisms were administered immediately, in any place, and often by 'lay' members of the church.

Interestingly enough, the practice of lay baptism finds greater recognition in Catholic and Orthodox churches, with a high sacramental theology, than in Protestant, Reformed and Evangelical churches. The official position of the Roman Catholic church is that 'bishops, priests and deacons are the ordinary ministers of baptism, although in the case of imminent danger of death, anyone with the right intention may administer the sacrament of baptism.'[9] In 1215 the Fourth Lateran Council decreed as valid baptism by whomsoever, properly conferred; that is conferred with the intention 'of doing what the church does' and with the necessary matter and form of the sacrament. It is interesting that in terms of this decree the *whomsoever* can be a non-Catholic or even a non-Christian and the baptism still be valid. The only criteria are that the person baptising should have 'the use of reason "with the intention of doing what the church does." '[10]

Although various Catholic theologians have alluded to this dimension of the lay administration of baptism, either directly or by implication, they very rarely develop it in any way. Hans Küng declares quite boldly: 'The entire Church is given the power to baptise; every Christian has the power to baptise (and to teach).'[11] The Orthodox priest, Paul Lazor, makes the following comments in describing details of the liturgy of the Orthodox rite of baptism:

> It should be noted that several of the liturgical actions performed at Baptism and Chrismation are the same as those done at ordinations. The laying on of hands, the giving of a vestment and the circling procession are all executed at ordinations to the Orthodox Priesthood. . . . The use of these liturgical actions in Baptism and Chrismation indicate that these sacraments, too, involve a consecration to royalty, an ordination to priestly service to God . . . The entire Church is a priestly race. Therefore, all Services and Sacraments are performed by the whole Church.[12]

As has already been mentioned above, this little excursus on the subject of lay baptism has been inserted here for the sole purpose of emphasizing the considerable gap that exists between the normal pattern of baptismal practices in the New Testament and today. The issues of the proper minister of baptism and the venue of baptism are closely related to the question of the function of baptism. Today, there are considerable differences between various church traditions in the understanding of the function of baptism. And it needs to be realized that in all church traditions there has been a development in the understanding of the meaning and function of baptism. In the next chapter an attempt will be made to trace developments in the early church in the understanding of the function of baptism. Further insight in this area will hopefully enable us to consider more meaningfully, in Chapter 5, the central theme of this book: baptism, reconciliation and unity.

Notes

1 D. Jenkins, 'Baptism and Creation', in B.S. Moss (ed.), *Crisis for Baptism* (London, SCM, 1965), p.59.

2 A. König, 'Eager to maintain the unity', in A. König, H.I. Lederle, & F.P. Möller, *Infant Baptism? The arguments for and against* (Roodepoort, CUM, 1984), p.1.

3 F.S. MacNutt, 'A proposed, practical solution to the controversy between proponents of Believers' Baptism and Infant Baptism', in A. König, H.I. Lederle, & F.P. Möller, *Infant Baptism? The arguments for and against* (Roodepoort, CUM, 1984), p.1.

4 D. Deane, 'Truth and the Flight from Unity,' *Studies* 301(1987):54–5.

5 L.G. Walsh, *The Sacraments of Initiation* (London, Geoffrey Chapman, 1988), p.88.

6 K. Clements, 'Baptist theology,' in A. Richardson & J. Bowden, *A New Dictionary of Christian Theology* (London, SCM, 1986), p.62.

7 G.W. Bromiley, 'Lay Baptism,' in W.A. Elwell (ed.), *Evangelical Dictionary of Theology* (Grand Rapids, Baker, 1985), p.115.

8 Ibid., p.117.

9 J. Upton, 'Baptism,' in J.A. Komonchak (ed.), *The New Dictionary of Theology* (Dublin, Gill & Macmillan, 1990), p.79.

10 J.L. McKenzie, 'Roman Catholicism,' *Encyclopedia Britannica Vol. 15,* (Chicago, Encyclopedia Britannica, 1977), p.997.

11 H. Küng, *The Church* (London, Search, 1976), p.380.

12 P. Lazor, *Baptism* (New York, Orthodox Church in America, 1983), p.14.

Chapter 4

Developments in the Early Church: the historical question

In literature dealing with baptismal practices in the early church there are two approaches discernible, a theological approach and a historical approach. Those emphasizing a theological approach claim that historical evidences can be interpreted in various ways and a sound theological grasp of the context in which the evidences occur is needed as a guide to a correct interpretation. Other writers have put more emphasis on research into primary sources, calling for the suspension of theological presuppositions so that the evidence of the primary sources can be followed, without bias, to their own conclusions.

The theological approach

The phenomenon of household baptisms recorded in the New Testament, where whole households were baptised on receiving the gospel, has been the source of not a little discussion by scholars. Paedobaptist scholars have suggested that these households, in some cases at least, must have contained infants and so infants were obviously baptised in New Testament times. Baptist scholars have responded that careful examination of these passages shows that it is impossible that infants could have been included in these household baptisms. König makes the following perceptive remarks concerning the expression, 'He and his whole household were baptised':

> If infants [*kinders*] were baptised in the book of Acts, then this expression means that the infants in each household were also baptised. If infants were not baptised, then this same expression does not mean that infants in the household were baptised. In order to know if the expression 'he and his household were baptised' includes infants, it is first necessary to know whether infants were baptised or not.[1]

The point König is making is that to know if a certain statement refers to all or only some of a group, one must know beforehand to whom in that group the statement *can* refer. Infants cannot run, so the statement, 'the whole household ran away', obviously excludes small infants. Infants can be killed, so the statement, 'the whole household was killed', would include infants. Accordingly, the meaning of the statement, 'the whole household was baptised' is determined by the answer to a prior question, 'Was it the practice of the apostles to baptise infants?'

Having made this comment, König goes on to express his conviction that the infants in such households were indeed baptised because of the covenantal way of thinking that prevailed in the minds of the believing Jews who constituted the very earliest church.

> In a context where people had been accustomed for centuries to family circumcision and for at least one century to family baptisms (proselyte baptism), one can hardly doubt that 'he and his house' would have been understood to include infants where infants were actually present.[2]

But the theological argument is used equally by Baptist scholars who stress the centrality of faith in the New Testament and maintain that in the teaching of Paul the emphasis is on 'faith as the sole mode of appropriation of the Gospel.'[3] Therefore, they reason, the expression, 'he and his house were baptised', can only refer to those capable of being baptised, that is, those capable of exercising faith.

The historical approach

Does the study of early church history, in the apostolic and post-apostolic periods, furnish any evidence that can provide answers for some of the vexed questions that surround the understanding and administration of baptism? Historical research has provided evidence in abundance, but the interpretation of this evidence has given rise to fiercely conflicting claims.

In the 1950s and 1960s the historical question was debated with great erudition by two outstanding German scholars, Joachim Jeremias and Kurt Aland. In 1958 *Die Kindertaufe in den ersten vier Jahrhunderten* was published by Jeremias (English translation 1960, *Infant Baptism in the first four centuries*). In 1961 Kurt Aland replied to Jeremias in *Die Säuglingstaufe im Neuen Testament und in der alten Kirche* (English translation 1963, *Did the early church baptise infants?*). In 1962 Jeremias responded to Aland with *Nochmals: Die Anfänge der Kindertaufe* (English translation 1963, *The origins of Infant Baptism*). Jeremias interpreted the evidence in favour of the apostolic practice of infant baptism, while Aland concluded that infant baptism was a post-apostolic development. It would not be possible to repeat all their various arguments here. Some of their arguments are based on the New Testament, including discussions of Jewish proselyte baptism, the household baptisms in Acts, and various New Testament texts.

Jeremias and Aland also discuss various references (or possible allusions) to baptism occurring in the writings of early Christian writers such as Polycarp, Justin, Aristides, Irenaeus, Clement of Alexandria, Tertullian, Hippolytus, Cyprian and Origen. They also discuss the inscriptions found on the tombstones of children, dating from the third and fourth centuries.

It is generally reckoned that one of the first references to infant baptism is found in Tertullian's *De Baptismo,* written some time between 200 and 206, in which he advocates the postponement of the baptism of children and unmarried people:

> It is true that the Lord says, 'Forbid them not to come unto me.' Very well, then, let them 'come' when they are bigger (*dum adolescunt*). They may 'come' when they can learn, when they are able to be instructed whither they should 'come'; they may become Christians when they can know Christ. (Tert. *Bapt.*18.3f)

Jeremias sees here a witness to infant baptism in the fact that Tertullian is arguing 'against an established usage'.[4] Aland, on the other hand, discerns in the situation a significant tendency in Carthage towards the baptism of infants:

> About AD 200 there was a movement in that area that desired the baptism even of infants, a movement that was manifestly not very old, for Tertullian's polemic is directed against something *new;* and yet it was so powerful that Tertullian had to enter into open discussion with it.[5]

The Christian inscriptions found on the tombstones of deceased children after the year AD 200 are especially interesting, although, again, Jeremias and Aland draw opposite conclusions as to their significance. These inscriptions contain phrases such as '*Dei servus*' (slave of God), 'Χριστου δουλος' (slave of Christ), 'ἁγνον παιδον' (holy infant), 'νηπιος ἀκακος' (innocent infant) and '*decesset in pace*' (died in peace). Jeremias concludes that such attributes and symbols 'allow us to infer that we are dealing with baptised children'[6]. Among these epitaphs there is a group of four which explicitly mention the time and date of baptism – in each case shortly before death. The children of this group were of different ages at the time of baptism, from eleven months to twelve years old, and with respect to this group Jeremias concludes 'that these emergency baptisms were administered to children of non-Christians . . . whose parents were in all probability pagan'.[7]

Aland sees the tombstone inscriptions as bearing clear witness that infant baptism was not obligatory in the third century.[8] The fact that where baptismal dates are given they are all shortly before death points to the phenomenon of emergency baptism which was common in the third and fourth centuries. Aland therefore concludes that in every case where infants and young children were baptised, these were emergency baptisms administered to those in danger of death.[9]

Areas of agreement

Despite the fact that Jeremias and Aland came to opposite conclusions concerning the practice of infant baptism in the early church, one of the most valuable and interesting fruits of their discussions was the large body of information on which they were in agreement, and of which there can be said to be general consensus in the scholarly world. It will be useful to summarize these areas of agreement.

1. Lack of conclusive evidence before AD 200

Both authors are agreed that the sources from the second century do not provide conclusive evidence that infant baptism *was* practised or that it *was not* practised. The tombstone inscriptions referred to above all date from the beginning of the third century and in the early Christian writings Tertullian is generally reckoned to be the first to refer to infant baptism. Indeed, in his reply to Aland's book *Did the early church baptise infants?* Jeremias begins by protesting that he never claimed that there is any direct evidence for infant baptism before the third century, and he affirms 'the incontrovertible fact that direct evidence for the baptism of children starts only with Tertullian.'[10]

2. Existence of various baptismal practices after AD 200

Both authors are agreed that the sources provide indisputable evidence that in the third and fourth centuries both infant baptism and a delayed believers' baptism were practised side by side. Indeed we find an extraordinary range of baptismal practices in the third and fourth centuries, ranging from infant baptism to deathbed baptism and including a number of varieties in between.

3. A sacramental theology

The early church was characterized by a strongly sacramental theology of baptism. In and through baptism the various benefits of redemption were obtained: the forgiveness of sins, regeneration, the gift of the Holy Spirit and full entrance into the church. The failure to receive baptism was considered in a most serious light.

4. The catechumenate

The catechumenate was a class in which instruction was given to those desiring baptism. Both authors are agreed that from at least the third century onwards those desiring to enter the church were first enrolled as catechumens for a period of about two or three years before being baptised and received as full members of the church.

5. Emergency baptism

From the third century, at the very least, emergency baptism was administered to catechumens and unbaptised children who were in danger of death. Seeing that baptism was essential for salvation and also efficacious for salvation, it was universally agreed that it should not be withheld from those in danger of dying without it, even if they did not fulfil the normal ecclesiastical requirements for baptism.

It can be seen from the above that there is a considerable area of agreement between Jeremias and Aland concerning baptismal practices in the early church. This agreement constitutes a body of facts that can be said to have been established beyond reasonable doubt and which commands general assent throughout the Christian world. In this way Jeremias and Aland have rendered the church valuable service in establishing a body of facts about which there is general agreement and which can serve as a basis for ongoing ecumenical discussion. Having agreed on the parallel existence of various baptismal practices in the third and fourth centuries, both Jeremias and Aland are obliged to provide an explanation as to how such a situation could have arisen. It is in this interpretation of the known facts that they diverge.

Jeremias's interpretation

Jeremias identifies a crisis developing in the fourth century in a 'tendency to delay one's conversion to Christianity, if possible, to the hour of death in order to die *in albis* [free of guilt].'[11] This crisis arose in the decades following the recognition of Christianity as the religion of the state, that is in that period during which countless numbers of pagans were flocking into the church, bringing with them a superstitious conception of baptism which also had an influence on Christian circles. As a result even Christian parents began to postpone the baptism of their children. Jeremias notes: 'Gregory of Nazianzus would not have found it necessary . . . to exhort parents to have their children baptised without delay, if that had then been the general practice.'[12]

As further witness of this crisis 'in the middle of the fourth century a new phenomenon occurs on the tombstone inscriptions – the description of dead persons as neophytes (newly baptised)'.[13] Jeremias lists eight examples of children from ages one to nine on whose tombstones was inscribed *neofitus*, indicating that in all these cases baptism was administered shortly before death. Jeremias also notes that while Basil the Great and his younger brother Gregory of Nyssa sharply criticized those who go on postponing baptism, they did not baptise infants except in cases of emergency.

However despite the crisis in the fourth century and the widespread practice of delayed baptism, Jeremias finds evidence for the survival of infant baptism in the numerous Church Orders dating from that time, in the decisions of the Synod of Elvira in southern Spain (c. 306) and, above all, in the tombstone inscriptions 'concerning infants who obviously were baptised at birth'.[14] Proof of the last mentioned is the inscription '*in pace*' on the tombstones of children from seven months to four years. Further proof of the continuance of infant baptism is that heretics were said to have practised it just as the orthodox did.

Jeremias discerns an ecclesiastical reaction against the postponement of baptism beginning from about 365. After that date more witnesses in favour of infant baptism are found, such as Optatus of Milevis, Ambrose of Milan (who justifies infant baptism by appealing to the Old Testament ordinance of infant circumcision), Chrysostom, Cyril of Alexandria and Didymus the Blind. Traces of the crisis are found in the teaching of Gregory of Nazianzus who as late as 381 advises that children should normally be baptised at about the age of three 'when they can take in something of the mystery, and answer [the baptismal questions]' (Gr. Naz. *Or*.40). However Gregory's advice seemed to have had little influence on church practice, and by the time of the Pelagian controversy in the early decades of the fifth century infant baptism would appear to have been the unquestioned norm of the universal church.[15]

Aland's interpretation

In Aland's view the practice of infant baptism has its origin and rise towards the end of the second century, as testified to by sources in North Africa, Palestine and Rome. Yet even in the third century infant baptism is plainly not the rule everywhere, for in those very areas where it had secured a firm place in the church, the custom of baptising children after attaining a maturer age remained in force alongside it, as the inscriptions testify. [16] Hence the fourth century custom of 'postponing' baptism, a usage observed in circles of deep spirituality, did not originate *ex nihilo* but bears witness to the practice of baptising children of a mature age, which met with no ecclesiastical objection. Aland points out the complete unaffectedness with which Gregory of Nazianzus, at that time patriarch of Constantinople, recommended the baptism of children at the age of three years; surely he must have been conscious of remaining within the limits of what was possible and usual in the church. So the 'postponement of baptism' in the fourth century is not something new and unheard of but indeed represents the last epoch of the practice of the ancient church. However this epoch came to an end in the fourth century, and by the time of Augustine infant baptism is an established custom that cannot be gainsaid. [17]

But how is the change to infant baptism to be explained? Aland finds the key to answering this question in the doctrinal development in the early church with respect to the innocence of infants.

> So long as it is believed that children are without sin, infant baptism is not needed. For baptism is a bath of cleansing, in which a man is washed clean from his sins. If a child born of Christian parents is sinless, it does not need this bath of cleansing. As soon as the conviction becomes prevalent, however, that an infant participates in sin, even when born of Christian parents, infant baptism as a requirement or practice is unavoidable. [18]

Aland maintains that the New Testament and the Apostolic Fathers show that the primitive church regarded infants and small children as innocent. The Gospel sayings of Jesus about little children, as well as 1 Cor.7:14, are adduced. In the *Letter of Barnabas* and the *Shepherd of Hermas* he finds the presumption of the innocence of children unambiguously intimated, as indeed it is throughout the Apostolic Fathers. [19] This belief in the sinlessness of infants was held continuously till the time of Tertullian. But from the moment that the taint of original sin was believed to apply to the newborn child, its baptism became a necessity, as witnessed to in the arguments of Origen in favour of infant baptism. Echoes of the earlier view concerning the innocence and purity of children persisted in considerable areas of the church, as is hinted by the opposition of the Pelagians in the fifth century to the idea of original sin implanted in the newborn child from Adam. However, infant baptism had become so well established by that time that Augustine could argue: If children have no sin when they are born, why are they baptised?[20]

Other possibilities?

It seems to me that the explanations provided by Jeremias and Aland both have serious flaws. A key element of Aland's explanation is his theory that the early church regarded infants and small children as being without sin and therefore in no need of baptism, which was essentially 'a bath of cleansing, in which a man is washed clean from his sins.'[21] As part of the evidence cited in favour of his thesis, Aland refers to Paul's description of the children of believers as 'holy' (1 Cor.7:14) and therefore in no need of cleansing by baptism. But then what of the children of pagans? According to the same teaching of Paul, they were unclean. But if those pagan parents were then converted and cleansed of their sins by baptism, would not their children who were born in uncleanness also surely need cleansing? However, Aland makes no provision for the baptism of any infants and small children in the primitive church, and this would seem to be an inconsistency in his theory. Furthermore, Jeremias is surely correct in pointing out that the ἅγια (holy) of 1 Cor.7:14 denotes consecration to God rather than moral integrity.[22] In his writings the Apostle Paul continued the rabbinical doctrine of an evil impulse inborn in man, and although it is true that the doctrine of original sin was only worked out logically in the fourth century, yet even the Apostolic Fathers and the earlier writers were aware that 'we are not simply born into a sinful world, but we are born with a propensity toward sin'.[23]

But if Aland's explanation for the baptismal anomalies of the third and fourth centuries is flawed, the same is true for Jeremias. According to his explanation, the period following the recognition of Christianity as the religion of the state in the fourth century saw countless numbers of pagans flocking into the church with a superstitious conception of baptism which led them to delay their baptism as long as possible. This in turn influenced the Christian families to delay the baptism of their children.[24] This explanation, however, raises several problems. The first is that clear evidences that Christian children were not always baptised in infancy begin to appear from the start of the third century, more than a hundred years before the state recognition of Christianity. Moreover, the third century saw some of the fiercest persecutions of the church by the state, so it would be impossible to attribute any baptismal developments in that period to the influence of 'countless numbers of pagans flocking into the church'.

Jeremias's interpretation of the tombstone inscriptions is not always consistent, as, for example, when he states that certain children who were baptised shortly before their death were probably the children of pagan parents baptised by an emergency baptism. Why not the children of Christian parents baptised by an emergency baptism? And why would pagans be baptising their children anyway?

A further problem with Jeremias's explanation is that if the practice of infant baptism had been the rule and norm in the church for more than two centuries, it is difficult to conceive how the scruples of pagan converts in the fourth century could have induced Christian families to abandon so suddenly a custom of such long-established usage. The sheer novelty of delaying the baptism of Christian children until adulthood (which was so widespread in the fourth century as to be almost normal) when previously they had always been automatically baptised as infants is very difficult to reconcile with the high value the early church attached to customs reckoned as apostolic.

Indeed, the argument that no novelty could possibly be suddenly introduced into the church, especially in a usage of such fundamental importance as baptism, can be used against the explanations provided by both Jeremias and Aland. Against Aland it can be argued that if the primitive practice of the church was to baptise only adults, or, at the best, more mature children and adolescents, then the introduction of infant baptism would have been a sheer novelty which would certainly have been opposed vigorously and with much debate. However, there is no sign of such opposition and debate in the sources.

So if the explanations put forward by Jeremias and Aland are both unconvincing at certain points, what did then actually happen? What is the reason for the coexistence in the third and fourth centuries of infant baptism, believers' baptism and delayed baptism? How did that situation come about? Surely the apostolic church either did, or did not, baptise the infants of believers, and there cannot be any third alternative? There are modifications of Jeremias's and Aland's explanations that can be considered. Perhaps the early church baptised the children of believers at a very young age, much younger than envisaged by Aland, as soon as they were able to answer the baptismal questions themselves, and that child baptism later developed into infant baptism. Or perhaps the early church did baptise infants with their parents, but with the delay of baptism a few years for the purpose of instruction, the baptism of infants was also delayed a few years. In this way the postponement of baptism came about, not as a result of pagan influence, as suggested by Jeremias, but as a result of internal developments within the Christian church. At this point in this book it will be useful to consider more carefully some of the known developments that occurred in the baptismal practices of the early church, to see what light they throw on the question in discussion.

Developments and variations in the baptismal practices of the early church

We have already seen that the baptism of the New Testament was an immediate baptism. Whatever else we might know, or not know, about the apostolic practice of baptism, this much is certain: there was no delay in its administration; it was given immediately to those desiring it, wherever they were, whatever time of the day or night it was, and by whoever was available to administer it. Every recorded instance of baptism in the New Testament bears out this fact. This is why baptism in the New Testament was so closely tied to all the richness implied by Christian salvation. Baptism was baptism into Christ and all the benefits of his redemption, adoption, forgiveness, cleansing from sin, eternal life. Baptism was incorporation into the body of Christ, a baptism of the Holy Spirit into the one body of the risen Lord. And seeing that Christian salvation is by grace through faith (Eph.2:8), baptism is linked to these too. The immediacy of baptism, given without conditions or testing, manifests the grace of the gospel, the gift of God given freely to all who believe. The role of faith in salvation is manifested in the baptismal confession that Jesus is Lord, the Son of God who died to save us.

1. Delay

The first significant development to be observed in the baptismal practice of the church was the delay of the baptism of converts, and the imposition of certain tests both of a doctrinal and practical kind. This development might well have been the fruit of a growing spirit of asceticism and legalism in the early post-apostolic church. The following description by Lietzmann of the procedure followed when a convert requested baptism is probably true already of the second century:

> If he were converted, he reported himself to the 'teachers' of the church as a catechumen. Then there came a serious testing; he had to declare what moved him to make the change and become a Christian, and his Christian friends had

to give a sort of guarantee for him. Then his outer relationships in life were tested, and the first requirement laid upon him was that he should avoid every form of non-conjugal intercourse. If he were the slave of a Christian master, he must be recommended by that master as worthy of reception; if he served a pagan, faithful labour became a duty for him for the sake of the good reputation of the Christians.[25]

Clearly the conviction was developing in the church that those desiring baptism must first prove themselves worthy to receive it.

2. *Elaboration of the rite*

The spontaneity and immediacy with which baptism was first administered meant of necessity that the rite was kept simple; a simple washing in water as the latter was available. The pragmatic instructions of the *Didache*: 'If no running water is available, immerse in ordinary water. This should be cold if possible; otherwise warm. If neither is practicable, then sprinkle water three times on the head' (*Did*.7) bear witness to the primitive practice. If an adequate quantity and quality of water are not immediately available, then the best must be done with what there is so that baptism be not unnecessarily delayed. Concerning the performance of baptism there seems to be no restriction in the New Testament as to who did it. On the contrary, as has already been observed, baptism by lay persons (to use an anachronism for apostolic times) would seem to have been normal.

However, as the practice of delaying baptism gained favour it is understandable that a psychological need arose to 'improve' upon the simplicity of the earlier rite so that the ceremony that climaxed the period of careful testing and instruction should be suitably awesome and impressive. Naturally, as Ignatius instructed the Smyrnaeans, only the bishop could be entrusted with the performance of the rite, or at least those authorized by him (Ign. *Smyrn*.8). The following description by Lietzmann gives an idea of the considerable elaboration of the baptismal rite that had occurred as early as the second century:

> The candidate for baptism was made ready by a fast which lasted one or two days, and which was shared by certain friends. Then the baptismal water was purified by exorcising the elemental spirits which dwelt in it, and was prepared for the sacred ceremony . . . [in a special rite of exorcism] the priest placed his hand upon him, blew on him, anointed his forehead, ears, and nose: this was followed by a renewed fast for the night. Early in the morning, at cock-crow, the baptism began; . . . after the candidate had undressed, he was required first of all solemnly to abjure Satan and all his service and works, to which hitherto he had been subject; thereupon he was once more anointed with the exorcising oil. Then he went down into the water, and gave the new oath of service, the

'sacramentum', to his new Lord by uttering the three-fold baptismal creed, whereupon he was plunged three times beneath the water . . . Afterwards, all passed from the place of baptism into the church, where the bishop transferred the gift of the Holy Spirit to the newly baptised by laying on of hands, anointing, making the sign of the cross, and a kiss.[26]

The *Apostolic Tradition* of Hippolytus, composed about 217, and many other baptismal liturgies dating from the third century onwards, all show that the baptismal rite had developed into a ceremony worthy of the great event it both signified and mediated. This, of course, could only happen when the delay of baptism made possible the necessary planning and preparation of the occasion. Among many other detailed instructions, the *Apostolic Tradition* of Hippolytus also contains the following: 'When they have removed their clothing, then first baptise the little ones. Those who can speak for themselves shall do so; if not, their parents or some other relative shall speak for them. Then baptise the men. . . .' Was this a reference to the baptism of infants, or simply to young children, able to speak, but overcome with shyness and needing some adult assistance? Arguments have been brought forward for both interpretations.

3.　Ritual efficacy

It has been seen that New Testament baptism is a rite of salvation, grace and faith. But in apostolic thinking the power of baptism is not so much in the outward rite, the washing of water, but in that which is expressed in and through the rite – the resurrection of Jesus Christ, the grace and power of the Holy Spirit, faith in the gospel. The apostle Peter deliberately plays down the purely outward aspect of washing with water alone (1 Pet. 3:21). One of the most significant developments in the baptismal teaching of the early church was the tendency to exalt the outward, material aspect of the baptismal rite as efficacious of itself in the bestowal of grace. In this way attention was focused on the power of the water, or the oil of chrismation, or the hands of the bishop, rather than on the efficacy of faith and repentance in obtaining the grace of God. An example of this can be seen in the following extracts from the *De Baptismo* of Tertullian:

> Thus the nature of the waters, having received holiness from the Holy, itself conceived power to make holy. . . . All waters, when God is invoked, acquire the sacred significance of conveying sanctity: for at once the Spirit comes down from heaven and stays upon the waters, sanctifying them from within himself, and when thus sanctified they absorb the power of sanctifying. . . . Thus when the waters have in some sense acquired healing power by an angel's intervention, the spirit is in those waters corporally washed, while the flesh is in those same waters spiritually cleansed (Tert. *Bapt.* 4).

Tertullian goes on to explain that the efficacy of the water extends only to the forgiveness of sins; the Holy Spirit is given with the act of chrismation and the laying on of hands of the bishop. Tertullian was certainly not alone in these sentiments, although there was some confusion and difference of opinion as to whether the Holy Spirit was given in the washing of water or the laying on of hands immediately after. That such confusion should arise was inevitable, given the elaboration of the rites and the exaltation of their efficacy. The significance of Paul's question to the Galatians, 'Did you receive the Spirit by observing the law, or by believing what you heard?' (Gal. 3:2) seems to have been lost in the post-apostolic church to a large extent. Baptism was the occasion of the Galatians' reception of the Spirit, and the vital element of *that* baptism was faith in the message heard.

When the understanding of baptism as a rite of salvation overshadows or even eclipses its function as a rite of faith then the New Testament balance between the human and the divine, between salvation, grace and faith, is upset. And when this is coupled with the conviction of the absolute necessity of baptism, the way is opened for further developments, some of them quite bizarre. Lietzmann, for example, reports a practice that developed in the case of a convert dying before baptism. 'The corpse was baptised, and another person gave the answers to the liturgical questions instead of the dead. In many places, even the Lord's Supper was administered to the dead man.' [27] Even those who were 'baptised for the dead' in Paul's time (1 Cor. 15:29) were probably guilty of a similar misunderstanding, confusing salvation with the rite of washing alone. Baptism is indeed a rite of salvation – when the washing with water signifies an appeal to God for salvation through Christ.

4. No forgiveness after baptism

With the elaboration of the rite to an impressive and awesome ceremony, and in the light of the careful and painstaking preparation for that momentous event over a prolonged period of time, it is unthinkable that the solemn vows and promises so made could be dishonoured by later unfaithfulness and sin. And if such should occur, the conviction grew that there could be no further forgiveness for such apostasy. And so it was that 'a powerful current of thought in the second-century church favoured the view that no remission was possible for sins deliberately committed after baptism'. [28] This view found scriptural justification from the passage in Hebrews, 'It is impossible for those who have once been enlightened ($\phi\omega\tau\iota\sigma\theta\epsilon\nu\tau\alpha\varsigma$) . . . if they fall away, to be brought back to repentance' (Heb. 6:4–8). Hence the pardon that was obtained in baptism, which effected an actual sinlessness, was to be carefully maintained. To lessen the harshness of such a teaching, in practice the custom became established of permitting the forgiveness of one failure after baptism, but only one, and that on condition of public confession.[29]

It is very understandable that belief in such a doctrine would make parents hesitate to have their children baptised, knowing that any falling away from the faith would be irredeemable.

5. Extended delay

It is easy to see the inevitable result of the previous development – a prolonged postponement of baptism, even until just before death, so that reasonable assurance might be had of dying in the purity of baptismal forgiveness, unsullied by any post-baptismal sin. The reason for this delay is quite different, of course, from the delay noted earlier. That delay was for the purpose of testing and instructing the candidate, and was imposed by the church. This extended delay was self-imposed and was the result of a fear that temptation to sin after baptism might prove too strong and thus cause the irreparable loss of baptismal grace and eternal life. This tendency to delay baptism for as long as possible became especially widespread in the fourth century, and was, for a time, very common. It was practised by pagans entering the church, fearful of falling back into old pagan habits, as well as by children of believers, wanting first to pass through the storms and temptations of youth before receiving a baptismal absolution that could never be repeated or renewed if once it was lost. In the latter case parental guidance and advice strongly influenced the delay of baptism. Clearly the concept of sin functioning behind this practice was very formalized and superficial, a view which regarded sin as certain outward deeds. This is usually the case when religion moves in a legalistic direction, as was the case, to a large extent, in the post-apostolic church.

6. Emergency baptism

We must now begin to take note of the simultaneous and parallel development of divergent practices in baptism. The trend towards the delay and even the extended delay of baptism has already been noted. There might also have been a trend in the opposite direction towards the baptism of children at an ever younger age for quite a different set of reasons. What we do know of, beyond any doubt, was the practice of emergency baptism.

Given the practice of delaying baptism and the conviction of the necessity of baptism for salvation, the problem inevitably arose of the catechumen who had not yet completed the required period of instruction and who then fell ill and was in danger of death. To die without baptism meant to die in one's sins unforgiven and unregenerate, and thus to suffer eternal loss. To avoid such a tragedy the one who was ill would hastily be baptised by an 'emergency baptism'. Augustine, for example, in his *Confessions* relates how as a boy he fell seriously ill, and being in danger of death, he was about to be baptised when suddenly he recovered so that his baptism was again postponed (Aug. *Conf*.1.11).

The same reasoning would have applied in the case of children. If and wherever it was the regular practice that children were baptised only after receiving a prescribed course of instruction so that they could answer the baptismal questions, what if they fell dangerously ill and were in danger of death? Several factors would have virtually demanded the administration of emergency baptism to children – the natural parental solicitude for the eternal welfare of their children; the prevailing notion of the necessity of baptism for salvation; and the growing belief in the efficacy and power of the rites themselves to convey the grace and blessings of redemption. It would have been impossible for the church to resist the popular pressure for the emergency baptism of sickly children, given the twin convictions of both the necessity and the efficacy of baptism. Mountain reports the case of Galetes, the son of the Emperor Valens, who died in the year 379. 'This child was evidently at the point of death; and his father "swore" with an oath that it should not forfeit eternal happiness for lack of baptism; and so he compelled an unwilling bishop to administer the ceremony.' [30]

One thing is certain: there were many children of varying ages who were baptised with an emergency baptism shortly before their death. Is this evidence that children were enrolled as catechumens, preparing for baptism at an appropriate time according to apostolic tradition, or is it evidence of a crisis in the church resulting in parents delaying the baptism of their children instead of having them baptised as infants according to apostolic practice?

7. *Infant baptism*

If infant baptism was a post-apostolic development, the step from the extraordinary, emergency baptism of children in danger of death to the regular baptism of infants would have been both a small and a logical one, especially when the high rate of infant mortality in the ancient world is taken into account. The anxiety experienced by Christian parents, for both the temporal as well as the eternal welfare of their children, is easy to imagine. Life was precarious and death often sudden. Although the provision of emergency baptism was made available by the church, yet unexpected death could supervene even before that gracious provision could be availed of.

Basil Moss describes an early woodcut which vividly illustrates the tensions and anxieties we have been referring to:

> On the right of the picture is the baptistery, where a bishop is plunging a naked infant into the font. . . . Parents, sponsors, acolytes stand around in various attitudes of edification. On the left is the nave of the church; here another christening party is seen, suddenly halted with expressions and gestures of horror and dismay, just before the entrance to the baptistery; in their midst a nurse holds the corpse of an infant, who was being brought to baptism, but has that very moment unexpectedly died on the very verge of receiving the sacrament of regeneration, and whose soul must therefore be presumed to have gone straight to hell, in virtue of original sin. The picture is surmounted by a scroll, bearing the inscription *Unus assumitur et alter relinqitur; Quia magna est gratia Dei, et verax iustitia Dei* [One is taken and the other left; how great is God's mercy, and true his judgement].[31]

Moss's interpretation might seem somewhat over-dramatic, yet it accurately captures something of the concern felt by many early Christians for the unbaptised, whether adults or infants. The very reason that baptism should be given to newly born infants on the second or third day rather than the eighth, wrote Cyprian to Fides, was: 'as far as we can, we must strive that, if possible, no soul be lost' (Cyp. *Ep*.64.2). As infant baptism became widespread, 'the less there was heard of the catechumenate. It was finally compressed into a brief rite to be performed at the church door before the baptism of an infant'.[32]

8. *Two baptismal practices*

As a result of developments in the understanding of the nature of baptism, there arose in the third and more especially in the fourth century two divergent baptismal practices existing side by side in the church. On the one hand, anxiety that baptismal grace might be lost by post-baptismal sin led to its prolonged delay. On the other hand, anxiety that sudden premature death would result in the eternal loss of an unbaptised child led to the baptism of infants as soon after birth as possible. We must note, of course, that while delayed baptism was clearly a post-apostolic development, we cannot with the same certainty identify infant baptism as a post-apostolic development. In the immediate baptisms of whole households recorded in the New Testament, infants might have been included. Philip Schaff made the following comments on the divergent baptismal practices found in the early church:

> It was in a measure the same view of the almost magical effect of the baptismal water, and of its absolute necessity to salvation, which led Cyprian to hasten, and Tertullian to postpone the holy ordinance; one looking more at the

beneficent effect of the sacrament in regard to past sins, the other at the danger of sins to come.[33]

In considering the *Apostolic Tradition* of Hippolytus, the Roman Catholic scholar Robert Grant comes to a similar conclusion concerning the development of two divergent practices in the church:

> Evidently, then, there were two developments in baptismal practice. On the one hand, adult baptism had been combined with an extended period of instruction, longer than what we could infer from the *Didache* and Justin. On the other hand, the practice of child baptism had arisen along with adult baptism. Apparently this baptism was as a rule for children rather than for infants, although infants seem not to have been excluded.[34]

It must be noted that no divergent practice (whether delayed baptism, infant baptism, or both) appeared in the church suddenly, as a complete novelty, but only gradually, in an evolutionary way. Therefore it is impossible to point to a clear date when a new practice was introduced. There is no such date. This explains why no evidence can be found of any violent debate or protest, objecting to the introduction of novelties in the church. There was no such debate. There was no reason for it. What can be found in the sources are cautionary exhortations against this or that tendency which was perceived to be divergent from the apostolic tradition. We find Tertullian, for example, cautioning against both tendencies. On the one hand he urges those unnecessarily postponing their baptism to get baptised. On the other hand he advises the delay of baptism in certain cases, namely young children and unmarried young adults. On balance we would have to class Tertullian among those who contributed towards the extended delay of baptism, and his advice possibly influenced the prevalence of that practice in the fourth century. In the fourth century there are many voices of protest against the prolonged postponement of baptism, and while some church leaders such as Chrysostom advocated the baptism of infants, others such as Gregory of Nazianzus advocated the baptism of children when they could make their own responses. All, however, were agreed that in the case of infants in danger of death 'It is better to be consecrated without knowing it than to depart unsealed and uninitiated.'[35]

9. *The triumph of infant baptism*

After the fourth century the practice of delayed baptism largely died away, at least in the catholic church, while the practice of infant baptism prevailed and became the norm for the children of believers. The following reasons can be advanced for this development:

(a) The earlier rigid discipline, which rejected the possibility of forgiveness for sins committed after baptism, gave way to a more lenient and reasonable discipline as the church grew in size and numbers, and especially after it became the favoured religion of the state with the conversion of Constantine. As the practice of penance for the forgiveness of sins after baptism grew in acceptance, so the pressure for the delay of baptism withered away.

(b) The continuing convictions concerning the absolute necessity of baptism and the efficacy of the rites in themselves provided both the logic and the motivation for infant baptism, before which the practice of delaying baptism gradually gave way.

(c) The last-named process was completed by the full development of the doctrine of original sin in the course of the Pelagian controversy. The following two conclusions of the Council of Carthage held in 417 make this point clear: 'If any one says that new-born children need not be baptised, or that no original sin is derived from Adam to be washed away in the laver of regeneration . . . let him be anathema . . . if any one says that there is in the Kingdom of Heaven, or in any other place, any middle place, where children who depart this life unbaptised live in bliss . . . let him be anathema.'[36] Clearly in the light of such convictions it would be cruelty itself to withhold salvation from helpless infants when it is in the power of the church to give it through baptism. It is not surprising that not long thereafter the baptism of infants became compulsory by imperial law.

In 1987 David Wright, then a senior lecturer in Ecclesiastical History at the University of Edinburgh, published an article in the *Scottish Journal of Theology* entitled *The Origins of Infant Baptism – Child Believers' Baptism?*[37] In it he examined the discussion between Aland and Jeremias on the issue of infant baptism in the early church and makes the following concluding remarks:

> So the baptism of babies in families converted to Christianity may have begun early in the apostolic age, although the baptism of babies born to Christian parents probably did not. The latter may have developed out of the emergency baptism of infants some time in the second century, or out of the practice of baptising very young children who could answer for themselves. In so far as more of the evidence points to young children belonging to the Christian community alongside their elders and hence presumably on the same basis of faith-baptism, the extension of children's baptism to baby baptism is becoming an increasingly attractive hypothesis.[38]

Wright's observations and reflections on the Jeremias/Aland debate are interesting as they again reflect the ambiguity of the earliest sources and the difficulty scholars have in interpreting them.

The cultural factor

Having reviewed the development of various baptismal practices, the question remains: why did these developments take place? How is it that changes can occur in the understanding and practice of baptism? There are no simple or easy answers to such questions. But one important factor must be the cultural factor, and in the case we are considering, the transition of the church from the Jewish culture of Palestine to the predominantly Greek culture of the Roman world.

An understanding of the complex psychological and sociological processes involved in the transference of religious ideas from one culture to another is a vital key to understanding the development of Christian doctrine in the early church. The Jewish mind in New Testament times had been trained up and conditioned by a two thousand year old heritage of biblical thinking that was pervaded by concepts of monotheism, revelation, grace and law, judgement and salvation. The Greek mind, on the other hand, had been deeply influenced by its own heritage of paganism, metaphysical speculation and philosophy. The very languages of Hebrew and Greek had been shaped by their cultural milieus. The difficulties of transferring religious concepts from the one to the other were immense. It is, in fact, impossible to translate concepts from one culture to another without those same concepts undergoing certain subtle changes. And this is precisely what happened with the transmission of Christian doctrine and faith from Jewish to Greek culture. 'In the process of transmission the expression of that faith changed beyond what many an outsider might recognise.'[39]

If we apply this principle now to baptism, it can be said that the Gentile Christians received customs and doctrines which they did not, indeed could not, fully understand.[40] And even though they could read and study the basic Christian documents, the Septuagint and the New Testament, yet 'too often they read the Greek Bible through the eyes of Greek philosophy without realising that they were wearing tinted – or tainted – spectacles'.[41] So it was that in the transmission of the gospel from Jew to Greek something of the original, finely tuned, theological balance could have been lost. The church continued to speak of baptism as salvation, as the apostles had done; but the focus was now more on the rite itself than on the faith and repentance expressed in the rite. The Pauline concept of grace, manifested in the immediate administration of baptism to those desiring it, was reinterpreted as a new law whereby proof of worthiness and purity of life was required as a condition for the grace of baptism. Baptism no longer witnessed quite so clearly to the good news of salvation by grace thorough faith.

Conclusions

Before closing this chapter a few remarks need to be made concerning its significance for the overall purpose and goal of this book. Although we do not have clarity about all the details, if the general pattern of development in baptismal practice outlined above is an accurate interpretation of the historical sources then it must be concluded that *all* contemporary baptismal practices are a development of the apostolic baptism of the New Testament, and that no church today can claim to be administering baptism 'as the apostles did in the New Testament'.

Certainly the vast majority of those churches practising believers' baptism (understood in the sense of rejecting infant baptism) cannot make such a claim, as their baptism is essentially a delayed baptism, whether the delay is a few days, a few months or a few years. Furthermore, their baptism differs in function from the New Testament baptism, being a baptism of witness, in which the candidate bears witness to salvation already received through Christ by a decision previously made, rather than a baptism of salvation in which the candidate actually receives salvation through Christ.

Delayed baptism is also practised by paedobaptist churches with respect to converts coming to Christ from a non-Christian background. The enrolling of such converts into a catechumenate to receive instruction and preparation for baptism is common to all churches, whether they be of a Baptist, Catholic or Reformed type. Furthermore, it can be said that in all Christian churches the administration of baptism is reserved to special ministers, special times and special places. Whether it be during a Sunday service by a minister (Baptist, Presbyterian), or in a baptistery by a priest (Roman Catholic), or in a river by a prophet (African Independent), or in a swimming pool at a charismatic fellowship meeting – all of these have a certain structure and planning about them which is remarkably lacking in the New Testament instances of baptism. As we have seen above, the pattern in the New Testament seems to be that baptism was administered to whoever desired it, wherever they happened to be, immediately, and by whoever was available to administer it.

Such a conclusion demands a certain humility on the part of all participants in the discussion and debate over baptism. None of us can claim:

'We practise New Testament baptism.' All of us must acknowledge that our practices differ from those in apostolic times. Does this mean that we are all wrong? Not at all. As already pointed out in Chapter 3, the categories 'wrong' and 'right' are not helpful in the area of contemporary baptismal practices. To explore strengths and weaknesses is more helpful. Furthermore, the possibility that certain developments were both legitimate and necessary cannot be excluded. The development of the catechumate, for example, in the early post-apostolic period, might well have been the correct thing to do in the given circumstances. In Aland's view the practice of infant baptism in the church today is 'both needful and legitimate',[42] even though he considers it a post-apostolic development.

Rather than conclude that we are all wrong, it would be better to conclude that we are all right, or partially right at least, insofar as every contemporary baptismal practice preserves some vital aspect of New Testament baptism. The Catholic approach to baptism with its strongly sacramental character preserves the New Testament emphasis that baptism is salvation, no mere symbol but the very means whereby the grace of Christ is received. The Baptist approach to baptism bears witness to the New Testament reality that acceptance of baptism is an act of faith, an appeal to God for salvation through Jesus Christ in the belief that Jesus is the Saviour. The Reformed approach to baptism underlines the primacy of grace in all God's dealings with human beings. Baptism is grace, the gracious act of a God who loved us before ever we loved him, who chose us before we chose him, and who gathers his people as a covenant community of redeemed people, a community that embraces all, from old to young, in the eternal covenant of grace.

From this basis, the humble acknowledgment that none of us is 'wrong' and that none of us has 'got it all', we can engage in authentic dialogue towards reconciliation and unity. This dialogue will then not be pursued from some lofty position of absolute truth, seeking ways in which we can tolerate the errors of weaker brothers and sisters, but from a common base of weakness, deeply conscious of our fragmentation, partial knowledge, and need of one another for wholeness.

Notes

1   A. König, *Die doop as kinderdoop én grootdoop* (Pretoria, NGKB, 1986), p.44. translation.
2   Ibid., p.46.

3   G. Beasley-Murray, *Baptism in the New Testament* (London, Macmillan, 1962), p.267.

4   J. Jeremias, *Infant Baptism in the first four centuries* (London, SCM, 1960), p.83.

5   K. Aland, *Did the early church baptise infants?* (London, SCM, 1963), p.69.

6   J. Jeremias, *Infant Baptism in the first four centuries* (London, SCM, 1960), p.80.

7   Ibid.

8   K. Aland, *Did the early church baptise infants?* (London, SCM, 1963), p.79.

9   Ibid., p.76.

10 J. Jeremias, *The Origins of Infant Baptism* (London, SCM, 1963), p.9.

11 J. Jeremias, *Infant Baptism in the first four centuries* (London, SCM, 1960), p.87.

12 Ibid., p.89.

13 Ibid.

14 Ibid., p.92–3.

15 Ibid., p.94–7.

16 K. Aland, *Did the early church baptise infants?* (London, SCM, 1963), p.100.

17 Ibid., p.101.

18 Ibid., p.104.

19 Ibid., p.105.

20 Ibid., p.107.

21 Ibid., p.104.

22 J. Jeremias, *The Origins of Infant Baptism* (London, SCM, 1963), p.81.

23 D.G. Bloesch, 'Sin,' in W.A. Elwell (ed.), *Evangelical Dictionary of Theology* (Grand Rapids, Baker, 1984), p.1013.

24 J. Jeremias, *Infant Baptism in the first four centuries* (London, SCM, 1960), p.95.

25 H. Lietzmann, *A History of the Early Church Vol. II* (London, Lutterworth, 1967b), p.151.

26 Ibid., p.132.

27 H. Lietzmann, *A History of the Early Church Vol. I* (London, Lutterworth, 1967a), p.141.

28 J.N.D. Kelly, *Early Christian Doctrines* (London, A & C Black, 1980), p.198.

29 A. Harnack, *History of Dogma Vol. II* (London, Williams & Norgate, 1896), p.109.

30 J. Mountain, *My Baptism* (London, James Clarke, [s. a.]), p.157.

31 B.S. Moss (ed.), *Crisis for Baptism; The Report of the 1965 Ecumenical Conference sponsored by the Parish and People Movement* (London, SCM, 1965), p.35.

32 P. Toon, 'Catechumens,' in J.D. Douglas (ed.), *The New International Dictionary of the Christian Church* (Exeter, Paternoster, 1974), p.201.

33 P. Schaff, *History of the Christian Church. Vol. 1* (USA, A P & A, [s. a.]), p.119.

34 R.M. Grant, 'Development of the Christian Catechumate,' in *Made, Not Born* (The Murphy Centre for Liturgical Research, Notre Dame, Notre Dame Press, 1976), p.35.

35 Ibid., p.37.

36 H. Bettenson, *Documents of the Christian Church* (Oxford, University Press, 1975), p.59.

37 D.F. Wright, 'The Origins of Infant Baptism – Child Believers' Baptism?' *Scottish Journal of Theology* 1 (1987):1–23.

38 Ibid., p.22.

39 A.F. Walls, 'Culture and coherence in Christian history,' *Scottish Bulletin of Evangelical Theology* 1 (1985), p.1.

40 Ibid., p.99.

41 D.F. Wright, 'Christian Faith in the Greek World: Justin Martyr's Testimony' *Evangelical Journal of Theology* 1 (1982), p.77.

42 K. Aland, *Did the early church baptise infants?* (London, SCM, 1963), p.110.

Chapter 5

Baptism and Unity

T.F. Torrance begins the foreword to his book, *Theology in Reconciliation*, with these words:

> Any theology which is faithful to the Church of Jesus Christ within which it takes place cannot but be a theology of reconciliation, for reconciliation belongs to the essential nature and mission of the Church in the world. By taking its rise from God's mighty acts in reconciling the world to himself in Christ, the Church is constituted 'a community of the reconciled', and in being sent by Christ into the world to proclaim what God has done in him, the Church is constituted a reconciling as well as a reconciled community. The task of theology is made more difficult, however, by the fact that although the Church has been sent into the divided world in the service of reconciliation it has allowed the divisions of the world to penetrate back into itself so its own unity in mind and body has been damaged, and its mission of reconciliation in the world has been seriously impaired. It is incumbent upon theology, therefore, to find ways of overcoming disunity within the Church as part of its service to reconciliation in the world, . . . Christian theology is thus inescapably evangelical and ecumenical.[1]

The work of God through Christ in the world is a work of restoration reconciliation, and reuniting into one that which has been broken and divided by sin. 'The reason the Son of God appeared was to destroy the devil's work' (1 Jn 3:8). The devil's work is sin, which has shattered the original unity of God's creation and fragmented humankind into countless hostile camps at war with one another: nation against nation, tribe against tribe, race against race, family against family, brother against brother. Every conceivable difference between people has become a potential flashpoint for hatred, alienation and conflict, whether the distinctions be linguistic, economic, ideological or religious. Christ came not only to destroy the works of the devil, but to reverse the tragic consequences of human sin; not only to heal the brokenness of individuals, alienated from God and one another, but also to heal humanity itself, to bring together the scattered children of God and make them one (Jn.11:52), 'to bring all things in heaven and on earth together under one head, even Christ' (Eph.1:10). There is a universal and even cosmic dimension to the saving work of Christ as well as the personal and individual one. The purpose of God is nothing less than through Christ 'to reconcile to himself all things, whether things on earth or things in heaven, by making peace through his blood, shed on the cross' (Col.1:20).

In the scriptural passages touching the purpose of God in Christ for the world we find a continual refrain of 'bringing together into one', emphasizing the restoration to unity and wholeness of that which was broken and divided by sin. This is why the issue of unity is of such profound importance for the Christian church. 'Its oneness is given by God precisely to restore into unity all the diversity of His creation; its Catholicity is precisely this capacity of unity to save, to fulfil, to bring back all humanity.' [2] Now if reconciliation and unity lie at the very heart of God's work in the world, through Christ and through the church, then baptism is pre-eminently the sacrament of reconciliation and unity. Through baptism men and women are being incorporated into the unity of the 'one new humanity' in Christ (Eph.2:15). 'For we were all baptised by one Spirit into one body – whether Jews or Greeks, slaves or free – and we were all given the one Spirit to drink' (1 Cor.12:13). But before we pursue this line of thought any further we need to reflect somewhat on the biblical emphasis on unity.

The biblical emphasis on unity

The ecumenical movement is generally reckoned to have had its beginnings at the International Missionary Conference at Edinburgh in 1910. Since that time many churches have been deeply involved in discussions around the theme of Christian unity and a considerable body of literature has grown up on the subject. But a significant number of churches, largely of a conservative evangelical nature, have remained outside this movement and are often hostile to, or, at the least, suspicious of it. There have been a number of reasons for this new evangelical/ecumenical divide – theological, sociological and political reasons. Professor Peter Beyerhaus of the University of Tübingen, for example, has charged: 'The goal of the boldest ecumenical thinkers and leaders has grown increasingly clear: to construct a world community embracing all races, classes, religions, and political systems, united as far as possible under a common world government whose business will be the establishment of world peace.' [3] In a book entitled *The*

Fraudulent Gospel, Bernard Smith, at that time National Secretary of the Christian Affirmation Campaign in the United Kingdom, wrote: 'For some Christians this fraudulent theology is sufficient proof that the WCC is Anti-Christ since it fulfils St. Paul's prediction (2 Thes.2:11) that even the believers shall believe a lie.'[4] Smith's book was chiefly concerned with the grant of financial assistance by the WCC, the chief vehicle of the ecumenical movement, to liberation movements employing violence in their struggle to gain power.

These two quotations illustrate how deeply emotive and contentious the issue of ecumenism has become in some evangelical circles. For many, the very word 'ecumenical' has strongly negative overtones, and one of the sad consequences of this is that many other words that have become associated with ecumenism have also become suspect – words like unity, dialogue, cooperation, and reconciliation. It is especially sad that Christians deeply devoted to the Bible should be blinded, to some extent, to the theme of reconciliation and unity, which is so deeply embedded in the very heart of the Bible. Because this book is written from a perspective that is deeply rooted in the conservative evangelical world, and for the sake of those readers who share this heritage, there follows here a brief consideration of the biblical emphasis on unity.

One God, one body

Like Israel of old, the church bears witness to the world: 'Hear, O Israel: the Lord our God, the Lord is one' (Dt.6:4). And a vital aspect of the church's testimony to the unity of God is its own unity. In the words of Hans Küng:

> The unity of the Church is a spiritual entity. It is not chiefly a unity of the members among themselves, it depends finally not on itself but on the unity of God, which is efficacious through Jesus Christ in the Holy Spirit. It is one and the same God who gathers the scattered from all places and all ages and makes them into one people of God. It is one and the same Christ who through his word and his Spirit unites all together in the same bond of fellowship. It is one and same baptism by which all are made members of the same body of Christ and with one another. It is one and the same confession of faith in the Lord Jesus, the same hope of blessedness, the same love, which is experienced in oneness of heart, the same service of the world. The Church *is* one and therefore *should be* one.[5]

It was because of this powerful link between Christian unity and the unity of God that the Apostle Paul urged the Christians in Ephesus so strongly to be 'endeavouring earnestly (σπουδαζοντες) to keep the unity of the Spirit through the bond of peace' (Eph.4:3). Disunity among Christians amounts to a denial of the very message of the church, which is a message of reconciliation. Paul was entirely realistic about the forces at work in the world and in the church to bring about division and disunity, 'the cunning and craftiness of men in their deceitful scheming' (Eph.4:14). Hence his reference to the extraordinary effort required to maintain the unity already acquired. Paul also recognized that this unity, in the horizontal dimension of human experience, was neither perfect nor complete. Rather, it was something growing, even as the body of Christ was being built up 'until we all reach unity in faith and in the Son of God and become mature, attaining to the whole measure of the fullness of Christ' (Eph.4:13). The unity attained and experienced by believers was something to be cherished, maintained and increased. We can see a certain parallel here between unity and holiness. Each is both the gift of God to his people *and* their status in Christ. Both are a goal after which believers strive. The spiritual unity of the church is both real and to be realized.

Unity and evangelism

A major plank in the platform of Evangelicals has always been a strong and enthusiastic commitment to missions and evangelism. Indeed, the conviction is sometimes expressed in such circles that all the effort and time spent in ecumenical deliberations is really so much wasted time that could more profitably be employed in reaching out to the lost to win them for Christ. Yet in biblical thinking it is a false dichotomy to posit evangelism over against unity. The two are inseparably connected. Nowhere is this more clearly illustrated than in the prayer of Jesus recorded in John 17. There he prays for the church of the future, those 'who will believe in me through their message, that all of them may be one, Father, just as you are in me and I am in you. May they also be in us so that the world may believe that you have sent me' (Jn.17:20,21). It is precisely the unity of the church, a unity in love, a unity in God and in Christ that gives the church credibility in its message to a divided and broken world. How can a divided and quarrelling church speak convincingly of the love of God and reconciliation in Christ?

Like Paul after him, Jesus foresaw a process of growth and development in unity. Thus he prayed: 'May they be brought to complete unity to let the world know that you sent me and have loved them even as you have loved me' (Jn.17:23). It is not so much the perfection of Christians as their ability to work together in seeking solutions to the problems threatening to divide them that is the evidence of the power of the Holy Spirit among them and of the divine origin of their faith. In the tough ideological market place of the world, it is not noble ideas that count so much as solid, concrete evidence of a love and unity that can transcend the petty, banal and persistent forces of division and hatred which so fragment and impoverish the world.

The scandal and sin of disunity

If Christian unity – real, visible, practical and experiential unity – was so important to the apostolic community in the New Testament, then clearly schism and disunity was a scandal and a tragedy. Schism would be akin to divorce, a tearing apart what God has joined together, something which cannot occur without sin and damage to all parties, something which grieves the Holy Spirit. Hence we can understand the deep indignation felt by Paul when news reached him of the quarrels and party spirit in the church at Corinth, leading him to lament: 'One of you says, "I follow Paul"; another, "I follow Cephas"; another, "I follow Apollos"; another, "I follow Christ" ' (1 Cor.1:12). In 1 Corinthians Paul deals with many important and weighty matters, but it is striking that the very first issue he addresses is that of divisions in the church. He begins with a strong appeal for unity: 'I appeal to you, brothers, in the name of our Lord Jesus Christ, that all of you agree with one another so that there may be no divisions among you and that you may be perfectly united in mind and thought' (1 Cor.1:10). A little later he berates them for their lack of growth towards maturity: 'You are still worldly. For since there is jealousy and quarrelling among you, are you not worldly? Are you not following human inclinations? For when one says, "I follow Paul," and another, "I follow Apollos," are you not merely human?' (1 Cor.3:3,4). Paul continues to deal, directly or indirectly, with the issue of Christian unity in the first four chapters of this letter. Then, after he has turned his attention to other serious matters – such as gross immorality in the church, lawsuits among believers, problems relating to mixed marriages, food offered to idols, propriety in worship, and the eucharistic meal – Paul returns once more to the subject of unity. Although chapters 12 to 14 ostensibly deal with the issue of spiritual gifts in the church, at a deeper and more profound level they are concerned with maintaining unity and love in the context of a diversity of gifts and ministries. We may conclude that the one issue that stands out above all others in this letter is Paul's concern 'that there may be no divisions among you and that you may be perfectly united in mind and thought' (1 Cor.1:10).

The justification of disunity

In the face of the powerful biblical exhortations in favour of unity and love, and against schism and division, it is astonishing how Christians (especially Protestants) have lightly justified ecclesiastical divisions. Gordon Rupp, for example, one of Methodism's most eminent historians, once spoke of the 'painless extraction' of Methodism from within the Church of England. But Methodism's separation from Anglicanism was far from painless, and, furthermore, was followed by a process of ongoing fragmentation into further divided bodies, so that by the time of the first international Methodist Conference held in London in 1881, there were ten separate denominations from the British Isles, and eighteen from America – all Methodist!

Küng has analysed four ways in which Christians have sought to justify the unjustifiable and evade facing up to the scandal of disunity:

1. A first evasion is to retreat from the disunited visible church to an undivided invisible church;
2. A second evasion is to see the divisions in the church as a normal divinely intended development and to postpone the reconciliation of the church to the time of eschatological fulfillment.
3. A third and related evasion is to regard the different churches which have arisen as a result of schism as the three or four great branches of the one tree.
4. A fourth evasion is to explain the schisms by saying that there is only one empirical church identical with the church of Christ, which does not recognize any of the other churches as churches. [6]

Having discussed each of these evasions and exposed the essential bankruptcy of them all, Küng concludes with the following comments:

> If we wish to avoid all these evasions, there is in fact only one alternative: not to look for any theological justifications for the divisions in the Church. We should not justify these divisions, any more than we justify sin, but 'suffer' them as a dark enigma, an absurd, ridiculous, tolerable yet intolerable fact of life, that is contrary both to the will of God and the good of mankind. And in so far as it is against God's will and man's good, it is at the deepest level failure, guilt, sin – whether of individuals or of the community – and rarely of one 'party' alone. However great the misunderstandings, however understandable the historical genesis of the separation and the circumstances of the break, it should never, never among Christians, have come to a division in the Church. A division in the Church is a scandal and a disgrace.[7]

The cost of unity

The Apostle Paul was under no illusions concerning the very real and practical difficulties in the way of Christian unity. He himself experienced a difference of opinion with his fellow labourer Barnabas that led to 'such a sharp disagreement that they parted company' (Acts 15:39). Happily, that particular disagreement and separation did not lead to a permanent schism in the church, and later references to John Mark in the letters of Paul show that healing and reconciliation had taken place between those who had so sharply differed. The fact is that whenever Christians come together there will always be a thousand reasons for dissatisfaction on all sides. This means that Christian unity always calls for immense forbearance and forgiveness. Paul's exhortation to the believers in Colossae was: 'Clothe yourselves with compassion, kindness, humility, gentleness and patience. Bear with each other and forgive whatever grievances you may have against one another. Forgive as the Lord forgave you. And over all these virtues put on love, which binds them all together in perfect unity' (Col.3:12–14). Paul's words make it clear that love, patience and forgiveness are the cords that bind Christians together in unity. Or, to change the metaphor, unity is a tender plant that can flourish only in an environment of humble patience, forbearance and forgiveness. The importance of such an attitude has been emphasized and exhibited by Küng:

> The Churches themselves can do nothing to free themselves from guilt in the sight of God, they can only seek to be freed: they are dependent on forgiveness. So the first step in healing the breach must be an admission of guilt and a plea for forgiveness addressed both to God, the Lord of the Church, and to our brothers: 'Forgive us our trespasses, as we forgive those who trespass against us.' In asking for forgiveness, we ask for the healing of the division and in asking for forgiveness we declare that we are ready to do whatever is God's will to remove the division: Metanoia![8]

Spiritual renewal and unity

Nothing of what has been said above is really new. Indeed, for many readers of this book it will all be 'old hat'. Yet it has to be admitted that there are many Christian circles, often characterized by a high regard for the Bible and a deep devotion to its teaching, in which the matter of Christian unity has been strangely neglected or even regarded with suspicion and fear. But the Holy Spirit, whose task it is to lead the faithful into all truth, has a way of overcoming the barriers of human prejudice, even when they have been constructed over centuries of mistrust and hostility. The charismatic movement of recent decades, while it has produced even further divisions among Christians in many places, has also been instrumental in bringing together in remarkable unity Christians long separated by mutual rejection and misunderstanding. An interesting example of the latter phenomenon is the testimony of Michael Harper, former director of the Fountain Trust and for many years a leading figure in the charismatic renewal among British Anglicans. In his book *This is the Day*, he speaks of the 'three sisters' who had a profound influence in his life, Evangeline (Evangelicalism), Charisma (the Charismatic movement) and Roma (Catholicism). Developing this metaphor, he describes how his encounter with Evangeline led to his Christian conversion, soon after which he discovered however that the three sisters were not on speaking terms. Evangeline was suspicious of Charisma and positively hostile to Roma. Friendship with Charisma led to a rift between him and Evangeline. Both Evangeline and Charisma had strongly prejudiced him against Roma, even calling her a 'whore', so that when he eventually met the third sister he was surprised to find 'that she was related to the other sisters, and was chaste.'[9] Harper than describes the debt of gratitude he owed to all three sisters:

> To the evangelical sister for teaching me the gospel and introducing me to Jesus Christ. To the pentecostal sister for helping me to experience the spiritual dynamic of the Holy Spirit and to explore many neglected areas of the Holy Spirit's activity in the Church and the world. To the catholic sister for ushering me into a whole new world especially to understand the corporate dimensions of Christian life and to balance the spiritual with the human aspects of Christian truth, the Cross and the Incarnation, Word and Sacraments.
>
> I must confess to a deep longing to see these sisters reconciled to each other; to see them united in Christ and the Spirit, learning from one another and humbly listening to each other. If these sisters could be brought together on a large scale, there is no knowing the blessings that could follow.[10]

In his book Harper admits that there is yet another sister in the family, Orthodoxa (Eastern Orthodoxy), whom he has never really met. He has seen her 'sometimes in the distance' and feels that 'somehow the rest of the family seems incomplete without her.'[11] These excerpts from Harper's book have been included because in them we may see something of how a man with his roots in conservative evangelical Christianity set out on his pilgrimage towards a conviction of the vital importance of Christian unity while fully retaining the love and respect for the Bible so characteristic of that tradition. After penning the above words, Harper's pilgrimage of faith was to take an even further interesting path. He did indeed make acquaintance with 'Othodoxa' and was so struck with her that today he is an ordained Eastern Orthodox priest!

The significance of Christian unity for baptism

Baptism, like the Lord's supper, is a sacrament of unity. It is the sacrament of reconciliation whereby we are incorporated into the one body of Christ and made to drink of one Spirit (1 Cor.12:13). In baptism we are united with Christ and with one another (Rom.6:5, Gal.3:26–28). Indeed, it could be said that in baptism we are united with ourselves, as one of the destructive consequences of sin is the disintegration of the human personality into a battleground of conflicting passions and desires (Jas. 4:1, 1 Peter 2:11). Drawing us out of a sinful humanity characterized by alienation and hostility and consisting of multitudinous factions at war with one another and with God, baptism reintegrates us into the unity and harmony of God's new creation in Christ. In short, baptism is, *par excellence*, the sacrament of unity and reconciliation. What a supreme irony is it, therefore, that baptism, the sacrament of unity and reconciliation, should have become a source of division and estrangement. What a massive theological inconsistency that baptism should be a stumbling block to Christian unity. What an astonishing perversion of purpose that baptism should serve to estrange people from one another. That which was given by God to unite and bring together becomes an instrument of division and separation. What a sad illustration of T.F. Torrance's observation that the church 'has allowed the divisions of the world to penetrate back into itself so that its own unity in mind and body has been damaged, and its mission of reconciliation in the world has been seriously impaired'.[12]

We cannot minimize the extent of alienation and division that has been brought about by baptismal differences. In the words of Bridge and Phypers:

> . . . perhaps no command of Christ has occasioned so much controversy, division, bitterness and mistrust as this one. Indeed, as we shall show later, at times it has caused Christians to destroy each other with a ferocity, cruelty and hatred at variance with him who constantly exhorted his disciples to 'love one another.'[13]

This extraordinary inconsistency in the life of the church should be a source of shame and sorrow to all Christians. Like the Corinthians of old, we have been boasting when we should have been mourning. Various baptismal doctrines and practices have been fiercely maintained with little thought of the damage being done to the body of Christ or the consequences of disunity and division. These consequences are of such a serious nature that it is necessary to be reminded of some of them.

The consequences of disunity and schism

Church splits, which can happen in a moment, are very rarely healed – if ever – and certainly not without great difficulty. The reasons for this are not only spiritual but also psychological and sociological and it is necessary to consider some of the complex phenomena which accompany divisions among Christians, especially those which lead to schism, a break in the corporate life and fellowship of the church.

Because baptism involves actions, rites and ceremonies and not just ideas, it is inevitable, perhaps, that differences in baptismal doctrine and practice should more easily give rise to divisions. Not that other areas of Christian doctrine are merely ideas with no practical implications for life and practice. But these implications are not so immediately obvious or visible as is the case with baptism, which by its very nature has an immediate and necessary visibility. Christians, for example, can hold to conflicting views on the interpretation of the millennium and yet maintain a reasonably united front in their worship, service and fellowship, so that an observer from outside a church might not even be aware of some of the tensions and differences existing within it. If there are reasonably good relations between the protagonists of the different views, such a situation can continue for years without the issue ever resulting in a split. Indeed, has the church ever, in its entire history, been without such tensions and differences threatening unity and fellowship? Certainly not, in this writer's view. But in the case of baptism, it is just so much more difficult to hold conflicting views and still remain together.

Once points of conflict and tension lead to actual schism among Christians, the possibility of calm, honest and fruitful discussion virtually disappears altogether. Formal schism brings powerful psychological factors into play. Deep down inside, Christians are aware that schism, with all the hostility and trauma involved, cannot be pleasing to God, so there arises in each group a need to justify their action. Legitimate grievances are exaggerated. It becomes vitally important for each side to be able to demonstrate convincingly that the blame for the schism lies largely with the other side. Discussion becomes debate in which neither protagonist can concede any points to the 'enemy'. Then, once the two groups are separated from one another, they continue to grow even further apart from one another, as M.J. Congar has shown in his study of the major divisions in Christendom:

> There is the dead weight of prolonged separation, the growing accumulation of prejudices, the almost irremediable remoteness between divergent developments in each Christian group. Difference and division have been woven into the fabric of social and national life: Orthodoxy is identified with the national and cultural forms of the East: the Protestant Reforms are closely bound up with modern forms of the State. . . .[14]

In the major divisions considered by Congar, whole communities, societies and nations develop a culture deeply formed by the prevailing religion among them, so that we speak of a 'Protestant' culture, a 'Catholic' culture or an 'Orthodox' culture. One could easily add to that list a 'Baptist' culture, a 'Pentecostal' culture, a 'Reformed' culture and many other even smaller subdivisions of religious cultures. Religious differences become reinforced by social and cultural realities so that they, rather than purely theological considerations, become the most powerful factors keeping Christians apart. Congar himself is an illustration of this point. Being a Catholic theologian of pre-Vatican II vintage he was deeply suspicious of the ecumenical movement which was then still in an early stage of development. With reference to the *Faith and Order* conference held at Lausanne and Edinburgh he wrote the following:

> The position of the Catholic Church in face of all these Conferences is that of knowing with certainty that she possesses in its fullness the truth which all their participants hold but partially and therefore distortedly. It is precisely because she possesses and *is* this fullness, that the Catholic Church cannot become involved in such meetings: they are sectional affairs and she is the whole.[15]

If the above quotation represents a rejection of the ecumenical movement because of an intransigent Catholic insistence that she is the one true church in which alone unity exists and can be found, many quotations could be made from staunch Protestant sources rejecting the ecumenical movement precisely because of its perceived Romeward trend. In a strongly polemical book against the ecumenical movement, Donald Gillies, an Irish Presbyterian minister from Belfast, issues the following warning:

> Courtesy visits and pathetic appeals for union and peace talks are to Rome signs of the weakening of Protestant faith and resistance. . . . We seem to be preparing for a 'Munich' Agreement – at best a mere delaying action – which will prepare the way for the eventual destruction of Protestant resistance before the guile and might of Rome. Whether or not Protestant churches will continue to be betrayed by their leaders, or will turn to a strong Churchillian approach towards evil before it is too late, remains to be seen. . . . The rank and file of Protestantism must be warned. The ecumenical climate is depressing and soporific. It is slowly drying up our evangelical fervour. The soft winds of false doctrine are lulling us to sleep and carrying us slowly but surely in a Romeward direction. The cause of true Protestantism is at stake. The work and sacrifice of Reformers and martyrs are in danger of being brought to naught. . . . Better even that the Protestant Church should perish than be reunited with 'Catholic' error, superstition and idolatry.[16]

It is interesting that Gillies does not hesitate to liken the 'Roman Catholic dictatorship' to that of Adolf Hitler, and Protestantism's struggle against Rome to the British struggle against Nazism. This line of argument would have a very special appeal to Northern Ireland Protestants who oppose any thought of the return of Northern Ireland by the British to the government of Ireland. Thus we see the powerful way in which themes of national and social history are drawn in to bolster and affirm Christian divisions, illustrating the sober fact that schisms, once affected, are not easily healed. The above quotations from Congar and Gillies illustrate that when it comes to divisions among Christians much more is involved than differences over certain doctrines. There is a mentality of hostility and fear that makes it exceedingly difficult even to discuss the doctrinal differences involved. Bearing in mind Gillies's emotive references to the 'sacrifice of Reformers and martyrs' it is interesting to note the perceptive observations of a fellow British Protestant and evangelical, David Watson:

> We tend to cling to our traditions, and in particular to those distinctive traditions that have separated us from the other churches. We therefore magnify out of all proportion the secondary issues which have become the *raison d'être* of our particular group. No doubt we justify these positions by a strong appeal to Scripture or tradition; but often it is more a crisis of group identity. We fear lest we change the boundaries within which we feel safe. The barriers may separate us from other brethren, but at least we know where we belong; it would be too risky, too vulnerable, trying to live without those barriers. Moreover, some of those barriers were erected by the Reformers at the cost of their own lives. They are rooted deep into history and cemented with the blood of martyrs. Can we pull down those divisions for which they gave the ultimate sacrifice? Can we betray the past and deny our heritage? So the argument goes.[17]

Such are the difficulties of trying to dismantle those barriers of which Watson speaks, and such are the hostilities aroused by the mere suggestion of such an action that the temptation is to leave all such matters well alone rather than stir up a hornet's nest of problems. It seems safer and wiser to simply remain in those enclaves inherited from our spiritual forefathers and pursue our activities safely within their protective boundaries. But this is the tragedy of schism. It separates Christians into isolated groups, severely limiting meaningful contact between them, and thus condemning them all to the spiritual impoverishment that results from estrangement and the lack of fellowship and interaction. MacNutt speaks as follows of the moral dilemmas produced by divisions:

> Moral dilemmas such as this make you sympathetic to the desires of the churches to remain apart, to protect their flocks from doctrinal confusion by contamination. Such separation and the forming of protective enclaves is the simplest solution, but I believe that ordinarily it prevents us from discovering the synthesis of Christian truth that we need to draw us together. Where I used to believe that I didn't need other Christian churches, I now find that they often have seen some areas of Christian truth more clearly than I, and that I need these other groups, precisely in their otherness.[18]

But however strong the temptation might be to form, or simply to remain in, the 'protective enclaves' of various ecclesiastical blocs, each gathered around its own particular doctrinal distinctive, it is Christian truth that is ultimately the victim of such *laager* mentalities. It is ironic that while 'defence of the truth' is so often the watchword justifying the separation of Christians from one another, the result of such schisms is the impoverishment of that very truth supposedly being defended. As Deane has pointed out, the flight from unity can only hinder the process by which truth is apprehended.

> The insight that Christ through the Holy Spirit guides his followers towards the truth *only insofar as they grow in respect for and unity with each other* has been more or less ignored by theologians. But not entirely ignored. Somewhere in the writings of Jürgen Moltmann there is the phrase, 'Only an ecumenically united Christianity can become the body of Christ's truth.'[19]

We can summarize the consequences of disunity and schism as follows. When differences between Christians lead to their formal separation from one another and the formation of opposing bodies, then the original points of difference become hardened into deeply entrenched denominational positions. Meaningful discussion becomes almost impossible as theologians from neither side are able to concede any points in an argument without being considered disloyal to their denomination. Indeed, if any should change their mind on certain issues they would be obliged to go through the embarrassing and painful process of resigning from their church and going over to the 'other side' – an experience so traumatic as to effectively deter most from even considering it. And when, from time to time, individuals do 'defect to the other side', the result is one of deep dismay from those 'deserted', together with a stiffened resolve to tighten up the ranks and to defend the cause even more passionately. Churches become victims of the cruel logic that any doubt concerning certain doctrinal positions brings into question the entire *raison d'être* of the church itself. This is especially threatening when it is remembered that churches and ecclesiastical institutions develop a life and momentum of their own with a fierce instinct for survival. For those at home within them, the thought of a beloved denomination ceasing its separate existence is a thought worse than death. It is the end of the world. Hence ways need to be found towards creating an environment in which dialogue and discussion can be promoted without the above-mentioned threatening aspects being brought into play.

The need for an environment conducive to fruitful dialogue

As long as the baptismal issue is such a divisive one, demanding either allegiance to or the repudiation of a particular church or denomination, the broad patterns of defence and hostility, as we have described them, are likely to remain. What is needed is the creation of an environment that would be more conducive to honest dialogue, a non-threatening environment in which Christians could feel free to discuss and think through issues without fear. In such an atmosphere not only could Christians develop their thinking and understanding of the sacrament of baptism, but they could even change their minds on certain issues without their church membership being called into question and without all the embarrassing and humiliating consequences that would normally follow such changes in conviction. When Christians have the opportunity to meet together to discuss differences in the right kind of environment, they are often surprised by the positive results of such dialogue. One outstanding example of such dialogue has been the extensive and valuable work on the subject of baptism done by the Faith and Order Commission of the World Council of Churches. The BEM document produced at Lima, Peru in 1982

> . . . has become the most widely distributed, translated, and discussed ecumenical text in modern times. Some 450,000 copies translated into 31 languages have been studied in a huge variety of situations around the world. Over a thousand written reactions have so far been published. Never before have more than 180 churches reached out to each other by responding officially to an ecumenical document.[20]

The positive value of the achievement of the Faith and Order Commission in the production of the BEM document cannot be overestimated. The generally positive response to and the lively discussion stimulated by the BEM document have been truly amazing, and one can understand why the authors of the above-mentioned paper describe the BEM event as 'an outpouring of God's blessing'. Yet possibly the most urgent task now is for that blessing to filter down from the levels of church leadership to the ordinary members in local congregations. How many ordinary church members have ever heard of the BEM document? Indeed, how many of the regular clergy have heard about it – especially those whose busy lives in the round of church and parish affairs leaves them little time to keep track of current theological developments? Among the ranks of those churches that are not connected in any way to the WCC, churches with which the writer of this book is most familiar, it is safe to say that very few indeed have ever even heard of the BEM document. This brings us back to the need of stimulating authentic dialogue and discussion on the subject of baptism, and in order to do this, the need of creating an environment that is conducive to such dialogue. The need for ecumenical discussion and experience, not just in the higher echelons of church leadership, but also at the local level is widely recognized. Hans Küng and Jürgen Moltmann, for example, have written:

> Official ecumenism, whether at a *universal* or *national* level, is of only *secondary* importance. Ecumenical experience at the *local* level is not just the point of departure but the aim of *all ecumenical endeavor*. . . . Ecumenical activity at the local level has shown that often the real barriers to collectivity and mutual encounter between Christians are not so much doctrinal differences as an emotional attachment to particular devotional practices and a fear that their individual identity is threatened.[21]

A non-threatening atmosphere might well lead Christians of all traditions to reflect more calmly and critically on the baptismal doctrines and practices of their churches, without fear and anxiety. Such reflection could lead to a realization of the need in *every* tradition for reform and renewal in this area. Out of such deliberations there could well emerge the possibility of allowing greater diversity in various alternative rites and practices. Küng and Moltmann have expressed their opinion that 'the *greatest possible* diversity in the practical application of theological thinking' should be allowed in the local church to the end that it 'no longer admits the practice of excluding *any* Christian from *any* parish service'.[22] In the next chapter we shall consider ways in which this might be implemented, practically, in the various church traditions which have baptismal practices widely divergent from one another.

Notes

1 T.F. Torrance, *Theology in reconciliation* (Grand Rapids, Eerdmans, 1976), p.7.

2 M. J. Congar *Divided Christendom: a Catholic study of the problems of reunion* (London, Geoffrey Bles, 1939), p.98.

3 P. Beyerhaus, *Bangkok '73: the beginning or end of world mission?* (Grand Rapids, Zondervan, 1974), p.107.

4 B. Smith, *The Fraudulent Gospel: Politics and the World Council of Churches* (Sandton, Valiant Publishers, 1977), p.113.

5 H. Küng, *The Church* (London, Search, 1976), p.273.

6 Ibid., p.281–282.

7 Ibid.

8   Ibid., p.284.
9   M. Harper, *This is the Day* (London, Hodder & Stoughton 1979), p.14.
10 Ibid., p.15.
11 Ibid., p.15.
12 T.F. Torrance, *Theology in reconciliation* (Grand Rapids, Eerdmans, 1976), p.7.
13 D. Bridge & D. Phypers, *The water that divides* (Leicester, IVP, 1977), p.7.
14 M. J. Congar *Divided Christendom: a Catholic study of the problems of reunion* (London, Geoffrey Bles, 1939), p.39.
15 Ibid., p.133.
16 D. Gillies, *Unity in the Dark* (London, Banner of Truth, 1964), p.25.
17 D. Watson, *I believe in the Church* (London, Hodder, 1989) p.338.
18 F.S. MacNutt, 'A proposed, practical solution to the controversy between proponents of Believers' Baptism and Infant Baptism', in A. Künig, H.I. Lederle, & F.P. Möller, *Infant Baptism? The arguments for and against* (Roodepoort, CUM, 1984), p.161.
19 D. Deane, 'Truth and the Flight from Unity,' *Studies* 301(1987):59.
20 Faith and Order Paper No. 149, *Baptism, Eucharist & Ministry 1982–1990: Report on the Process and Responses* (Geneva, WCC, 1990), p.155.
21 H. Küng & J. Moltmann (eds.), *An Ecumenical Confession of Faith?* (New York, Seabury, 1979), p.xi.
22 Ibid.

Chapter 6

Can we get closer?

If the general thrust of the previous chapter on baptism and unity is accepted, the following points emerge as a foundation for this present chapter:

1. The reconciliation of humans to God and to one another through Christ lies at the heart of the Christian mission to the world.
2. The visible unity in love of this reconciled fellowship is a vital witness to the power of the gospel to save, heal and reunite that which has been marred and divided by sin.
3. Baptism, the sacrament of union with Christ and union with all other believers in the body of Christ through the power of the Holy Spirit, is pre-eminently the sacrament of reconciliation and unity.
4. There is, therefore, a profound contradiction of purpose, if not plain absurdity, that baptism should become a source of division and alienation between Christians.

Given the above points, it follows that one of the chief failures of most churches in the area of baptism is not the omission or the promulgation of this or that point of doctrine or practice, but rather the allowing of baptismal differences to result in division. If we are looking for something to brand as a baptismal heresy, surely this is the chief and most serious baptismal heresy – neither infant baptism nor rebaptism nor baptismal regeneration, but the rejection of fellow-believers on the grounds of baptismal differences. This is the most serious heresy precisely because it is a sin against the chief and greatest commandment of Christ, the commandment to love one another. As Declan Deane has put it: 'There can surely be no greater deviation from the truth than the formal abandonment of love.'[1] This means that whatever group holds to the 'correct baptism' (whatever this is and if there is such a group), that same group is wrong, and unfaithful to the gospel of Christ when it uses its 'correct baptism' as an instrument to exclude fellow Christians on account of their 'incorrect' views. Their very zeal for the truth can become a stumbling block to their obedience to Christ just as their zeal for God and the Law became a stumbling block for so many Jews in the time of Paul (Rom.10:2).

> If remaining in the truth is essentially a question of discipleship in the Spirit of Jesus Christ, this is *more a matter of orthopraxy than of orthodoxy:* it is realized more in the Christian life than in teaching, more in the deed than merely in word. . . . In the passages on Jesus' calling of his disciples he never asks first for a profession of faith. The profoundly disturbing Sermon on the Mount is centred not on orthodox belief but on radical observance of God's will in service to one's neighbour. Why? Because Christian truth is concrete.[2]

Many questions can be raised in connection with some of the above statements; questions concerning truth, convictions of truth and the implications of such convictions. Not all of these questions will necessarily have easy or straightforward answers. What of those who have no baptism at all, and are resistant to any form of baptism, yet desire acceptance in the church on the basis of faith in Christ? What of those with bizarre, strange forms of baptism that could not be classified under any of the Baptist/Reformed/Catholic forms of baptism?

Truth, convictions and dialogue

What then is the way forward if the divisive barriers of baptismal differences are to be overcome? Is it by abandoning any firmly held convictions concerning baptism? Must truth be sacrificed in the interests of unity and reconciliation? Such a course would prove utterly fruitless as nothing is accomplished by a mere indifferentism, least of all the cause of Christian unity and reconciliation. In the words of Hans Küng, truth must not be sacrificed, but rediscovered.

> The Churches cannot be unified satisfactorily on the basis of indifferentist faith and half-hearted allegiances. Diplomatic settlements and compromises in dogma are not the right way. We must be mistrustful of formulas or forms of unity which conceal our differences rather than overcoming them. If unity is to be genuine, dogmatic differences must be settled theologically. They will not be solved by pretending that they are not there or that they do not matter. Unless they are genuinely overcome, they will remain a constant source of infection, the more dangerous for being hidden. We must reject 'unity at any price'. A Church which abandons the truth abandons itself.[3]

Küng goes on to say: 'Our faith must be stronger, not weaker, our judgement must be clearer, not obscurer, our ability to draw distinctions must be truly critical, not uncritical: this must be the basis of our efforts for unity.'[4] Again it must be said, nothing is to be gained by concealing differences or abandoning convictions. On the contrary, open, frank, honest discussion, debate and dialogue are all essential if the quest for truth is to be vigorously promoted.

It is important to make this point very firmly at this stage in view of some of the suggestions that will be made later in this chapter and in this book. Some will tempted to think that such suggestions could be seriously entertained only by those with dangerously liberal views, having no clear convictions of truth. 'We do not want a watering down of truth to bring us together at the lowest common denominator', as MacNutt has put it, 'we need to come to a level higher, where both truths can be joined without compromise to either position.'[5] If this expansion of truth is to be achieved, room must be made for the full discussion and sharing of various views. Any suppression of the process of honest and open dialogue can only inhibit the growth of truth. It can hardly be denied that the present structures of many churches do not serve to promote an honest dialogue on the subject of baptism but rather serve to inhibit such dialogue. Therefore in the interests of truth it is essential that attention must be given to the question of church structures and how they can promote or inhibit the full and free discussion that is necessary for the growth of truth and understanding.

Two models of church relations

It must be stressed that the two models of church relations discussed below are in no way models of church union. No attempt is being made here to propose or discuss models of church union. All that is being discussed is how different church bodies relate to one another, and two different kinds of relationship are considered. A discussion of models of church unity would require a very much more exhaustive treatment. The following paragraphs deal quite simply with the way churches (as separate denominations) can relate to one another, together with certain suggestions towards more fruitful patterns of inter-church relationships.

The 'laager' model

Traditionally much baptismal discussion has been of the 'laager mentality' or 'trench warfare' type, each ecclesiastical body being strongly entrenched in its position and suitably fortified by a well constructed doctrinal barricade. Erudite books or forceful pamphlets are produced demonstrating with a theological *tour de force* the correctness of one point of view. The intention of such literary artillery pieces is twofold: firstly, that the faithful may be confirmed in the truth, and, secondly, that those in error might be persuaded of the error of their ways, embrace the truth, and join up with those adhering to the truth. This would imply, of course, separating from the body in error and converting to the body maintaining the true doctrine. This model of church relations could be represented diagrammatically thus:

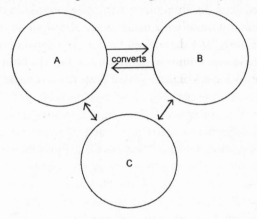

The distance between each position is quite clear and the movement from one position to another requires a conversion, not only of doctrinal conviction, but also of ecclesiastical affiliation. If the one body is able to make considerable more converts than the other bodies, after a while the relative positions of the ecclesiastical bodies could be represented as follows:

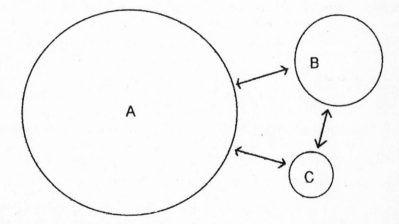

In practice, converts are made only with difficulty. One of the problems is that the literature produced to convince those in error is very rarely read by those in error. Instead, it is largely read by those holding the same convictions as the author. Because such literature does not usually attempt to portray the opposing view in a sympathetic light, its chief achievement, therefore, is the strengthening of prejudices on either side. This makes the process of conversion even slower and more difficult. The possibility of one body being able to convert all the members of another body to their point of view is a very slim one. Credobaptists are not going easily or quickly to persuade paedobaptist churches to abandon their practice of baptising infants. And paedobaptist churches are not going easily or quickly to persuade credobaptist churches to adopt the practice of baptising infants. So the process of conversion, on this issue, is likely to be very protracted. In terms of Christian witness to the world it will be a costly process, as it will inevitably result in the unedifying spectacle of Christians battling one another, often with acrimony and bitterness.

If the question at issue was one of fundamental importance, so that error in it threatened the very heart of the gospel and its saving efficacy, then there could be no other alternative than the model described above. No church can consider compromising the gospel or its mission to bring the salvation of God to the ends of the earth. But in the question of baptism this is not the case. The overwhelming majority of credobaptist churches do not question the saving efficacy of the faith of those believers within paedobaptist churches. Neither do the latter question the sincerity of faith of the former. So whatever may be the case in other issues, in this particular issue there must be another model in which churches and Christians can relate to one another in a better and more edifying way.

Growing together

The underlying concept in this model is that each group or body should expand its basis, not surrendering its own truth convictions but making room for other truth convictions, and in this way allowing a process of growing together, or convergence towards one another from within. This model could be represented diagrammatically as follows:

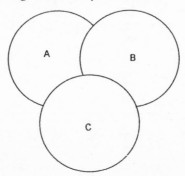

Again it must be stressed that this is not a model of church union. That is not being considered at this place. Each of the churches or denominations, A, B and C, retains its separate and autonomous existence. But each one also allows some of the practices of the other two, creating a certain 'overlap' in the practices of the different churches. In this model, the traumatic and acrimonious process of conversion from one camp to another is eliminated, as members of group B can move towards the position of C, or A, or both, without having to abandon their identity as B. In this way a growing unity can be forged while the discussion and the debate continues. Furthermore, an environment is created in which dialogue and discussion can be carried out in a far more fruitful and constructive way. Instead of the debate being a witness to the world of the failure of Christians to reconcile their differences, it can become a shining example of how legitimate differences can be discussed and debated by Christians within a fellowship of genuine reconciliation.

Perhaps the most powerful witness of the church in the world is not some perfect and problem-free society (such a society would be unearthly, unbelievable), but the witness of a community of people, struggling with very human problems, but enabled to pursue their struggle in a spirit of authentic love, mutual acceptance and reconciliation. As Küng has observed: 'Even in the Church conflicts are unavoidable. They are signs of life and in any case are to be preferred to the deathly silence of totalitarian systems. Conflicts must be endured and a fruitful settlement attempted.' [6] In a world deeply divided into alienated, hostile, prejudiced and conflicting camps, the struggle of the church patiently to endure conflicts and to work with determination towards a fruitful settlement of every division is both a salutary witness to the power of the gospel and a valuable contribution towards establishing the *shalom* of God in the world.

The convergence model considered above is quite open-ended as to where the process might lead. The passage of time might see the emergence of:-

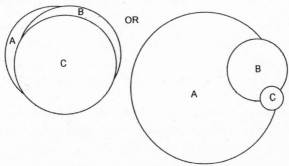

It must be noted that in this model there always remains room for those, whether individuals or congregations, who are strongly convinced of the correctness of their practices and do not approve of any other practices. They, too, must be fully provided for, even if they should become a minority, if genuine unity between all believers remains the goal.

The promotion and implementation of such a process of growing together or convergence could be a profound act of faith in the power of the Holy Spirit to lead Christian believers into all truth, and a demonstration of the conviction and confidence that God's truth will prevail in the end. Hans Küng has spoken of the indestructibility of the church, by which he means that the church is maintained in truth by divine power. 'Christians are confident that there is a living God and that in the future this God will also maintain their believing community in life and in truth. Their confidence is based on the promise given with Jesus of Nazareth: he himself is the promise on which God's fidelity to this people can be read.'[7]

The doctrinal barriers referred to above when considering the 'laager' model, which serve to maintain a rigid distance between the churches, are the work of human hands. Indeed, it must be emphasized that those hands are holy hands, stretched out in genuine concern to the protect the ark of God's truth. Yet such actions are manifestations, all too often, of fear rather than faith, a fear that human frailty and error will undermine God's truth unless the latter is suitably protected and hedged around by doctrinal fences. But God is surely able to defend his own cause, and the truth is able to stand on its own and even prevail over error by virtue of the divine power inherent in it.

> . . . if truth is to be continually in the Church, this will not be because the members or at least certain members in certain situations do not make mistakes or because their liability to error is sometimes excluded by higher influence. The reason why truth remains in the Church is because, in the face of all human failings and mistakes, God's truth proves to be stronger and because the message of Jesus continually produces faith, so that Jesus remains in the community of believers and his Spirit constantly guides them afresh into the whole truth.[8]

This, then, is what is meant by 'growing together' and 'ways of convergence'. The intention of this model of church relations is not an attempt to suppress the truth but rather to liberate it and to promote it, in the firm conviction that there is a divine power lodged in truth that will cause it to prevail in the end.

It could be asked at this point if it is the intention of this book to suggest that room should be made in the church for any and all kinds of error in the belief that truth will prevail in the end anyway? Certainly not. In keeping with sentiments expressed in various places in this book, the writer believes that Christians are duty bound to decisively oppose errors that strike at the heart of the gospel. They must do this, not because God's truth is dependent on their actions, but because the duty of combating anti-Christian error is directly commanded by God's word. The distinction between primary and secondary issues within a hierarchy of truths is the special subject of discussion of chapter 7. Suffice to say at this point that it is only in those secondary issues in which the gospel itself is not at stake that a policy of openness and flexibility is being advocated. But how can this be applied to the three baptismal approaches we have been considering? What practical steps can be taken by churches in each tradition towards growing together? How could such steps be justified?

Steps that credobaptist churches could take

Generally speaking, Baptists do not recognize the validity of infant baptism. They do not practise it and in most cases do not receive people into church membership unless they have been baptised as believers. But it is equally true that Baptists do not doubt the authentic Christian status of those believers in other communions who trust in Christ as Saviour. For this reason the great majority of Baptists hold to an 'open table' policy when it comes to the eucharistic meal. This means that all Christians are welcome to share in the Lord's Table, or Holy Communion, whether they be members of that church or not.

There are some Baptists who feel there is an inconsistency involved in a church having an 'open table' and a 'closed membership', that is, gladly receiving other Christians at the Lord's table to share in the sacrament of the Holy Communion on the basis of their faith in Christ while refusing to receive those same Christians into the membership of the church. Thus there are also Baptist churches who have an 'open membership' policy whereby believers are received into membership of the church on the basis of faith in Christ alone. Occasionally this leads to the further anomaly of believers being received into membership who have never been *baptised* in any way at all! Generally speaking, both in South Africa and in other parts of the world, such 'open membership' Baptist churches are a fairly small minority in Baptist Associations – but a significant minority nevertheless. However, while such 'open membership' churches might be a minority among Baptist churches, they are a majority in other credobaptist associations. The International Fellowship of Christian Churches (IFCC) in South Africa, for example, is committed in its statement of faith to the position 'that baptism is the immersion of the believer in water as a confession of identification with Christ in burial and resurrection.'[9] Yet the majority of IFCC churches (with a total membership considerably larger than that of the Baptist Union of Southern Africa) have an 'open membership' policy. Of course this does not prevent these churches from putting considerable pressure on members to be baptised as believers.

On the basis of the above *status quo* in Baptist circles, a few proposals will here be made concerning steps Baptists could take towards convergence. In addition, an attempt will be made to provide a theological justification, from a Baptist perspective, for such steps.

To come directly to the heart of the matter, let it be suggested that Baptists accept infant baptism as a legitimate, though defective, baptism. This does not mean endorsing or promoting infant baptism. Neither does it mean being compelled to practise it. It simply means accepting fully and unconditionally fellow-Christians who are convinced in their own minds of the validity of their baptism without relegating them to some second-class status in the body of Christ. That means accepting their baptism as a legitimate baptism, while honestly holding reservations about certain aspects of its mode and administration. 'But what scriptural grounds', it could be asked, 'do such Christians have to justify their infant baptism as a true baptism?' In answer to such a question we can only point back to Chapter 2 of this book, where the paedobaptist position from both a Catholic and Reformed perspective was summarized. Clearly a great many Christians are convinced that there are good scriptural grounds for infant baptism; and these include some Christians who are held in the highest esteem by Baptists for their integrity, sanctity and scholarship. This fact alone, surely, must compel Baptists to consider the *possibility* that there is some substance to the case for infant baptism. Could so many Christians of unquestionable spirituality and sound learning support a position for which there is not a trace of support in Scripture? Such considerations, of course, fall short of any proof of infant baptism. But it does point to the fact that Baptists cannot simply write off infant baptism as a position unworthy of serious consideration, but ought rather to give it some recognition, though retaining the right to criticize aspects of it. The respected British Baptist scholar, Alec Gilmore, has made the same point:

> The very inconclusiveness of the arguments for and against both forms of baptism ought to make us stop and think, and also ought to deliver us from a dogmatism that ill-becomes the scholar searching for the truth. No one who has read the literature on baptism during the last fifteen years could honestly feel that either side has really proved its point beyond a peradventure.[10]

Gilmore follows on this observation by coming to a conclusion similar to that being suggested in this thesis, namely, that Baptists should give some kind of recognition to infant baptism, whatever reservations they might honestly have in connection with it.

> . . . if infant baptism is 'no baptism', then the Church that practises it is 'no church'. Few Baptists will want to go so far, and fewer still find it possible to support such doctrines in practice. It is better to acknowledge that infant baptism, though partial in its expression of the truth and though involving serious theological distortion, is nevertheless baptism, and cannot therefore be followed by believers' baptism being administered to the same person.[11]

The second part of Gilmore's conclusion, that infant baptism 'cannot' be followed by believers' baptism, is not part of what is being suggested here. All that is being suggested here is that infant baptism be given some kind of recognition and that a further baptism be not insisted upon in every case. The point made by Gilmore that infant baptism involves a serious theological distortion is very similar to the position that Karl Barth came to:

> It is certain that no rejection of the order and practice of baptism through the fault of the Church, or through fault or lack on the part of the candidate, can make the baptism of a person, once it has been performed, ineffective and therefore invalid, or can lead to or justify a call to re-baptism according to a better order or practice . . . . Baptism without the willingness and readiness of the baptised is true, effectual and effective baptism, but it is not correct; it is not done in obedience, it is not administered according to the proper order, and therefore it is necessarily clouded baptism. It must and ought not to be repeated. It is, however, a wound in the body of the Church and a weakness for the baptised. . . .[12]

Many years later, in the last major work he was to write, Barth had refined his understanding of baptism somewhat but still maintained that despite the doubtful and irregular nature of infant baptism, 'Nevertheless, one cannot say that it is invalid.'[13]

What would be the practical implications for Baptists accepting infant baptism as a legitimate, though defective, form of baptism? What are the answers to some of the objections that could be raised? Firstly, it must be stressed that both pastors and church members would remain perfectly free in their preaching and practice to maintain with all vigour their credobaptist convictions. They would remain free, too, to engage in honest dialogue and debate with fellow Christians of other convictions, to seek to persuade them, if possible. But they would do all this in an attitude of love, respecting the views of fellow church members, even when they disagreed with them, and respecting their right to hold them. Paedobaptist members of the church would also not be restricted in any way in their service in the church. They would not be barred from any office in the church, such as deacon or elder. To such a proposal the concern is often expressed: 'That would allow people of paedobaptist convictions to occupy important teaching posts and undermine the Baptist character of the church.' To such a concern it could be answered: 'If Baptist truths are so weak that they cannot be maintained in an environment of honest dialogue but must be defended by excluding paedobaptists from certain positions in the church, then are those truths worthy of faith? Are they from God?'

What is being proposed is quite simply a greater freedom within Baptist churches to hold divergent views on baptism without being penalized in any way on account of those views. This freedom would have to include the possibility of parents having their infant children baptised if they so choose. This would certainly be a departure from historic and contemporary Baptist practice. 'But why do we call ourselves Baptists, if we should permit the baptism of infants in our churches?' could well be a genuinely puzzled protest to such an idea. Such an inquirer could be reminded that the term 'Baptist' was not coined by Baptists, but by their enemies. The first 'Baptists' were simply Christians who desired the freedom to act according to their conscience in the matter of baptism. On being refused this freedom they were cast out of the church and branded as heretics and 'Baptists'. It is actually strange that Baptists should be unwilling to allow the same freedom of conscience in their churches that their spiritual forefathers originally desired in the churches from which they came. There is the fear, of course, that such a 'lax' policy in the administration of baptism might lead, in time, to a church ceasing to be a Baptist church. But again it must be asked: if Baptists are convinced of the truth of their convictions, what do they have to fear? Surely in an environment where those of Baptist convictions have the fullest freedom to promote their views, the majority will be convinced of the truth of those views. If they are not, then do such views deserve special protection? It is generally the mark of a weak position that people seek to prop it up by artificial means and protect it from any honest exposure to open debate and discussion. That is surely not how Baptists wish to defend their convictions.

Yet another question could be: 'Who would administer baptism to infants in a Baptist church?' Certainly it would be quite wrong to oblige the pastor of the church to administer baptism to infants if such an action was impossible for him on the grounds of conscience. But are there not others in the church who could administer baptism? As was pointed out in Chapter 3, in the early church baptism was administered by a wide variety of believers and not only by the 'ordained' leaders. Why should not the believing parents themselves administer baptism to their children? Indeed, should baptisms necessarily be performed in the church, or in the presence of the congregation? These are important questions and will be returned to later.

To summarize this section on steps that Baptists could take towards convergence: these would amount to simply allowing church members greater freedom to hold to divergent views on baptism and to act according to their conscience, without being excluded from fellowship and church membership or discriminated against in any way in the church. This proposal is entirely in line with the principle of freedom of conscience which is strongly cherished as a central tenet of Baptist faith. It is also in line with what some of the earliest Anabaptist pioneers wanted from their Reformed fellow believers – simply the freedom to act according to their conscience. It was a Baptist scholar, who, contemplating the possibility of permitting both infant baptism and believers' baptism in one congregation, wrote: 'Is there not room in the providence of God for both forms of baptism to co-exist, and might not this inconclusiveness be one means by which God is seeking to lead His Church into something richer than our forefathers ever dreamed of?'[14]

Steps that Reformed and other Protestant paedobaptist churches could take

It would be quite wrong to suggest that Reformed churches do not practise believers' baptism. The baptism of adults on the confession of their faith is administered quite regularly to those who have never been baptised before. In addition to this, baptism is also administered to the infants of believers, whether they be new believers coming into the church by baptism themselves, or believers who grew up in the Christian community. If such a church was engaged in vigorous outreach to non-Christian peoples, resulting in many being brought to faith and baptism, the baptism of adults on the confession of their faith and the baptism of the infants of believers would both be common occurrences in the church. But when the church grows chiefly by its own biological growth, then clearly the vast majority of baptisms witnessed in the church will be infant baptisms.

What is unacceptable to Reformed and other paedobaptist churches is the rebaptism of those who have already been baptised, and also that believing parents do not offer their infants for baptism. Those members who accept rebaptism are liable to be disciplined by the church and perhaps even to be put out of the church, unless, of course, they should admit and repent of the error of their rebaptism. Parents in the church are expected to have their infants baptised and those who fail to comply could also face disciplinary measures, although of a much milder nature.

There are two steps that Reformed churches could take to enhance the process towards convergence. The first would be to permit parents to defer the baptism of their children if, for reasons of conscience, they are not convinced of the correctness of infant baptism. Such children would be baptised at a later stage when able to make a profession of personal faith at their baptism. The pastor and any others in the church would remain free, of course, to seek to persuade such parents to have their infants baptised. Their freedom to teach and share their convictions concerning the validity of infant baptism would not in any way be impaired. But it would mean that they would have to recognize and respect the right of parents to choose in this matter according to their conscience.

The objection could be raised: 'Would not the delay of baptism be an act of cruelty to the infants involved, depriving them of the sacramental grace of baptism?' Two answers can be made to this objection, one practical and the other theological. On the practical level it could be argued that nothing would be gained by the church rigidly insisting upon the baptism of infants without exception. Such an attitude would probably result in the dissident parents leaving the church, which – from a paedobaptist perspective – would hardly improve the situation for the infants involved. A more flexible approach by the church on the other hand, would more likely result in the parents remaining in the church, which in turn would provide greater opportunity for others to convince them of what is best for their children. On the theological level it can be argued that the Reformed tradition has generally hesitated to insist on the obligatory nature of baptism in any absolute way. While Reformed theology embraces quite a wide range of views on this issue, the following remarks of Hendrikus Berkhof are probably representative of mainstream Reformed theology:

> Though we may not say that children 'ought to be baptised', we may say that they too may be given the rite of incorporation if they grow up in a community (family, village, institution) in which they are involved in God's salvation. In every instance it depends, however, on a pastoral decision, not on a general dogmatic principle. In principle the incorporative rite is possible at any age, either before a profession of faith or already earlier as a stage on the way within the congregation toward conscious faith.[15]

Berkouwer also refers to repeated statements that can be found in Reformed theology 'that the sacraments are not necessary for the obtaining of salvation. This is not said about the sacraments *in general*, but with respect to *salvation*. The intention of the Reformers is clear: they wished to deny the Roman

Catholic doctrine that the sacraments are necessary because they infuse supernatural grace.'[16]

Finally it can be argued that sheer honesty concerning the ambiguities and complexities of the questions surrounding the issue of infant baptism demands a flexible approach rather than a rigidly dogmatic one. We have already noted the admission of a Baptist scholar, Alec Gilmore, of the 'inconclusiveness of the arguments for and against both forms of baptism'. We can also note similar remarks by an Anglican scholar made during a conference on the subject of baptism:

> In these last months I have tried to read widely and deeply on baptism, and I must admit I am somewhat mystified at the way some people at the Conference have been so certain on the subject. For instance, you cannot read Jeremias on infant baptism, followed by Kurt Aland on Jeremias, followed by Jeremias's reply to Aland, and believe that anyone can say all that much certain about infant baptism in the Early Church. . . . I have been mystified by the way so often those who clearly want the biblical evidence to be in favour of no infant baptism find that it is so; and *vice versa*. Honesty must not only be required in one department of our thought about baptism, but in all. And I should have thought that there was one thing that was really certain to those who are concerned for honesty in our thought about baptism: a vast area of uncertainty.[17]

Such frank admissions of uncertainty are rarely found in baptismal discussion, but perhaps more would be more willing to make them if some of the barriers of fear and prejudice surrounding the subject were to be dismantled.

The second step that Reformed churches could take to enhance the process towards convergence would be to allow room for those who have already been baptised as infants to be baptised as believers if they so wish. This is, admittedly, a difficult proposal and one which touches upon a very sensitive area. Rebaptism is often seen in paedobaptist circles as the rejection of a previous infant baptism and therefore, by extension, a rejection of the church and community which administered that baptism. But does rebaptism necessarily and always imply the rejection of something? Should it not rather be seen as the desire to affirm something? There are many reasons why people desire rebaptism. In some cases there might have been a profound conversion experience after a long period of having lapsed from any active Christian practice, and there is then a deep desire to testify of this conversion in some significant way. In other cases there might be serious reservations about the validity of the original infant baptism because of the failure of the parents to even attempt to provide a Christian upbringing – and the list could be extended. But the point that needs to be made is that it is in the interests of the church to create space for those who are convinced of the need to be rebaptised. Often their desire is to remain in the church, and if handled with sensitivity and understanding they have the potential to remain or become active and useful members of the church, even learning to respect others who have not felt led in the same way in the matter of rebaptism. Furthermore, their rebaptism could be viewed by the church as a celebration or renewal of their baptismal vows. Some churches in the Reformed tradition (e.g. the Presbyterian Church in New Zealand) have already made use of this concept of the 'celebration of baptismal vows' by allowing members to be immersed in water in the name of the triune God as a celebration of the baptismal vows taken on their behalf as children (the formula used is slightly different from that used in regular baptisms).

A further objection could be made that if such laxity in baptismal matters were to prevail a situation of total confusion could result characterized by widespread rebaptisms and numbers of infants remaining unbaptised. But the answer to this objection would be essentially the same as that given earlier in this chapter to Baptists who feared the consequences of too much freedom in their churches, namely, that if the case for infant baptism is so weak that it cannot be maintained in an environment of free and open discussion (in which anyway it would be preached from the pulpit), then does it really deserve to be maintained by the questionable means of simply outlawing all contrary opinions and practices and excluding them from the church?

As was the case with the proposals concerning steps Baptists could take towards convergence, so here in the case of Reformed and other paedobaptist churches the proposals discussed above can be summarized quite simply as allowing for greater freedom of conscience in baptismal matters, believing that the truth of God will surely ultimately prevail in an atmosphere of open and honest study and discussion. In an eloquent passage on the precious gift of liberty which is 'both a gift and a task for the Church' Küng concludes as follows:

> No one in the Church has any right openly or secretly to manipulate, suppress or still less to abolish the basic freedom of the children of God and, instead of the rule of God, to set up the domination of men over men. This freedom should be manifested particularly in the Church in free speech (frankness) and the free choice of action or refraining from action (liberality and magnanimity in the widest sense of the terms); and it should be evident also in the Church's institutions and constitutions. The Church itself should be a *realm of freedom* and at the same time the *advocate of freedom in the world.*[18]

The kind of freedom being advocated by Hans Küng is always a little unnerving, if not downright threatening, to Christians concerned for the purity of the faith and the unity of their particular church. Yet at a deeper level the granting of such freedom to fellow-believers is a profound act of faith in the power of the Holy Spirit to guide his people and in the wisdom of God in the management of his church. And if situations of confusion arise in the church with apparently conflicting baptismal practices contending with one another, the end result could well be an enrichment of the church rather than its destruction.

> We have to recognise differences that exist amongst us about baptism, and the nature of the confession of faith. These, however, are issues that will be resolved as we draw closer together. In particular we believe that in a united Church the co-existence of patterns of initiation, including both believers' baptism and infant baptism, will itself lead to a fresh appreciation of the insights they reflect, without being destructive of the unity we wish to attain or compromising the question of achieving a common practice subsequently.[19]

Steps that could be taken by churches holding to a Catholic and sacramental understanding of baptism

By 'Catholic and sacramental' is meant here those churches holding to a 'high' baptismal theology in which baptism is held to be the direct and ordinary means whereby individuals are regenerated to eternal life and become children of God – *ex opere operato* (by the performance of the rite). These churches would include the Roman Catholic Church and the Eastern Orthodox Churches as well as many churches in the Lutheran and Anglican traditions. The proposals concerning steps which these churches could take towards convergence are essentially the same as those suggested above for Reformed and other Protestant paedobaptist churches. However, although the proposals might be the same, the problems and difficulties involved with such proposals would be different on account of the nature of Catholic baptismal theology.

A decision to allow Catholic parents to delay the baptism of their children, if they so choose, until such time as they are able to make a personal profession of faith would be especially problematical in view of the Catholic doctrine of baptismal regeneration and the belief that infants left unbaptised would be deprived of baptismal grace. The omission of baptism would even jeopardize the eternal salvation of the infants concerned, so how could the church be expected to sanction, however grudgingly, such an act? These are serious considerations, and need to be taken seriously by anyone genuinely interested in promoting reconciliation and a convergence towards unity. The writer is persuaded, however, that there are compelling theological arguments, drawn specifically from Catholic theology, that can help to answer these difficulties.

Before considering any theological answer, there is a compelling practical reason why it would be in the church's interest to permit a more flexible approach in baptismal matters. If certain parents should come to have doubts about the validity of infant baptism, a rigid and inflexible response from the church would tend only to drive them into the arms of another church perhaps more sympathetic to their doubts, and that would not improve the situation for any infants involved, from a Catholic perspective. But if, on the other hand, room is made in the church for alternative baptismal practices for those not convinced about infant baptism, then there always remains the opportunity of persuading them, in time, of the merits of infant baptism. This pragmatic approach is more or less a repetition of what has already been said in connection with Reformed churches.

The teaching that an unbaptised infant is in danger of eternal loss is strongly dependent on the Augustinian doctrine of original sin. While the theology of Augustine has played a powerful role in western Christianity, both Catholic and Protestant, some of the implications of the doctrine of original sin have been the subject of considerable debate, also in Catholic circles. The Augustinian view has never found widespread acceptance in the Orthodox Church, which understands itself to be the 'One, Holy, Catholic and Apostolic Church' of the creed and is, at least, an important component of the 'catholic world' in the wider sense.

> Most orthodox theologians reject the idea of 'original guilt', put forward by Augustine and still accepted (albeit in a mitigated form) by the Roman Catholic Church. Men (Orthodox usually teach) automatically inherit Adam's corruption and mortality, but not his guilt: they are only guilty in so far as by their own free choice they imitate Adam. . . . And Orthodox have never held (as Augustine and many others in the west have done) that unbaptised babies, because tainted with original guilt, are consigned by the just God to the everlasting flames of Hell. The Orthodox picture of fallen humanity is far less sombre than the Augustine or Calvinist view.[20]

As a result Orthodox Christians, while strongly maintaining the validity and desirability of infant baptism, do not normally experience the anxiety that is often found in western Catholic circles concerning the fate of unbaptised infants. So in this body of Catholic Christendom, at least, the possibility of some parents delaying the baptism of their children might not be regarded as totally unacceptable. But in Roman Catholic theology, too, there has been a long tradition of scholars who have looked 'for a way of affirming the salvation of unbaptised infants that will not contradict the tradition of the universal necessity of Baptism, and the correlative universality of original sin.'[21] Walsh himself admits:

In truth, it is hard to believe that a God who so loved the world as to give his only-begotten Son for the salvation of all, and who is believed to take more delight in the saving of one lost soul than in the ninety-nine who are already safe, would set a baptismal requirement so rigid that it would exclude from salvation an infant who, through no fault of its own, does not fulfil it literally.[22]

Walsh then proceeds to survey a number of attempts by Catholic scholars to provide a theological and biblical foundation for the affirmation of the salvation by Christ of infants (especially of believers), whether baptised or not. All this demonstrates, surely, that the possibility of permitting some parents to delay the baptism of their infants, for reasons of conscience, is not completely outside the bounds of contemporary and ancient Catholic thinking. Indeed some of the early Fathers, such as Tertullian and Gregory of Nazianzus, *advocated* the delay of the baptism of children until they were able to grasp something of the meaning of the rite. While it may be conceded that their views on infant baptism did not represent the mainstream of Catholic thinking at that time, it must be equally conceded that such views were not excluded from the Catholic church of the time. And if the Catholic church of the fourth century was flexible enough to make room for a variety of baptismal views and practices, why cannot the Catholic church of the twentieth century do the same? It would seem that at least some contemporary Roman Catholic scholars are thinking along these lines, as evidenced by the following remark in a Faith and Order Paper:

In view of the notable agreement on the meaning of baptism, it is not surprising that there are replies which explicitly state that it is possible for infant and believers' baptism to co-exist in one church. This raises the question of whether this practice could be expanded in order to promote wider consensus.[23]

The above-mentioned document, of course, is not an official Roman Catholic document. Catholic scholars, however, work in such close co-operation with scholars from other traditions on the Faith and Order Commission that the above remarks surely carry the endorsement of significant Catholic theologians – and those who have been officially delegated by their Church to their work on this Commission.

There is an even more powerful theological reason why Catholics should be in favour of greater flexibility in baptismal practice, a principle which would lie close to the heart of every true Catholic. It is the principle of catholicity. The Catholic church stretches out its arms to embrace all the faithful in Christ throughout the world and eschews, in principle, any tendency to sectarianism or exclusiveness that would divide the body of Christ. In his study on the church in the New Testament, the Catholic scholar Rudolf Schnackenburg speaks of the 'catholicity of spirit' of the apostle Paul as follows:

> But the great missionary and theologian also based this openness of the Church to all who wished to be saved and this bringing together of natural contraries in the one community of belief and love on ideas which he derived from the concept of the Church's nature. He himself wished 'to become all things to all men' and he made little account of external manner of life, whether according to Jewish Law or without it, adapting himself to the mentality of as many as possible (1 Cor.9:19–22). He took the idea seriously that in Christ a new man comes to be, with whom neither circumcision nor uncircumcision is of any importance (Gal.6:15) . . . The universality of the Church was not therefore promoted merely on missionary or opportunistic grounds but was profoundly rooted in its essential idea.[24]

Would it be too bold to suggest that the contemporary application of this truly catholic spirit of Paul would lead to the statement: 'Neither paedobaptism nor credobaptism is of ultimate importance, but a new creature in Christ and a fellowship of reconciliation and love centred on Christ'? Of course such a statement would not and could not have been made in the first century. But is it not the dynamic equivalent in the twentieth century of similar statements in the first? In his study of denominationalism and Christian unity, Wolfhart Pannenberg – not a Roman Catholic, but a man of catholic spirit – draws the following conclusions:

> The unity of the church is not primarily a unity of doctrine. It rests on a common confession of Jesus Christ. Differences and even contradictions in the way that Christians understand the faith do not necessarily negate the fact that we share a common confession of faith. Such contradictions could be regarded as contrasting expressions of what is basically the intention to hold the same faith, expressions that correct and supplement each other. To be sure, they could also be regarded as expressions of contradictions that invalidate our confession of Christ, that is, expressions that the other person is confessing something other than faith in Jesus Christ. Which of these is the case must finally be decided by a spiritual verdict on the situation in which such contradictions arise. In terms of a doctrinal confession, contradictions that we previously tolerated in our understanding of the faith can come to be seen as contradictions in our confession of Christ himself. On the other hand, disagreements that were once regarded as crucial to our confession of faith in Christ may, in the light of a later time, lose their force and validity.[25]

Pannenberg is not advocating some bland inclusivity that dispenses with any criteria whatever concerning what is Christian, but rightly distinguishes between those differences that can and ought to be tolerated within a catholic unity and those which cannot. And the different baptismal traditions considered in this book surely do not constitute such a contradiction of the confession of Christ that it is impossible for them to be included in a Christian unity.

No specific mention has yet been made of the issue of rebaptism. As in the case of churches in the Reformed tradition, Catholic churches view the question of rebaptism with grave concern and strong disapproval. Arguments that could be brought forward for the allowance of the possibility of rebaptism would be essentially the same as those cited above (for Reformed and other paedobaptist churches), so they will not be repeated here. Only a few comments can be added concerning the concept of 'the celebration of baptismal vows'. As has already been stated, some churches in the Reformed tradition have made room for those having a strong desire to be baptised as believers by permitting them to receive a rite of washing as a celebration, or renewal, of the vows made by the sponsors on their behalf when they were baptised as infants. This is a recent development in Protestant churches, but the Roman Catholic Church has had for centuries a liturgy for the celebration of baptismal vows involving the sprinkling of the whole congregation with water by the priest while the congregation repeat their baptismal vows. Seeing that such a 'celebration of baptismal vows', complete with sprinkling of water, already exists in the Roman Catholic Church, the way is surely open for individuals to be washed (by immersion or some other way) in water in the name of the Triune God on confession of their faith, as a celebration, or renewal, of their baptismal vows.

Concluding remarks

In all the above suggestions and proposals there is a common theme: greater freedom for individual Christians to be able to act according to their conscience in baptismal matters, together with the cultivation of a spirit of tolerance between Christians and respect for each other's views. This would apply, naturally, to all parties involved. Those dissenting from the official position of their church would need to respect the views of the majority who adhere to that position, if they in turn wish to be allowed freedom to act in accordance with their own convictions. Again it needs to be emphasized that the freedom that is being advocated here never implies any endorsement of views contrary to the official and traditional views, but only and simply a recognition that those holding to irregular views might well be, and often are, sincere Christians, zealous for the glory of God, and therefore ought not to be excluded from the church but rather received and respected, however defective their personal views on baptism might be.

It must be pointed out what real advantages there would be for every church and for the Christian cause in general in the adoption of a greater flexibility in baptismal policy. At the present time it often occurs that Christians from different traditions get married and then find great difficulty finding a spiritual home on account of the inflexibility of their respective churches. Let us take, for example, the case of Christians from a Baptist and a Reformed tradition. The Baptist partner would feel uneasy about joining the Reformed church in which they would obliged to have their children baptised in infancy. The Reformed partner would be unwilling to join the Baptist church if rebaptism was a condition for membership. As a result the family is alienated, to some extent, from both churches with the very real possibility of lapsing altogether from any regular pattern of worship and Christian fellowship. They would be lost, in the end, to both churches. It is to be feared that this is no mere hypothetical possibility but an actual reality in many cases. Bridge and Phypers also describe as 'common' cases where Christians from different denominational backgrounds get married and then experience difficulties in finding a spiritual home on account of the inflexibility of their respective churches.

If we refer back to the two models of church relations considered at the beginning of this chapter, it can be seen that the 'laager' model has clearly demarcated spaces between the various church bodies. It is precisely in these 'spaces' that many are lost to the church. The convergence model, on the other hand, has no such spaces between the churches, allowing for a gradation of views between the official positions of the different bodies. In this way those who do not comfortably fit into the traditional and official patterns of any of the existing churches can nevertheless find themselves a spiritual home on account of the flexibility permitted. All churches would benefit in the end as the total number of Christians 'falling through the cracks' of ecclesiastical divisions would be fewer. Mention could also be made of the possible enrichment of each tradition precisely through the exposure to views and practices other than the regular ones.

Yet another benefit that could well result from a policy of greater flexibility would be the reduction of the number of new Christian denominations being formed, as those with new insights and non-traditional views might find a sympathetic ear and a spirit of tolerance in their churches rather than an unyielding rigidity resulting in rejection and schism. As a case in point we could take the Disciples of Christ, a major Protestant denomination in the United States of America. Thomas Campbell, one of the founders of the Disciples and a man 'possessed of a truly catholic spirit', [26] found himself censured by his fellow Presbyterians on account of his welcoming at the Lord's Table various believers who did not adhere to the Presbyterian organization to which he belonged. Others joined with him and this group became associated with the Baptists having adopted baptism by immersion. But their stress on a baptism 'unto remission of sins' and their practice of a wide open communion led to their separation from the Baptists too. Hence the formation of the Disciples of Christ, from which in time other schismatic groups developed. And all this from Christian leaders who were deeply concerned for Christian unity! If the Presbyterians had only been more understanding and flexible, how much could they have benefited by retaining this man of clearly outstanding gifts. If the Baptists had been more far-sighted they could have been the beneficiaries. As it was, neither group benefited and the division of Christian ranks was further aggravated.

Many further examples could be enumerated. What if the English bishops of the eighteenth century had been more flexible and sympathetic towards Wesley and the early Methodists, all loyal Anglicans? What if the sixteenth century Reformers had been more tolerant and understanding of the Anabaptists, who also desired to reform the church according to the word of God? Indeed, what if Pope Leo X had been able to discern the voice of the Spirit in the voice of Martin Luther, who desired nothing other than to be a faithful Catholic? What if tenth century Latin and Greek Christians had been able to listen to one another in a spirit of understanding and charity rather than hurl anathemas at one another over issues such *as filioque*, clerical tonsures and the bread used in the eucharist? What if all Christians, like the apostle Paul, were able to rejoice in the preaching of Christ, however defective that preaching and false the motives behind it (Phil:1.18)? How much the church has lost in the past by an unbending and inflexible rigidity in matters which should never have been allowed to divide Christians from one another and thereby cause public schisms which have seriously undermined its message of reconciliation and its witness to the work of God which is 'to bring all things in heaven and earth under one head, even Christ' (Eph.1:10).

The whole thrust of the development of the church throughout history has been in the direction of greater variety as the church has expanded to fill the nations and cultures of the world. Coupled with this has been a continual movement towards greater freedom – not a freedom to indulge the flesh (although it has often degenerated into that) but a freedom in Christ. Where the structures and prevailing attitudes of the churches have been unable to cope with this movement towards greater variety and freedom, divisions have resulted. It must be realized, however, that this trend will not be reversed. The future will see even greater variety and greater freedoms. The church must recognize this and be prepared for it, so as not to react negatively to every new thing but to be willing to examine all things carefully so as to discern whether what is new is completely incompatible with the gospel or whether it can at least be tolerated in the church.

It might be thought that in the realm of baptism all the possible variations in doctrine and practice already exist in some or other Christian church today. But this would be a mistake. It has already been pointed out earlier in this book (Chapter 3) that the contemporary practice, hallowed by centuries of usage, of administering baptism at fixed places (usually in a church) and at fixed times (usually on certain Sundays) by an ordained minister of the church has no real foundation in New Testament practice. On the contrary, the evidence available to us, chiefly in the Acts of the Apostles, led to the suggestion of the following thesis: that *baptism in the New Testament was administered by any Christian to any person desiring to become a Christian at any place and at any time*. What if this practice were to be revived today? What if regular Christian believers, taking their stand on the priesthood of all believers, were to claim their right to be the ordinary ministers of baptism? Would the church regard this as a threat? Would the regular clergy fear that such a movement might take out of their hands altogether the exclusive right to administer the sacrament of baptism? Would such a movement lead to the formation of yet another Christian sect, characterized by novel and strange baptismal practices and duly shunned by regular Christian churches? Or could the churches reserve judgement and allow room for such a new development, however many reservations they might have about its correctness or desirability? Could they even see in such new developments the possibility of a new and powerful tool in the hands of the 'laity', equipping them more effectively in the task of evangelism? In the world today there are many people, Muslims for example, for whom public baptism is a deterrent to conversion to the Christian faith. The possibility of private baptism might well open a new door in helping the church to break through in some of the difficult challenges it faces in its evangelistic task. The practice of administering baptism immediately to those desirous of receiving salvation though Christ, without waiting for any special person, time or place would surely restore to the sacrament of baptism the full and rich meaning it has in the New Testament. It might help to restore also a more widespread perception of baptism as the way in which we are united to Christ and receive through him all the benefits of redemption.

Such thoughts might seem to be speculative and rash and in contradiction to the whole aim and tenor of this book, namely, baptism, reconciliation and unity. But the point being made is that the tendency of the church in the past to reject any deviation from the standard and accepted doctrines and practices in baptism, has led to division. In making a decision to be more flexible and tolerant of varying baptismal convictions, it must not only take into account those variations in baptismal practice presently existing but also other variations in administration that might still appear.

A final comment on the content of this chapter. The primary focus has been on the steps various churches in different traditions could take in order to grow towards one another. Clearly anyone concerned with Christian unity cannot avoid the subject of how churches and denominations might actually join together, and such a discussion would necessarily involve a consideration of various possible models of ecclesiastical unity. But that has not been the subject of this chapter. In a sense what has been the focus of this chapter could be seen as preparation for the more serious business of actual church unions. Before churches can even begin to want to discuss unity plans there must be a desire for such a union, and before there can be a desire for such a union there must be some kind of respect for one another. The development of some kind of respect (in the midst of disagreement) has been the thrust of this chapter. The 'models' spoken of here have not been models of church union, but simply models of how churches can relate to one another while still separate and autonomous. If churches from within themselves can begin to grow towards one another, then when the time comes to discuss the possibility of union (of whatever kind that may be) the chasms between them will not be so great or forbidding. Indeed, it even might be difficult to find any differences sufficiently serious so as to justify remaining apart!

Notes

1 D. Deane, 'Truth and the Flight from Unity,' *Studies* 301(1987):56.
2 H. Küng, *The Church – Maintained in Truth* (London, SCM, 1980) p.29.
3 H. Küng, *The Church* (London, Search, 1976), p.29.
4 Ibid.
5 F.S. MacNutt, 'A proposed, practical solution to the controversy between proponents of Believers' Baptism and Infant Baptism', in A. König, H.I. Lederle, & F.P. Möller, *Infant Baptism? The arguments for and against* (Roodepoort, CUM, 1984), p.161.

6   H. Küng, *The Church – Maintained in Truth* (London, SCM, 1980) p.61.
7   Ibid., p.11.
8   Ibid., p.15.
9   IFCC 1986 p.9.
10 A. Gilmore, *Baptism and Christian Unity* (London, Lutterworth, 1966), p.82.
11 Ibid., p.81.
12 K. Barth, *The teaching of the Church regarding baptism* (London, SCM, 1959), p.35 & 40.
13 K. Barth, *Church Dogmatics, Vol. IV, 4* (Edinburgh, T & T Clark, 1969), p.189.
14 A. Gilmore, *Baptism and Christian Unity* (London, Lutterworth, 1966), p.83.
15 H. Berkhof, *Christian Faith. Revised Edition* (Grand Rapids, Eerdmans, 1986), p.359.
16 G.C. Berkouwer, *The Sacraments* (Grand Rapids, Eerdmans, 1981), p.106.
17. J. James, 'Reflections on the Conference,' in B.S. Moss (ed.), *Crisis for Baptism* (London, SCM, 1965), p.138.
18 H. Küng, *On being a Christian* (Glasgow, Collins, 1978), p.482.
19 M. Hurley (ed.), *Ecumenical Studies. Baptism and Marriage* (Dublin, Gill & Son, 1968), p.45.
20 T. Ware, *The Orthodox Church* (Harmondsworth, Penguin, 1980), p.229.
21 L.G. Walsh, *The Sacraments of Initiation* (London, Geoffrey Chapman, 1988), p.106.
22 Ibid.
23 *Towards an Ecumenical Consensus on Baptism, the Eucharist and the Ministry: A Response to the Churches* (Geneva, Faith and Order Paper No. 84, 1977), p.7.
24 R. Schnackenburg, *The Church in the New Testament* (London, Burnes & Oates, 1981), p.138.
25 W. Pannenberg, *The Church* (Philadelphia, Westminster Press, 1983), p.81.
26 J.E. Orr, *The Light of the Nations* (Exeter, Paternoster, 1965), p.55.

Chapter 7

A Hierarchy of Truths?

This book contains a number of references to concepts such as freedom of conscience, religious liberty and flexibility of action. When Christians who take their faith seriously hear talk about freedom of conscience and absolute religious liberty they sometimes begin to entertain unsettling suspicions that somehow the very substance of the faith is under attack and the foundations are perhaps being eroded. This is especially true of conservative Christians, from whatever tradition they come, be it conservative evangelical or traditional catholic or orthodox. For this reason it might be useful at this point to consider briefly the issue of a 'hierarchy of truths'. What are those beliefs and practices in the Christian faith which are non-negotiable, concerning which there can be no room for variation of thought, since they constitute the very essence of the faith? What, on the other hand, are those beliefs and practices in which it is perfectly legitimate for Christians to differ among themselves? What kind of gradation can be made between those doctrines and rites of more or less importance within the Christian faith? Such questions are not easy to answer but they point to the existence of a hierarchy of truths and it is probably true that most Christians would freely acknowledge that in the whole range of Christian teaching there are some aspects that lie closer to the heart of the Christian faith while others are more on its periphery. The Decree on Ecumenism, *Unitatis Redintegratio,* for example, produced by Vatican II reminds Catholics that 'in Catholic doctrine there exists an order or "hierarchy" of truths, since they vary in relation to the foundation of the Christian faith' (*U.R.*II.11).[1]

The following chapter does not contain an exhaustive discussion of a hierarchy of truths. Such a discussion would require a separate book on its own. On the contrary it will only touch very lightly on certain broad aspects of the subject with a view to affirming the idea or concept of a hierarchy of truths. There are considerable allusions in other chapters in this book to the concept of a hierarchy of truths, and there is no need to repeat unnecessarily material contained in those chapters.

The concept of a hierarchy of truths

From time to time various Christian bodies, have issued doctrinal statements which imply the existence of a hierarchy of truths. Needless to say, their views on which things are most important, as well as the implied hierarchy of truths, are not always the same.

Towards the beginning of the twentieth century conservative Protestants in the USA produced a series of 'Fundamentals of the Faith' as an expression of what they considered to be vital to an authentic Christian faith. These 'fundamentals' included doctrines such as the inerrancy of Scripture, the virgin birth of Christ, his deity, his atoning death on the cross, his resurrection from the dead and his personal return.

In 1888 Anglicans adopted a four-point statement, known as the Lambeth Quadrilateral outlining those aspects of faith and order that could serve as an essential basis for a wider Christian unity. It identified: (1) the supremacy and sufficiency of the Scriptures; (2) the Apostle's Creed and the Nicene Creed as the sufficient statement of the Christian faith; (3) the two dominical sacraments; (4) the historical episcopate.

Eastern Orthodox Christians would point to the first seven ecumenical councils (held between 325 and 787) as expressing the catholic faith of the undivided early church and therefore essential to any statement of Christian truth today.

In 1968, in order to put an end to the confusion that was raging in the Roman Catholic Church after Vatican II, the Pope issued his profession of faith which became known as the Creed of Pope Paul VI.[2] This was a papal attempt to sum up those things central and vital to the faith of Catholics. It affirmed faith in the triune God, the incarnation of the divine Word, his birth of the Virgin Mary by the power of the Holy Spirit, his atoning death on the cross, his resurrection from the dead, his ascension into heaven and his coming again in glory to judge the living and the dead. It also included belief in papal infallibility, transubstantiation and purgatory.

While there is a certain degree of agreement between these various attempts to distil the essence of the Christian faith, there are also notable differences. The creed of Pope Paul VI has much in common with the 'fundamentals' of conservative Protestants – until it comes to the issues of papal infallibility, purgatory and transubstantiation!

What follows in the remaining part of this chapter is not so much an attempt to work out a fully developed hierarchy of truths or even an attempt to enter in any depth into the theological discussion around the subject. Rather it is more a personal exercise in dealing with the biblical material in the Old and New Testaments to establish the concept of a hierarchy of truths and in particular to point out the distinction between what may be called primary and secondary aspects of the faith. The purpose of this exercise is to help the reader understand what is meant in *this* book when mention is made of concepts such as freedom of conscience, religious liberty and flexibility, and what are the limits and parameters of such concepts.

Primary and secondary aspects of Christian faith

By primary aspects of the faith is meant those things which constitute the very essence of the faith and without which there would be no distinctive Christian faith at all. By secondary aspects is meant those things which play a valuable and important role in promoting, confirming and consolidating the faith but which nevertheless do not form part of the very essence of the faith so that their absence would not mean the absence of saving faith. It follows that error in such secondary aspects, or differences of understanding and practice are not destructive of the faith itself. The distinction here being proposed is much the same as the distinction between the *esse* and *bene esse* of the church used by some of the older theologians, that which consists of the being of the church itself and that which consists of its well-being.

What, then, is here proposed as essential to Christian faith? It is the conviction that the God who has revealed himself through the history of the Hebrew people and in the person of Jesus the Messiah is indeed the one true God – a Saviour, Redeemer and Helper of all who put their trust in him and keep his commandments. This is faith: faith in God, not any god but *this* God, the God of Abraham, the God of Israel who saved his people out of Egypt and brought them into their own land, and who in the fulness of time sent a Redeemer, Jesus, the Son of God, who suffered, died and rose again to save his people from their sins. To know this God, to believe and trust in him and to keep his commandments – this, it is proposed, is of the essence of Christian faith.

What then are the secondary aspects, important for the welfare and development of faith, yet not so essential that their absence would imply the absence of true faith? Secondary are all the external matters such as rites and ceremonies; structures, forms and customs. Since faith is something inward it will always be expressed in particular rites and ceremonies and will always give rise to particular structures and forms. It cannot do otherwise. Yet we must always remember that these outward aspects are but the outward manifestations of faith. The same faith may find expression in different and varying rites and give rise to different structures. Practically speaking, what is being referred to in terms of Christian practice? Forms of worship, the liturgy, styles of praying and singing; structures of church government and organization; styles and patterns of leadership; rites of salvation, confession, restitution, remembrance and thanksgiving; sacramental rites such as baptism, eucharist, penance, foot-washing, anointing with oil; the number of sacraments practised, whether two or seven or none; special days for worship and celebration; marriage customs, funeral customs, initiation customs, coming of age customs; customs of dressing and eating and fasting – all these and many other things could be mentioned as secondary matters, playing an important role in the life and order of the church and yet not to be confused with the very essence of the faith of the church.

These secondary aspects could themselves be further graded into another hierarchy. The rites of baptism and eucharist, for example, obviously play a more central and important role than marriage customs and customs of dress. The point being made, however, is that they are *all* secondary, in that faith can exist without them. Faith in God and Christ through the power of the Holy Spirit does come into being even without the rites of baptism and eucharist, valuable as the latter are for the well-being of the church.

In summary, then, it is suggested that primary to Christian faith is simply trust in God and his grace, as he has made himself known to his covenant people Israel through the prophets and apostles and supremely through his only begotten Son, the Lord Jesus Christ, the Word of God incarnate, the crucified and risen Saviour of the world. Always there is implicit to this trust, of course, the ethical element of commitment and obedience. But secondary to the Christian faith are all matters pertaining to the cult of this one true God, how he is worshipped and served by his people in the ordering of their lives as a community of faith.

But does this suggested hierarchy of truths reflect the central thrust of teaching contained in the Christian Scriptures, the Old and New Testaments? To this question the following brief consideration of certain scriptural passages will be offered as an answer.

The witness of the Old Testament

Does the Old Testament have something that can be considered its centre – one single unifying concept? This question is closely related to our concern to ascertain the essence of faith in the Old Testament. In his valuable work on Old Testament theology Gerhard Hasel[2] has provided something of an overview of the scholarly discussion around the above question, outlining the views of outstanding scholars such as Eichrodt, Sellin, Kohler, Wildberger, Seebass, Klein, Fohrer, Vriezen, Schmidt, Zimmerli and others. After surveying this scholarly discussion, Hasel concludes that the Old Testament is in its essence *theocentric* just as the New Testament is *christocentric*. In short, God is the dynamic, unifying centre of the Old Testament, who introduces and identifies himself by great events in deeds and words, and it is around them that Israel responds in praise and worship, and that Biblical literature originates.[4]

If God is the centre of the Old Testament who identifies himself by great events, then the greatest of these events in the history of the people of Israel was undoubtedly the exodus event. This was the event recalled in so many of the rites, prayers and feasts of Israel, the event to which so many of the Hebrew scriptures bear witness. Thus it is that the summary of the whole law which we commonly call the Ten Commandments is introduced by a preamble in which it is declared: 'I am the LORD your God, who brought you out of Egypt, out of the house of slavery' (Dt.5:6). Israel's faith is directed towards God, the only living and true God, Yahweh, the God of Abraham, the God of Isaac, the God of Jacob, the one who came down to save his people out of their distress and bondage in Egypt, who took them out of that land and gave them a land of their own where they might serve him in holiness all their days. The implications for ancient Israel of what it means to trust and serve this God are spelled out in the ethical requirements that follow: the prohibitions against idolatry, blasphemy, murder, adultery, theft, deceit and covetousness and the injunctions to honour parents and keep the Sabbath rest. John Bright summed up the heart of Israel's faith as follows:

> Israel's notion of God was unique in the ancient world, and a phenomenon that defies rational explanation. Nevertheless, to understand her faith in terms of an idea of God is a fundamental error, and one that is bound to lead to a misreading of the entire Old Testament. Israel's religion rested in no abstract theological propositions, but in the memory of historical experience as interpreted by, and responded to, in faith. She believed that Yahweh, her God, had by his mighty acts rescued her from Egypt and, in covenant, had made her his people.[5]

The *shema* expresses the heart of Israel's confession: 'Hear, O Israel: the LORD our God, the LORD is one. Love the LORD your God with all your heart and with all your soul and with all your strength. These commandments that I give you today are to be upon your hearts' (Dt.6:4–6). A little later in the same book we find a similar exhortation to trust in Yahweh, the God of Israel, and to keep his ways:

> And now, O Israel, what does the LORD your God ask of you but to fear the LORD your God, to walk in all his ways, to love him, to serve the LORD your God with all your heart and with all your soul, and to observe the LORD'S commands and decrees that I am giving you today for your own good (Dt.10:12,13)?

In the practical outworking of Israel's faith in the life of the people there inevitably and necessarily developed a special cult of worship and service, centred on the temple in Jerusalem and supported by a chosen caste of priests who carried out a variety of sacrifices and other ritual acts on specially appointed days throughout the year. All of this was by divine command, according to detailed instructions in the sacred books. So important was this official cult of worship and sacrifice that a prophet such as Haggai could make the rebuilding of the Temple in Jerusalem the central focus of his prophetic ministry. Yet the possibility of performing the external rites of the cult without any real trust in God and true obedience to his commands was sharply pointed out by many of the later prophets:

> 'The multitude of your sacrifices – 'what are they to me?' says the LORD. 'I have more than enough of burnt offerings, of rams and the fat of fattened animals; I have no pleasure in the blood of bulls and lambs and goats. When you come to appear before me, who has asked this of you, this trampling of my courts? Stop bringing meaningless offerings! Your incense is detestable to me. New Moons, Sabbaths and convocations – I cannot bear your evil assemblies. Your New Moon festivals and your appointed feasts my soul hates. They have become a burden to me; I am weary of bearing them. When you spread out your hands in prayer, I will hide my eyes from you; even if you offer many prayers, I will not listen. Your hands are full of blood; wash and make yourselves clean. Take your evil deeds out of my sight! Stop doing wrong, learn to do right! Seek justice, encourage the oppressed. Defend the cause of the fatherless, plead the case of the fatherless, plead the case of the widow' (Is.1:11–17).

In this passage we see a clear distinction between the primary and secondary aspects of faith. Almost the entire cult – sacrifices, liturgical prayers, feasts and festivals – is dismissed as worthless because of the absence of what is primary to the faith of Israel, trust in God and an ethical lifestyle in the fear of the LORD. 'Every religion has its necessary outward forms,' comments Alec Motyer,[6] 'and every religion is susceptible to the same danger of defining the reality in terms of the form. . . . [Isaiah] was issuing a call to return to the primitive integration of the two elements of ethics and rite.' Hosea says the same thing when he declares on behalf of the Lord: 'I desire mercy, not sacrifice, and acknowledgment of God rather than burnt offerings' (Hos. 6:6). And virtually all the prophets struck the same note in their ministries (e.g. Mic. 6:8; Am. 5:21–24).

In a more positive way the psalms bear witness to the essence of Israel's faith. It is interesting to notice the lack of emphasis in the psalms on the sacrificial system in the temple cultus. Even those references that there are to the official cult are usually in the context of prayers of repentance, praise, intercession or thanksgiving. Far greater attention in the psalms is focused on God himself, Yahweh, the God of Israel, who 'remembers his covenant for ever, the word he commanded, for a thousand generations, the covenant he made with Abraham, the oath he swore to Isaac. He confirmed it to Jacob as a decree, to Israel as an everlasting covenant: "To you I will give the land of Canaan as the portion you will inherit" ' (Ps.105:8–11). Again and again the mighty acts of Yahweh are recounted, when he saved and delivered his people, especially the exodus event. These continual reminders were intended to encourage the people of Israel to put their trust entirely in their God and to seek his ways so that they too might experience his saving help.

> It cannot be said too often that the Psalter is a mirror which reflects not so much the religious experience of individuals as the experience of 'the religious soul of Israel' conceived as a corporate personality. . . . And this religion of the individual before God as reflected in the Psalter was supremely an expression of confident trust in the Lord, of praise to God, of acceptance with God. It was rooted in obedience to the law of God and of fellowship with God.[7]

The witness of the New Testament

The distinction between what is here being called the primary and secondary aspects of Israel's faith is brought out in sharp relief in the teaching of Jesus. When asked to identify the greatest commandment in the Law, Jesus simply quoted the words of the *shema*: 'Love the Lord your God with all your heart and with all your soul and with all your mind' (Mt.22:37). Then, to spell out clearly the ethical implications of what it means to love God and trust in him, he added: 'Love your neighbour as yourself. All the Law and the Prophets hang on these two commandments' (Mt.22.39). The preaching of Jesus is summarized in the synoptic gospels as 'the good news of the kingdom of God' (Lk.4:43), a message focused on God, who reigns over all in power and majesty. When it came to matters of ritual observance Jesus was no iconoclast. He did not reject all religious externals as a matter of principle; on the contrary, he adhered to the rites of religious observance as would any pious Jew. He refused, however, to subject the primary aspects of an ethically-oriented faith in God to the various details of cultic observance. Typical of his stance in this matter were his words to the Pharisees:

Woe to you Pharisees, because you give God a tenth of your mint, rue and all kinds of garden herbs, but you neglect justice and the love of God. You should have practised the latter without leaving the former undone (Lk.11:42).

In the same way, he refused to allow contemporary customs of Sabbath observance to take precedence over a ministry of mercy and healing. 'The Sabbath was made for man, not man for the Sabbath' (Mk.2:27). A secondary issue of ritual observance, valuable as it may be as an expression of faith and for the enhancement of faith, may not be regarded as being of the very essence of faith. On the issue of clean and unclean foods, again Jesus pointed to the primary issue of serving God from a pure and holy heart as being of greater importance than the secondary issue of the eating of clean foods (Mk:7.17–23). Similar instances could be quoted with regard to customs of fasting and cleansing and other ritual observances.

For the apostolic faith of the New Testament, then, the coming of Jesus was the supreme and definitive revelation of God to his people, the coming of God in mighty saving power to redeem his people from sin and bondage. The crucifixion, resurrection and ascension of Jesus constitute a new exodus event (*exodon* – Luke 9:31), laying the foundation for a new covenant whereby the Pentecostal gift of the Holy Spirit is poured out upon the Israel of God, destined now in a new and better dispensation to embrace all the various tribes and peoples of the earth. Subsequently, the apostolic message is still summarized as the good news of the kingdom of God (Acts 28:31) and the goal of that preaching is faith in Jesus as the Son of God, the incarnate Word of God who has come to make known the Father and to reconcile all people to the Father, the one true and living God, the God of Abraham, the God of Israel.

In this new community of faith, bound together by a common faith in Christ, some of the old rites fall away; they have become obsolete as they had primary reference to one particular ethnically-defined people, belonging to one particular geographically-bound land. By contrast, the new community of faith must develop new rites, new patterns of worship, new structures and new holy days of special observance. Therefore the distinction between primary and secondary aspects of the faith still remains. Primary to Christian faith is still faith in the one, true and living God, especially as he has made himself known through the marvellous and gracious salvation wrought through Jesus the Messiah. Inherent in that faith is still the ethical element, obedience to the law, now summed up as the law of love (Rom.13:8–10; Gal.5:14). Of secondary importance to the Christian faith are still all those outward matters of rites, customs, structures and observances, important for the initiation, celebration and renewal of faith and the good ordering of the life of the community, but not of the very essence of faith and trust in God.

Are there any evidences of this distinction in the apostolic writings? Certainly, despite the fact that the documents of the New Testament were produced in the time of the foundation of the church, a time of transition when many of the old rites were still being practised and the new rites just beginning to be developed. Nevertheless, the principle is clearly there. When reference is made, for example, to certain things 'without which no one shall enter the kingdom of God' the reference is always to matters of faith and morals. On the other hand there is always a certain flexibility when it comes to matters of rites and external practices, a tendency to downplay their importance in comparison to faith, love and righteousness. Commenting on Paul's statement, 'A man is not a Jew if he is only one outwardly, nor is circumcision merely outward and physical' (Rom. 2:28), Leon Morris observes:

> It was membership in the covenant of which circumcision was the sign that mattered. And covenant membership meant keeping the covenant. Without that, even the circumcised Israelite had no standing with God. Many commentators point out that Christian readers should remember that what is said here of circumcision applies with equal force to baptism.[8]

The New Testament documents consistently exalt the importance of faith. 'Without faith it is impossible to please God, because anyone who comes to him must believe that he exists and that he rewards those who earnestly seek him' (Heb.11:6). 'Whoever believes in the Son has eternal life' (Jn.3:36). 'Whoever hears my word and believes him who sent me has eternal life and will not be condemned; he has crossed over from death to life' (Jn.5:24). If it be asked what is the object of this faith, the answer is Christ himself, the good news of God's mighty act of salvation through Jesus the Messiah. Paul summed up this good news as follows:

> Now brothers, I want to remind you of the gospel I preached to you, which you received and on which you have taken your stand. By this gospel you are saved, if you hold firmly to the word I preached to you. Otherwise, you have believed in vain. For what I received I passed on to you as of first importance: that Christ died for our sins according to the Scriptures, that he was buried, that he was raised on the third day according to the Scriptures, and that he appeared to Peter, and then to the Twelve (1 Cor.15:1–5).

For Paul, the heart of saving faith was faith in God and his mighty acts wrought through Jesus the Messiah for the salvation of his people. Such faith was necessarily accompanied by an ethical lifestyle characterized by righteousness, love and holiness, without which 'no one will see the Lord'

(Heb.12:14). To the Corinthians Paul gave a solemn warning: 'Do not be deceived: Neither the sexually immoral nor idolaters nor adulterers nor male prostitutes nor homosexual offenders nor thieves nor the greedy nor drunkards nor slanderers nor swindlers will inherit the kingdom of God.' (1 Cor.6.9,10). Echoes of the decalogue can be heard in Paul's warning. In other places Paul stresses that all the commandments, whatever they may be, are summed up in this one rule: 'Love your neighbour as yourself' (Rom.13:9). Without this love, there is no Christian faith, there is nothing (1 Cor.13). Faith working through love is the burden also of the Johannine writings as well as the letter of James. For the Christian, faith in God is faith in Christ and love is the summary of the law.

If such faith working through love (which is faith in Christ as Saviour and Lord) is the primary aspect of the Christian faith, without which there is nothing, then what are those secondary aspects, concerning which differences and variations are legitimate? All outward matters of rites and observances. Matters concerning diet: 'Those who eat everything must not condemn those who do not, for God has accepted them. Who are you to judge someone else's servants? To their own master they stand or fall. And they will stand, for the Lord is able to make them stand' (Rom.14:3,4). The observance of special days: 'Some consider one day more sacred than another; others consider every day alike. Let all be fully convinced in their own minds' (Rom.14.5,6). As for the rite of circumcision: 'Neither circumcision nor uncircumcision means anything; what counts is a new creation' (Gal.6:15).

But would it be right to include the rite of baptism among those aspects of Christianity that are here being labelled secondary? In a way this whole book labours to answer that question, but a few preliminary observations can be made at this point. In the later ending of the Gospel of Mark (a postscript almost certainly not written by Mark, but reflecting nevertheless an early Christian tradition), the commission to evangelize the world is followed by the words: 'Whoever believes and is baptised will be saved, but whoever does not believe will be condemned' (Mk.16:16). It is surely significant that greater emphasis is laid on believing than on being baptised. While baptism would be the normal expression of faith, it is believing (or not believing) that determines one's eternal destiny. In one of the very few references to the baptising ministry of Jesus, it is explicitly mentioned that 'in fact it was not Jesus who baptised, but his disciples' (Jn.4:2). This reminds us of the remark of Paul to the Corinthians: 'For Christ did not send me to baptise, but to preach the gospel' (1 Cor.1:17). While we cannot press these isolated passages to tell us too much about baptism, neither can we ignore the clear impression that the administration of baptism is not ranked with the preaching of the faith in order of importance. The tentative suggestion, then, is that the rite of baptism can be included among those rites and observances that constitute a secondary aspect of Christianity, secondary in importance to the primary aspects of faith and love.

I realize how easily the last sentence above could be misunderstood, and emphasize yet again that my intention is not to minimize the importance of baptism. Baptism in New Testament times was the ordinary way of receiving salvation through Christ and to refuse baptism would have been to refuse Christ. Yet it remains true that certain instances in the biblical narratives (Cornelius; the thief on the cross) and in the history of the church (the Quakers; the Salvation Army) remind us that salvation and union with Christ are not necessarily dependent on the rite of baptism. Much as we may disagree with their views, we cannot exclude from the body of Christ those who, in accordance with their own Christian convictions, practise no rite of baptism at all.

Unitatis Redintegratio

Mention was made at the beginning of this chapter of a reference to a hierarchy of truths in the Decree on Ecumenism, *Unitatis Redintegratio (U.R.)*, produced by Vatican II. That document begins with the statement: 'The restoration of unity among all Christians is one of the principal concerns of the Second Vatican Council.'[9] Later it speaks of the existence in Catholic doctrine of 'an order or "hierarchy" of truths' (*U.R.*II.11). It is interesting to see how it develops this idea. With respect to the Eastern Churches the document notes 'the fact that the basic dogmas of the Christian faith concerning the Trinity and the Word of God made flesh from the Virgin Mary were defined in Ecumenical Councils held in the East. To preserve this faith, these Churches have suffered, and still suffer much' (*U.R.*III.14). Having referred to these matters of primary importance in the faith, the document then draws attention to the differences in ecclesiastical discipline between the Roman Catholic Church and the Eastern Orthodox Church and states that 'far from being an obstacle to the Church's unity, such diversity of customs and observances only adds to her beauty and contributes greatly to carrying out her mission' (*U.R.*III.16). What the document says about legitimate variety it is even willing 'to apply to differences in theological expressions of doctrine', observing that 'in such cases, these various theological formulations are often to be considered complementary rather than conflicting' (*U.R.*III.17). Concluding its comments on the Eastern Orthodox Church, the document states: 'In order to restore communion and unity or preserve them, one must "impose no burden beyond what is indispensable" (Acts 15:28)' (*U.R.*III.18). It is interesting to note that *Unitatis Redintegratio* also seems to draw a distinction between primary matters of faith, namely faith in the triune God according to the Scriptures, and those matters of customs and observances in which variety is not only legitimate, but even valuable, adding to the beauty of the Church and contributing to the carrying out of her mission.

In considering the Protestant churches which arose out of the sixteenth century Reformation, the document again identifies those primary aspects of Protestant faith with which it can identify, namely the confession of 'Jesus Christ as God and Lord and as the only Mediator between God and man for the glory of the one God, the Father, the Son and the Holy Spirit' (*U.R.*III.20). Furthermore the Council expressed its joy 'that our separated brethren look to Christ as the source and centre of ecclesiastical communion. Their longing for union with Christ impels them ever more to seek unity, and also to bear witness to their faith among the peoples of the earth' (*U.R.*III.20). Even the Protestant emphasis on Scripture is regarded positively, as 'the sacred Word is a precious instrument in the mighty hand of God for attaining to that unity which the Saviour holds out to all men' (*U.R.*III.21).

The question can be asked whether the Roman Catholic Church itself (or any other church for that matter) understands the full implications of its own stated principle: that 'in order to restore communion and unity or preserve them, one must "impose no burden beyond what is indispensable" ' (*U.R.*III.18). That which is indispensable is the faith itself, faith working through love, faith in the one true God who has made all things, who has redeemed all things through his Son Jesus Christ and who renews all things by his Spirit. Beyond this indispensable faith and love there are no matters of customs, rites and observances that are sufficient grounds to divide Christians from one another, for such a division would be a repudiation of that love which lies very high in the hierarchy of Christian truths.

Summary

In this chapter we have seen that there is a hierarchy of truths in the Christian faith. There are those aspects of primary importance which constitute the very essence of faith: faith in God, faith in the gospel, the good news of

God's redemption of the world through his Son. Also of primary importance are the ethical implications of faith: obedience to Christ's commands, a life of love. Aspects of secondary importance include all those matters of outward observance; special days and feasts; rites and ceremonies; structures and forms. While it is the life of love and faith that binds Christians together in one body through the power of the Holy Spirit, it is possible for Christians to differ from one another in secondary matters without being alienated from one another or from the life of God in the body of Christ. Indeed, secondary matters must not be allowed to separate Christians from one another. To tolerate this would be to grieve the Holy Spirit, who is the Spirit of love and unity.

Obligation is laid upon Christians to accept those whom God has accepted, 'without passing judgement on disputable matters' (Rom.14:1). Who are those whom God has accepted? Those who believe in his Son. Faith in Jesus Christ according to the Scriptures is the common bond between Christians, and though there be a thousand disputable matters, not one of them, or even all of them put together, can be adequate grounds for Christians to break fellowship and communion with one another.

Notes

1   A. Flannery, *Vatican Council II* (Bombay, St Paul Publications, 1992), p.417.
2   A. Flannery, *Vatican Council II: more post conciliar documents* (New York, Costello, 1982), p.387–95.
3   G.F. Hasel, *Old Testament Theology: basic issues in the current debate* (Grand Rapids, Eerdmans, 1982), p.117–43.
4   Ibid., p.130–40.
5   J. Bright, *A History of Israel. 2nd ed.* (London, SCM, 1976), p.144.
6   A. Motyer, *The Prophecy of Isaiah* (Leicester, IVP, 1993), p.45.
7   J.G.S.S. Thomson, 'Book of Psalms,' in J.D. Douglas (ed.), *The New Bible Dictionary* (London, IVP, 1970), p.1057.
8   L. Morris, *The Epistle to the Romans* (Grand Rapids, Eerdmans, 1992), p.140.
9   A. Flannery, *Vatican Council II* (Bombay, St. Paul Publications, 1992), p.408.

Chapter 8

Bridging the Waters that Divide

This chapter can be divided into three main sections. In the first section, four independent congregations in the Cape Peninsular region are examined. In the second section a major denomination in India in which both paedobaptist and credobaptist churches have united is considered, along with a few other similar schemes for church union which are still under discussion. The third section contains a consideration of the Faith and Order Paper No.111: *Baptism, Eucharist and Ministry* (BEM).

While the Cape Peninsular congregations studied are small, isolated and theologically unsophisticated, the BEM document and the Church of North India, on the other hand, are the product of theological experts representing major ecclesiastical traditions throughout the world. What they all have in common is the attempt to bridge the baptismal divide and to find a position in which people of differing baptismal convictions can co-exist in the same fellowship, worship and service.

Four congregations in the Cape Peninsular region

Practice is always more difficult than theory, and finding churches which genuinely made room for differing baptismal practices was not easy. There were many false leads. There are many united churches that unite different denominational traditions in one congregation yet adhere firmly to one baptismal tradition, either paedobaptist or credobaptist. The United Christian Fellowship was found to have no room for paedobaptists within its fellowship. The Noordhoek United Church (a fruit of the Church Unity Commission in South Africa) made no provision for the convictions of Baptists within its unity.

Appendix A supplies a fuller description of the four independent congregations in the Cape Peninsular area in which multiple baptismal practices can be found. What follows is a brief summary of the content of that appendix.

The **Kommetjie Christian Church**, first established in 1925, has a board of trustees who are predominantly paedobaptist, while the present minister (1996) is a Baptist. The Church constitution states the following concerning baptism:

> Baptism is an identification with the Lord Jesus Christ in His burial and resurrection as a sign of the gospel. Some understand this to refer to the baptism of believers and others to the baptism of the children of believing parents.
>
> The ordinance will be performed on request for:-
>
> - believers who wish to be immersed as a confession of their faith,
> - the children of believers as the parents promise to raise their children in the Christian faith.   *(Kommetjie Christian Church Constitution)*.

When parents wish to have their infants baptised, arrangements are made by the present pastor for the rite to be performed in the church by a paedobaptist minister. Sometimes, at the suggestion of the pastor, such parents opt to have their infants blessed in a rite of dedication. The baptism of confessing believers is carried out by the pastor himself in a Baptist church not far away.

While genuinely committed to maintaining the inclusive nature of the church's baptismal policy, the present pastor admits that the perspective of the incumbent pastor tends to prevail in the church. In the three years from 1992 to 1995 there have been four instances of infant baptism and twenty-five instances of believers' baptism.

The constitution of the **Hermanus United Church** makes no mention of baptism at all, and persons are eligible for membership 'by reason of being a member of any Christian Church, or by confession of faith'. [1] The church sees itself as uniting Methodists, Presbyterians, Congregationalists and Baptists in its membership and has sought to draw its ministers from one of these traditions. The most recent minister was a Baptist who reported quite a remarkable lack of tension over the question of baptism during the time he was there. Over a period of three years (1992–1995) some twenty infants have been baptised, and a number of others blessed in a service of dedication. Three people were baptised as believers.

The **Kleinmond Evangelical Fellowship** has a somewhat stronger Baptist ethos. The baptism of infants is permitted, though not encouraged. A paedobaptist minister in the area was invited to perform the few infant baptisms that have actually taken place. Many of those initially requesting the baptism of their infants agreed to a rite of infant dedication. For the baptism of believers, use is made of the private swimming pools of members.

The present pastor of the church reports that in the twelve years of the church's existence there has been no strife or conflict over the issue of baptism.

The **Hangklip Evangelical Fellowship** states the following in its constitution:

> We believe that Jesus Christ commanded that all Christians be baptised.
> **Believers' Baptism** is symbolic of the death and resurrection of our Lord, and expresses openly the inward experience of spiritual regeneration.
> **Infant Baptism** (followed later by confirmation) brings an infant, whose parents are Christians, into God's promised Covenantal relationship. On request, either form of baptism will be administered.[2]

The decision of a leading founder member of this church to be (re)baptised did give rise to some tensions for a while, but the inclusive nature of the church's baptismal policy has been maintained.

Of the four above churches, the Kommetjie Christian Church and the Hermanus United Church seemed to be the best examples of churches that permit Christians both to hold and practise differing baptismal positions. The other two churches were more pronouncedly credobaptist in their orientation. Features common to all four churches were:

- The autonomy of the local church
- An evangelical theological stance
- Adherents of paedobaptist and credobaptist convictions
- The possibility of infant baptisms and the (re)baptism of believers
- A prevalence of Baptists in church leadership

Church union schemes involving Baptist denominations

Instances of Baptist denominations becoming involved in church union schemes with paedobaptist denominations are very rare. Yet there is one notable such instance, namely, the Church of North India, and some attention will be given to this church and to how they were able to 'bridge the gap'. Furthermore, there are some other instances of discussions towards church union in progress in which Baptist churches are involved, and these too will be examined briefly.

The Church of North India

The churches that participated in the *Plan of Church Union in North India and Pakistan* included the Church of India, Pakistan, Burma and Ceylon

(Anglican), the Methodist Church, the United Church of Northern India, the Church of the Brethren in India, the Disciples of Christ, the Mennonites and the Council of Baptist Churches in North India.[3]

This union became possible because the plan of union provided that 'both infant baptism and believers' baptism shall be accepted as alternative practices in the Church of North India.' In fact, Baptists, Disciples and Brethren continue to practise only believers' baptism by immersion. However, if a member of a congregation requests the baptism of an infant, then the minister may, for conscience sake, call in a colleague to perform it.[4]

According to the *Plan of Church Union in North India and Pakistan*, full communicant membership in the Church of North India is limited to those who are baptised and 'give evidence of repentance, faith and love towards Jesus Christ . . .' This means a person may become a member either through infant baptism plus a 'public confession of faith' in which 'he affirms his acceptance of the baptism administered to him in infancy' (confirmation), or through infant dedication plus believers' baptism. In both cases (confirmation and believers' baptism) 'prayer for the gift of the Holy Spirit, the laying-on of hands by the bishop or presbyter, and acknowledgment of his attaining the full responsibilities of Church membership' are part of the liturgy.[5]

Also according to the *Plan of Church Union*, baptism in whatever form is a once for all event and therefore unrepeatable. 'Rebaptism' is ruled out. If any persons should persistently maintain that only their baptism as believers would satisfy their conscience, although they were baptised in infancy, the minister concerned will refer the matter to the bishop of the diocese for pastoral advice and direction. Ministers within the Church of North India may speak about baptism but they are instructed to refrain from any attempt to persuade those who were brought up in either of the accepted practices of the Church to adopt the alternative practice for themselves or for their children.[6]

The Church of North India represents an admirable effort to bring together in one visible fellowship Christians from differing baptismal traditions, and as such is an important ecumenical milestone in this process. A careful look at their *Plan of Church Union*, however, will show that Baptists and others in the credobaptist tradition have given up considerably more than those participating churches from the paedobaptist tradition. Baptists, for example, are free to change their minds on baptismal issues and to request the baptism of their infant children. And even if the Baptist pastor cannot personally administer this baptism, for reasons of conscience, he is able (and expected) to call in a colleague to perform it. Paedobaptists, however, are not given the same freedom. Should they experience a change of conviction on baptismal matters, they are not permitted to seek baptism in the way their conscience might lead them as any 'rebaptism' is ruled out. Although there is provision for such cases to be referred to the bishop for pastoral advice and direction, there is no indication that the individual involved might be granted permission to be baptised as he or she desires.

It is not surprising, perhaps, that many Baptists, including those with genuine ecumenical desires, would be wary of entering a union of churches such as the one outlined above, as it would appear to them unfairly to inhibit the free expression and practice of honestly held Baptist convictions.

The proposed Church of North-East India

In 1963 negotiations began to form the Church of North-East India which was expected to represent 93% of the non-Roman Catholic Christians of North-East India, most of whom are either Baptists or Presbyterians. Some of the key points of this proposed union, as far as baptism is concerned, can be seen in the following points of the suggested constitution:

1. The sacrament of baptism is a sign and seal of the covenant of grace, of union with Christ in his body, of forgiveness of sins in his blood, of death to sin and rebirth to eternal life through him. By this sacrament we are solemnly admitted into the household of faith for the lifelong service of Jesus Christ.
2. The Church of North-East India allows both infant baptism and believers' baptism but not both on the same person and shall receive as communicant members all those who have been baptised or confirmed. It assures freedom of expression for the particular convictions of different traditions.
3. All ministers of the church shall be free to administer either or both forms of baptism. A minister who, for conscientious reasons, is unable to administer baptism to infants shall be free to invite some other ministers of the Church to perform the rite.[7]

A strong point of the above proposed constitution is the freedom that is assured to be able to express the particular convictions of different traditions. It could be asked, however, whether this freedom could not be extended to be able to *put into practice* particular convictions, even if this meant, on occasion, the practice of what others would see as 'rebaptism'? The question of rebaptism is, of course, a deeply sensitive one to many – as is the question of infant baptism to others. No Baptist could want to enter into ecumenical relations with other Christians without being sensitive to this issue. Ideally, this sensitivity and concern not to offend others would, in most cases, be sufficient to refrain from what others would see as rebaptism. To allow complete freedom in the matter would be to run the risk of actions being taken that would offend some. But the question remains whether such a risky freedom is still not preferable to a prohibition (of rebaptism) that would violate the conscience of a few.

As long ago as 1934 discussions began concerning a proposed church union scheme for the churches of Ceylon. The proposals put forward are essentially the same as those discussed above in the case of the Church of North India and the proposed Church of North-East India. So no further comment will be made.

The report of the Churches of Christ and the United Reformed Church

This report was produced in England, and the particular issue of rebaptism is dealt with in the following paragraph:

> The Joint Committee recognizes, however, that such a dual practice will require respect for the rights of conscience at certain points and will only be possible if the adherents of each practice accept their common obligation to build up each other in the faith. It will be necessary to ensure that no one practice or mode of baptism will be forced upon either ministers or people contrary to conscience. Any attempt to do so would impede real union. More difficult is the case of someone baptised in infancy who comes to believe that baptism can only be administered to a believer and therefore requests believers' baptism. Such cases will have to be dealt with pastorally and the depth of the issues involved will have to be taken fully into account. Because baptism is more than an individual act, in such cases the conscientious convictions of ministers and congregations are involved as well as those of the individual. It would be inappropriate in a Basis of Union to try to make detailed provision for all the cases which might arise. The Committee therefore proposes simply the addition of a footnote to the paragraph on Baptism (of the Basis of Union of the United Reformed Church) requiring such cases to be handled pastorally.[8]

The above paragraph shows a fine sensitivity to and real appreciation of the issues involved with sympathetic insight to both sides. As such, the paragraph serves as a model for other Christians and churches seeking to bridge the gap between differing baptismal traditions. The possibility remains, however, that the one to whom 'such cases' are referred for pastoral guidance might not sympathetically understand the dilemma they find themselves in. If the possibility of a service of believers' baptism was precluded, then, as Mathews puts it, 'many Baptists would continue to affirm that to refuse to baptise someone in these situations challenges the freedom of that individual before God; it means the tacit acceptance of the complete validity and normality of infant baptism and involves Baptists in being asked to go beyond the proper demands of the charity of Christian fellowship.'[9]

The BEM document

Quite different from the above case studies, which have focused on individual congregations and regional church unions in their attempts to bridge the baptismal divide, here we examine an international effort involving some of the keenest theological minds in hundreds of different churches from every corner of the world. The fruit of this effort has been the production of a text which has sought to express the faith of the church through the ages. The final form of the BEM (*Baptism, Eucharist and Ministry*) text has attracted an attention unprecedented in the history of the modern ecumenical movement. The Faith and Order commission believed it had recognized and formulated 'a remarkable degree of agreement' in three areas where many points had been controversial among the churches.[10]

Here we shall consider briefly something of the process by which the BEM text came into being, the text itself, and some of the responses to the text from various churches world wide.

The development of the BEM document

From the very outset of the Faith and Order Movement, beginning with the first world conference at Lausanne in 1927, baptism and the eucharist have been the subject of theological discussions in the ecumenical movement. No important conference of the Faith and Order conference ever took place without at least some reference to these two sacraments. In 1961 a report entitled 'One Lord, One Baptism' was favourably received by the Montreal conference. The study on baptism was resumed in 1967 and after a number of consultations a report was submitted to the Commission on Faith and Order at its meeting in Louvain (1971) entitled 'Baptism, Confirmation and Eucharist'. At the Commission's request, the WCC executive committee decided to send the document to all member churches for their reactions and comments. In the light of the responses received from the churches, the text was then amended and again submitted to the Faith and Order commission at its meeting in Accra in 1974.[11]

The document produced by Accra was again sent to the churches for their reactions and the evaluation of the amendments proposed by the churches enabled a smaller steering group to bring the BEM text closer to the final form that it would receive at Lima in 1982.

The great majority of scholars involved in the production of the BEM text have been drawn from the great paedobaptist traditions. There has been, however, some Baptist involvement. The BEM steering group mentioned above comprised two Orthodox, a Lutheran, two Reformed, a Roman Catholic, a member of the Taizé community and a Methodist. A number of experts were also involved in the work of the steering group, including two Orthodox, two Roman Catholics, two Lutherans and a Baptist. [12]

It is important to remember that the Lima text was never intended to be a complete dogmatic statement claiming to be the perfect solution to the doctrinal differences that have developed between the churches in the course of history. It was rather intended as a theological service to the churches in ecumenical dialogue. The churches remain entirely free to accept, correct or reject the text. [13]

The part of BEM dealing with baptism is divided into five sections:

1. The institution of baptism,
2. The meaning of baptism,
3. Baptism and faith,
4. Baptismal practice,
5. The celebration of baptism.

The text of the BEM document

The full text of that portion of the BEM document dealing with baptism can be found in Appendix B. A few comments will here be offered on the text in the light of the theme of this book, to see to what extent, in the writer's view, this text succeeds in bringing together the major traditions of Catholic, Reformed and Baptist.

The first section describes baptism as both a 'gift of God' and a 'rite of commitment to the Lord', founded in a dominical command and apostolic practice (BEM 1991:2). [14] The expression 'gift of God' underlines the conviction of the divine initiative and action in baptism. The term 'rite of commitment' could be read by a Baptist as supporting the position that baptism is an act of faith and commitment. However the text does not spell out precisely whose commitment is in view here and this could be understood also as the commitment of the parents in bringing their children to baptism.

In the second section on the meaning of baptism the text emphasizes that baptism in the New Testament not only signifies certain blessings bestowed by God, but that it gives these blessings: participation in Christ's death and resurrection, cleansing from sin, the gift of the Holy Spirit, incorporation into the body of Christ. 'Through baptism, Christians are brought into union with Christ, with each other and with the Church of every time and place.' Many Baptists (along with some Paedobaptists) would feel uneasy about such a statement unless it could be made clear that the baptism being referred to is at one and the same time a rite of commitment to the Lord. This latter interpretation could be read into the sentence which follows the one quoted above: 'Our common baptism, which unites us to Christ in faith, is thus a basic bond of unity' – 'in faith' being the key phrase here. However, it is impossible that the framers of the text intended that baptism should have this restricted meaning (personal commitment to Christ) as this would exclude infant baptism.

So the wording of the second section remains problematical. While scholars in all traditions (Baptist, Reformed, Catholic) might well agree that it accurately describes those baptisms described and referred to in the New Testament, many will question whether the *same meaning* can be applied to baptisms today – whether they be the baptism of infants or the baptism of adults. It needs to be pointed out more clearly (perhaps in the official commentary accompanying the BEM text) that the same meanings cannot be ascribed to all baptisms without distinction, and that the meaning of any particular baptism is determined by the circumstances and function of that baptism in its context. The baptism of an infant born into a devout Christian home has a particular meaning; the baptism of an infant performed as a cultural custom has another meaning. The baptism of a teenager brought up in a Christian home has one meaning and the baptism of a Jew receiving the gospel of Christ has a somewhat different meaning. The meaning of baptism in the New Testament cannot be simply ascribed to contemporary instances of baptism unless those baptisms fulfil the same function and purpose as the New Testament baptisms.

The third section of the BEM document on baptism does much to allay any fears that the compilers of this statement were guilty of underplaying the role of faith in reception of salvation. Its key phrases are: 'Baptism is both God's gift and our human response to that gift. . . . The necessity of faith for the reception of the salvation embodied and set forth in baptism is acknowledged by all churches. Personal commitment is necessary for responsible membership in the body of Christ'. Some Catholic and Reformed people have felt uneasy with some of these phrases. In the case of the baptism of an infant, how is that baptism a 'human response' to the gift of God? Is not the gracious act of God here being diluted by an insistence on some human act of faith?.[15] Of course the 'human response' and 'faith' referred to does not have to refer only to the response of the one being baptised. In Catholic theology in particular great emphasis has always been placed on the faith of the church, the community which brings its infants to God and to baptism in faith, believing that such acts are efficacious precisely because they are performed in faithful obedience to his commands. And the faith of the church which brings the infant to baptism becomes the faith of the child as the child develops the capacity to understand and articulate that faith. Otherwise the child becomes an apostate, just as would be the case of an adult baptised into Christ and afterwards abandoning the faith.

The fourth section of the BEM document on baptismal practice deals in a direct and forthright fashion with some of the differences and tensions in baptismal practice. When one considers the overwhelming predominance of Paedobaptist scholars involved in the preparation of this document and the minimal Baptist involvement, a Baptist reader can only be impressed by the fairness shown to the Baptist position in this section. Indeed, some Paedobaptists could object that their position is being discriminated against. The section begins with the following paragraph:

> While the possibility that infant baptism was also practised in the apostolic age cannot be excluded, baptism upon personal profession of faith is the most clearly attested pattern in the New Testament documents.

The document then goes on to say that in the course of history the practice of baptism has developed in a variety of forms, with some churches baptising believers and their children and other churches restricting baptism to those who are able to make a personal profession of faith. The document makes no attempt to judge between these various patterns of baptismal practice and clearly regards them both as legitimate. Many paedobaptists, for sure, would prefer a stronger statement concerning the apostolic foundation of the practice of infant baptism, just as many Baptists would have reservations concerning even the possibility of the same. It is the conviction of this writer, in a study of the debate between Jeremias and Aland on this very subject, that the opening paragraph of this section accurately sums up the historical evidence available to us, namely, that the practice of infant baptism in the apostolic age can neither be established or excluded in an absolute way beyond any reasonable doubt.

Notwithstanding the admirable attempts, however, of the compilers of this document to mediate constructively between two historically opposing positions, certain problems remain. Christians of all traditions would agree that 'baptism is an unrepeatable act'. However the following statement: 'Any practice which might be interpreted as "re-baptism" must be avoided' does not adequately take into account the predicament of the person who, on grounds of conscience, is not convinced that his or her baptism as an infant was a legitimate baptism, and sincerely desires to confess Christ in baptism. The writer has already argued in Chapter 6 ('Can We Get Closer?') that in the interests of Christian reconciliation and unity Baptists need to be willing to grant some validity to infant baptism, when such is performed by believers in good conscience, and likewise paedobaptists need to allow for the possibility on occasions for believers to request 'rebaptism' when led in conscience to do so. Any attempt to exclude either infant baptism or rebaptism is not in the interests of Christian reconciliation and unity as it in effect excludes certain Christians who are acting in obedience to Christ's command as they understand it. This phrase in the BEM document (IV, 13) goes against the general spirit of the document which strongly favours mutual respect and conciliation between differing traditions. In deference to the compilers of the text it could be mentioned that their use of the word 'avoided' rather than 'rejected' or 'condemned' could possibly be interpreted by the Baptist as an acknowledgment that in some cases rebaptism could be allowed, but that in order not to give offence to other churches it should be avoided as far as possible.

Yet another questionable phrase in this fourth section is the sentence: 'Baptism should, therefore, always be celebrated and developed in the setting of the Christian community'. While this is not a point of controversy, as far as this writer is aware, between any of the major Christian traditions, yet surely it is an unnecessary restriction, especially in the light of the pattern of baptisms recorded in the book of Acts where baptisms were always administered immediately, irrespective of time or place, to those desiring to become Christians, whether individuals, families or larger groups. In fact it can be questioned if there is a single instance in the New Testament where a baptism is recorded as having taken place in the context of the regular gathering together of the church for divine worship.

The BEM document is accompanied by a brief commentary on the basic text, and before leaving this fourth section, attention can be drawn to an admirable attempt in this commentary to mediate in a conciliatory way between the infant-baptist and believer-baptist traditions:

> In some churches which unite both infant-baptist and believer-baptist traditions, it has been possible to regard as equivalent alternatives for entry into the Church both a pattern whereby baptism in infancy is followed by later profession of faith and a pattern whereby believers' baptism follows upon a presentation and blessing in infancy. This example invites other churches to decide whether they, too, could not recognize equivalent alternatives in their reciprocal relationships and in church union negotiations.

The spirit displayed in the above comment shows that the compilers of the BEM document were scholars truly committed to seeking reconciliation and unity between the differing baptismal practices in various churches.

In the fifth and final section of the BEM document (The Celebration of Baptism) attention is drawn to certain aspects of the different traditions with a view to encouraging mutual enrichment in the various rites connected with the celebration of baptism. Thus, for example, perhaps Baptists are in mind when the text declares: 'In the celebration of baptism the symbolic dimension of water should be taken seriously and not minimalized. The act of immersion can vividly express the reality that in baptism the Christian participates in the death, burial and resurrection of Christ.' And perhaps Eastern Orthodox practice is in mind in the following statement: 'As was the case in the early centuries, the gift of the Spirit in baptism may be signified in additional ways; for example, by the sign of the laying on of hands, and by anointing or chrismation'.[16]

Responses of the churches to the BEM document

So extensive have been the responses of the churches to the BEM document (186 official responses by 1990) that books have been and are being published to record and publicize them. Here only some broad outlines will be surveyed in order to get some idea of how various traditions have responded to this text.

In general a very positive response has come from churches of all traditions and from all parts of the world. The Roman Catholic response affirms that 'BEM is perhaps the most significant result of the (Faith and Order) movement so far'. The Ecumenical Patriarch of Constantinople greeted the Lima document 'with joy as the fruit of the efforts made during recent decades by the Commission on Faith and Order of the World Council of Churches'. From the Episcopal Church, USA, came the statement: 'We rejoice in the convergence of belief which this document represents and we regard it as a major step which the World Council of Churches has sponsored in the work of healing and reconciliation.' The Synod of the Reformed Church in Hungary welcomed the Lima document as follows: 'We are convinced that the Lima document is the best considered and elaborated paper in the whole history of the ecumenical movement in the service of the unity of the church as to these often discussed questions of decisive importance.'[17]

The above are just a few of the comments coming from churches in the Paedobaptist tradition. But there have also been positive comments from churches in the Credobaptist tradition. The Christian Church (Disciples of

Christ) could state: 'Because of the unity already represented in BEM and the ways in which differing theological positions are stated, Disciples join other Christians in appreciation for the significance of this document.' The American Baptist Churches in the USA responded: 'We give thanks to God for the "Baptism, Eucharist and Ministry" document – for the co-operation and the dialogue among Christians that made it possible, for the extensive biblical study and the insights which are represented in it, for the way in which many historical confusions and divisions among Christians are addressed in it.' In the same spirit the Burma Baptist Convention responded with a 'spirit of thanksgiving. We are grateful to God for the advent of BEM. Surely it is not by might nor human power that this historic "ecumenical milestone" has been reached. We express our thanks to all who have committed themselves to this unforgettable ecumenical task and laboured to bring this document into being.' The Baptist Union of Great Britain welcomed BEM as 'a notable milestone in the search for sufficient theological consensus to make possible mutual recognition among separated churches'. Even the Seventh Day Adventists (definitely not members of the WCC) have referred positively to BEM as 'unquestionably one of the World Council of Churches' most significant publications to date'. [18]

Of course there have also been some critical comments on the BEM document, and it is instructive to take note of some of them. Eastern Orthodox responses have contained critical comments, which can be summarized by the finding of the Finnish Orthodox Church that 'some parts of the document include theological terminology, categories and problematics of the Roman Catholic and Protestant churches of the West. In most cases the way the common faith of the undivided church is expressed is strange for us.' On the other hand, a number of Reformation and Free churches have spoken of a too 'Catholic' or 'High Church' orientation of BEM. Among this group of critical comments the strongest ones came from the Waldensian and Methodist Churches in Italy. Their synod pointed out that BEM 'indicates a convergence in a sacramental and clerical direction which is opposite to the direction in which the gospel calls the church in its witness in the world' and that 'this ecumenical document centres the faith, communion and Christian witness not on God and the gospel, but rather on the church as a structure that has and gives guarantees of the Spirit's activities through a caste endowed with priestly powers, mediatorial, and representing the divine.'[19]

It is inevitable that a document that seeks to promote reconciliation and unity between the various Christian traditions will be seen as having certain weaknesses by elements on different sides. Many more detailed criticisms of specific clauses in the text of the document could be mentioned. However these critical comments must not be allowed to obscure what is undoubtedly an overall positive appreciation of the BEM document by the broad spectrum of Christian churches in the world. 'We recognize in the document "the faith of the church throughout the ages" ' commented the Baptist Union of Denmark, 'though we find this expression more a description of the creative power of the ecclesiastical tradition than the norm of confession which alone can be found in the canonical scriptures.' The text on baptism was found by the Roman Catholic Church to be 'grounded in the apostolic faith received and professed by the Catholic Church.' The Reformed Churches in the Netherlands also recognized in the section on baptism 'fundamental elements of the church's faith through the ages.'[20]

Concluding comments

There is certainly a vast difference in ethos and theological understanding between the BEM document and the Church of North India on the one hand (both products of the ecumenical movement), and the faith and practice of the individual Cape Peninsular congregations examined at the beginning of this chapter on the other hand. Common to all the latter is a strongly evangelical understanding of the faith. Even where infant baptism is practised (or tolerated, as the case may be) it is within the context of an evangelical understanding of the sacrament. A catholic, sacramental approach to baptism has no real place in any of these churches. This is perhaps why these churches have a tendency to gravitate towards a Credobaptist position, a position possibly more consistent with the prevailing evangelical ethos characterizing these churches. The BEM document, on the other hand, has quite strongly catholic and sacramental overtones, to the extent that many evangelicals, whether Credobaptist or Paedobaptist, would consider it too 'High Church' in its tone. So the fact that Christians and churches might be sympathetic to both believers' baptism and infant baptism does not necessarily mean they have spanned the spectrum of baptismal views. The difference between Christians holding to baptism as a sign or symbol of grace and those who see baptism as a means whereby grace is actually mediated is probably greater than the difference between those who accept and those who reject infant baptism.

There do remain, therefore, very real gaps between Christians in their understanding and practice of baptism, despite the fact that some congregations seem to have developed a very inclusive policy on baptism.

Nevertheless, the positive gains that have been made must not be ignored. It is striking that it is generally churches of a Protestant evangelical kind that have often made most practical progress in bridging quite different baptismal traditions, though their theological understanding of the issues has often been unsophisticated. The BEM document, however, must not be seen only in terms of its 'high' doctrine of baptism. The framers of that document made real efforts to incorporate into it an emphasis on the elements of repentance, faith and personal commitment, so important to those of evangelical convictions. It is the conviction of the writer that careful study of the BEM document could do much to promote a deeper understanding and appreciation of the different baptismal traditions present in some of the churches studied above. Indeed, churches seeking consciously to create a fellowship that would include believers having differing baptismal convictions would do well to incorporate the BEM document into their constitutions; if not as a dogmatic confession then at least as a basis for dialogue, discussion and mutual understanding.

The BEM document has sometimes been criticized as a compromise document, trying to include bits and pieces from various baptismal traditions in an attempt to please as many as possible. It may be suggested, at the conclusion of this chapter, that that is not necessarily a bad thing, and that compromise documents can play a valuable role in bringing alienated parties into closer contact and dialogue. Consider, for example, the pivotal role played by the Definition of Chalcedon in the year 451 in bringing to some kind of conclusion the endless arguments in the fourth and fifth centuries concerning the person of Christ. The formula of the Chalcedonian decree was not an original and new creation but rather like a mosaic, assembled almost entirely from stones that were already available. The two antagonistic theological schools that it sought to reconcile were those of Alexandria and Antioch and the document was made up almost entirely of excerpts from leading theologians of both schools. Some found the compromise nature of the statement unacceptable, and the Nestorian and Monophysite Christians have remained unreconciled to the definition of Chalcedon to this day. But many others accepted Chalcedon, though it might have been 'an agreement to disagree', and it has continued to function as a symbol of unity for the vast majority of Christian churches to this day.

Perhaps the BEM document today can be viewed in a similar way. If it cannot command the unqualified support of every church as a completely adequate statement of the doctrine of baptism, then at least it can be seen as an 'agreement to disagree', but to disagree in a spirit of Christian love and respect, all the while remaining in dialogue and fellowship with one another.

The prevailing tone of the BEM document is strongly sacramental and therefore more easily acceptable to those of 'High Church' sympathies, whether Roman Catholic, Eastern Orthodox, Anglican, Lutheran, Reformed or other. Credobaptists, generally speaking, do not feel comfortable with the sacramental way of speaking that is characteristic of BEM. They cannot help but ask themselves: 'Should not all these blessings being attributed to baptism – the washing away of sin, a new birth, renewal by the Spirit, incorporation into Christ – more properly be attributed to faith and repentance?' But that interpretation is possible for the Credobaptist. Credobaptists are perfectly free to interpret every reference to baptism in BEM as the sacramental actualization of repentance towards God and faith in Jesus Christ. There is nothing in the document that precludes such an interpretation, although it is obvious that not everyone will interpret it in such a way. Indeed, Credobaptists could even appeal to certain sections of BEM in support of their interpretation, such as section 8:

> Baptism is both God's gift and our human response to that gift. It looks towards a growth into the measure of the stature of the fullness of Christ (Eph. 4:13). The necessity of faith for the reception of the salvation embodied and set forth in baptism is acknowledged by all churches. Personal commitment is necessary for responsible membership in the body of Christ.

In addition, Baptists could refer to section 11 of BEM where it states: 'While the possibility that infant baptism was also practised in the apostolic age cannot be excluded, baptism upon personal profession of faith is the most clearly attested pattern in the New Testament documents'. Catholics, of course, could immediately answer that BEM clearly accepts the validity of infant baptism and so every spiritual blessing attributed to baptism in BEM must also be attributed to infant baptism, as the document makes no attempt to exclude infants from the blessings of salvation given by God in and through baptism. But it is these contradictory and conflicting possibilities of interpretation that makes BEM something of a compromise document, a document that can play a valuable role in bringing into dialogue and creative tension two conflicting approaches to baptism.

Notes

1 Trust Deed of United Church, Hermanus 1990. Revised Constitution of the Church. Hermanus

2 Hangklip Constitution, *Declaration of Faith and Constitution of the Hangklip Evangelical Fellowship* (Betty's Bay, [s.a.]).

3 T. Lorenzen, 'Baptists and Ecumenicity,' *The Ecumenical Review* (1978) 257.
4 Ibid., p.258.
5 Ibid.
6 Ibid.
7 Ibid., p.259.
8 J.F. Mathews, *Baptism: A Baptist View* (London, Baptist Union of Great Britain and Ireland, 1976), p.25–6.
9 Ibid., p.26.
10 M. Thurian, 'Baptism, Eucharist and Ministry', in N. Lossky *et al* (eds.), *Dictionary of the Ecumenical Movement* (Grand Rapids, Eerdmans, 1991), p.80.
11 Ibid., p.81.
12 Ibid., p.82.
13 Ibid.
14 Faith and Order Paper No. 111, *Baptism, Eucharist and Ministry* (Geneva, WCC, 1991).
15 Faith and Order Paper No. 149, *Baptism, Eucharist and Ministry 1982–1990. Report on the Process and Responses* (Geneva, WCC, 1990), p.44.
16 Faith and Order Paper No. 111, *Baptism, Eucharist and Ministry* (Geneva, WCC, 1991).
17 Faith and Order Paper No. 149, *Baptism, Eucharist and Ministry 1982–1990. Report on the Process and Responses* (Geneva, WCC, 1990), p.18.
18 Ibid., p.19–21.
19 Ibid., p.30
20 Ibid., p.33–4.

Chapter 9

Towards a Model for Reconciliation

In 1995 research was done by the author among the students of five theological institutions in South Africa: the Dutch Reformed Faculty of Theology at the University of Pretoria, the Baptist Theological College (BTC) in Cape Town, St. Joseph's Theological Institute at Cedara (Pietermaritzburg), the Cape Evangelical Bible Institute (CEBI) in Cape Town, and the Bible Institute (BI) at Kalk Bay. A copy of the questionnaire may be found at the end of Appendix C.

A total of 182 responses to the questionnaire were received from students representing at least twenty denominations in South Africa. The theological institutions differed considerably from one another. Some were more ecclesiastically 'homogeneous', such as the Dutch Reformed students at Pretoria and the Baptist students at BTC. St. Joseph's students were predominantly Roman Catholic, with a sprinkling of other churches represented. CEBI and BI included a wide variety of (Protestant) churches among their students who responded to the questionnaire. The full analysis of the various responses to the questionnaire appears in Appendix C. This chapter begins with a brief summary of that analysis.

Of the 182 students who responded to the questionnaire, 69 belonged to credobaptist churches and 112 to paedobaptist churches. A strong majority of both groups (69 percent of paedobaptists and 66 percent of credobaptists) thought it possible to accommodate differing baptismal convictions in one congregation. From this it can be inferred that the great majority of all the respondents were in favour of a unity that could transcend the baptismal differences that tend to divide Christians. Notwithstanding this desire for unity, however, it appears from some of the other responses that not all of the respondents had thought through what the implications of such a unity might be.

Of those in whose churches the baptism of infants was the norm, 50 percent agreed that parents should be allowed by the church to delay the baptism of their children if they so wished, and if we add those who agreed to this option being permitted under certain circumstances, the total percentage rises to 66 percent. An equally strong majority (65 percent), however, were opposed to what they saw as rebaptism being permitted by the church.

Of those in whose churches infant baptism was not normally (or never) practised only 20 percent were willing to accept infant baptism as having some validity. If we add to this percentage those who were willing to accept infant baptism under certain circumstances and those who were uncertain, the total percentage rises to 50 percent. This indicates a significant number of credobaptist respondents who were at least open to the possibility of granting some recognition to infant baptism. As for the church allowing parents to have their infant children baptised if they so wished, a clear majority (53 percent) were opposed to it and only 37 percent in favour. Equally, a clear majority (57 percent) were opposed to church membership being open to those (only) baptised as infants.

About half of both groups were in favour of pastoral freedom in the administration or non-administration of certain kinds of baptism. With respect to the possibility of the 'lay' administration of baptism most of those in credobaptist churches were in favour while most of the paedobaptist respondents felt that in most cases, at least, the administration of baptism should be restricted to ordained ministers.

In summary we note that while the great majority of all the respondents desired a unity that would transcend baptismal differences, yet most of those belonging to credobaptist churches were reticent about granting any recognition to the validity of infant baptism. As for the paedobaptist respondents, while they were sympathetic to the possibility of parents delaying the baptism of their children if they wished, they could not countenance any rebaptism of those baptised in infancy.

One striking fact emerging from this research is that only 13 percent of the respondents thought it *not* possible for Christians having differing baptismal convictions to be accommodated within one congregation. It is surely a reasonable inference that those who considered such an accommodation *possible*, would also consider it *desirable*.

This result points to the existence of a deep instinct among Christians that baptismal differences ought not to be divisive. Yet the responses studied also showed that only a few were prepared seriously to consider the practical implications of such an accommodation. After living so many years in isolation from one another behind strongly entrenched positions, it is a costly and difficult thing for Christians seriously to consider making some kind of accommodation of positions traditionally rejected by their churches. In this chapter attention will be given to those kinds of costly decisions needed to bring about reconciliation and unity between Christians holding differing baptismal views.

Reconciliation between estranged persons or bodies is always a costly business. For this reason the cross is the primary symbol of the Christian faith, pointing to the sacrificial price paid by Christ to bring about the reconciliation of humans to God and one another. There are many parallels between reconciliation in the religious realm and reconciliation in the secular and social realm. In contemporary South Africa, where this book is being written, much attention is being given to the need of reconciliation between estranged communities and ethnic groups, with the realization of how difficult this is. In 1988 the National Initiative for Reconciliation produced a book entitled *The Cost of Reconciliation in South Africa*,[1] to which a number of Christian leaders in South Africa contributed articles grappling with the need and the way to promote genuine reconciliation in a deeply divided and suffering land. A constantly recurring theme in the articles is the pain and the difficulty of facing up to past patterns of injustice and the cost of taking effective action to end them. Exactly the same dynamics operate in the religious and ecclesiastical world. Centuries of prejudice and sub-Christian attitudes and actions have to be faced and decisive actions taken to break down the dividing walls perpetuating theologically indefensible divisions within the body of Christ. There is simply no easy way of doing this, and progress will not be made without the willingness to give serious consideration to difficult and even 'impossible' actions.

There is no simple solution to the problems of baptismal differences between Christians and churches. The only way of reconciliation is one which Christians and churches will pursue by seeking solutions together in a spirit of mutual respect and love while resisting the temptation to allow their differences to divide them into opposing camps of antagonistic and hostile combatants. All references to a 'proposed model' in this chapter are simply references to this, a way of facilitating mutual dialogue and discussion in a non-threatening environment characterized by mutual respect and Christian fellowship.

Freedom of conscience and the diaconal nature of baptism

Foundational to any way of reconciliation is recognition of the freedom of conscience granted to the Christian believer, and willingness to implement this in practical ways. This freedom of conscience is deeply rooted in the

Christian tradition and in the Scriptures – particularly in the writings of the apostle Paul, the 'apostle of the free Spirit', as F.F. Bruce describes him in his major work on Paul.[2] Bruce deliberately chose this phrase as the title of his book to emphasize the remarkable breadth of freedom for the Christian believer inherent in Paul's understanding of the gospel. Concerning this freedom Bruce elsewhere writes:

> Christian freedom is subject only to the self-imposed constraint of Christian charity. No-one may dictate what Christians must do in indifferent matters such as food or the observation of special days; it is for them to restrict their freedom voluntarily if its exercise may harm the spiritual life of others. Plainly, true spiritual freedom will not lead Christians into courses of action which enslave them, nor can it encourage practices which are generally unhelpful and not conducive to the healthy upbuilding of the whole believing community.[3]

Luther, too, in his liberating discovery of the essence of the Pauline gospel, also had occasion to exult in *The Freedom of a Christian* as his well-known tract on the subject was entitled. It was in that treatise that Luther enunciated his famous paradox: 'A Christian is a perfectly free lord of all, subject to none. A Christian is a perfectly dutiful servant of all, subject to all.' In the context of his times Paul was willing to grant freedom of conscience to Christian believers in a wide variety of issues that were at that time highly contentious: freedom in matters of food and drink, freedom with regard to the observance of special days, freedom from the law, freedom in certain marital matters, freedom with regard to circumcision – as long as these freedoms were not abused to undermine the gospel or Christian morality.

In an age when his fellow Jews had a horror of being defiled with unclean foods, Paul could counsel: 'Eat anything sold in the meat market, without raising questions of conscience, for "the earth is the Lord's, and everything in it" ' (1 Cor. 10:25,26). Such freedom was moderated in practice by a concern for the scruples of other believers and the desire not to cause unnecessary offence (1 Cor. 8:9). In the matter of the observance of special days, including the Jewish sabbath, Paul was content to leave the matter to the conscience of the individual. 'Some consider one day more sacred than another; while others consider every day alike. Let all be fully convinced in their own minds' (Rom. 14:5). This extraordinarily liberal position has been simply too much to swallow for generations of Puritan-influenced Protestant commentators who have laboured eruditely to show that 'the Lord's day cannot be included in what is here said'.[4] But Paul simply reflects here the attitude to days, rites and outward ceremonies displayed in the words of Jesus, when challenged on technicalities of sabbath observance: 'The Sabbath was made for man, not man for the Sabbath' (Mk. 2:27). In saying this Jesus drew attention to the diaconal nature of divine ordinances, even such a hallowed ordinance as the sabbath, enshrined in the ten commandments, central to the covenantal relationship between God and his people, and a major pillar of Jewish religious practice. Such ordinances are servants, not tyrants. They are instituted to promote the salvation, well-being and comfort of God's people. To use them as instruments of oppression, condemnation and division is to miss the purpose for which God ordained them. Hence the significance of the phrase 'the diaconal nature of baptism' in the heading of this paragraph. Baptism is given as a servant to the church, to promote the salvation, well-being and unity of God's people, and to be used as such with freedom of conscience. When baptism becomes a means to condemn fellow-believers and to divide the church it is no longer serving the function for which it was given. For baptism to fulfil its divinely given function, it must be used with great freedom of conscience, as befits the use of all those 'servants' given for the benefit of humans.

To return to the freedom of conscience granted by Paul (and the rest of the New Testament writers, although not always with such clarity), it is necessary to consider briefly the issue of circumcision and its possible implications for our thesis. When circumcision was insisted upon as a *sine qua non* for salvation, Paul resisted it (in his letter to the Galatians) with all the ferocity of one fiercely determined to defend the gospel of the grace of God, freely available to all who believe in Jesus. Yet on another occasion Paul himself circumcised Timothy (Acts 16:3), precisely because he perceived that such an action might promote the progress of the gospel. Paul was certainly not opposed to circumcision as such and would surely have opposed any attempt to ban it, just as he opposed attempts to enforce it. He simply wished believers to enjoy complete freedom of conscience in this matter, convinced that 'in Christ Jesus neither circumcision nor uncircumcision has any value. The only thing that counts is faith expressing itself through love' (Gal. 5:6). Would it be heretical to suggest that if Paul were present with us today, our intricate and prolonged controversies over baptism might provoke him to say, in the interests of Christian unity and fellowship, 'Neither infant baptism nor believers' baptism is anything. Keeping God's commands is what counts'? Certainly God's commands seem to speak far more clearly to the primary issues of Christian unity and love and fellowship than to the finer points of baptismal practice so acutely debated.

Many who may have read with sympathy the contents of this chapter so far will possibly have found the last couple of sentences completely unacceptable. There is a deliberately shocking element in them (Paul, too, sometimes used shock expressions for effect in driving a particular point home), so it is necessary to examine more carefully the intention behind them. The objection could be raised: 'Is there not in this book a tendency towards trivializing baptism, of the kind that has marred so much Protestant "evangelical" thinking about the sacrament, especially discernible among Baptist and Pentecostal groups?' Such an objection must be taken seriously and adequately answered as it is certainly not the intention of this book to trivialize baptism but rather to develop and promote such an understanding of the sacrament that its saving and beneficial function in the ministry of the church might rather be enhanced. However, this goal is not to be attained by exalting baptism at all costs, but rather by seeing it in its right perspective and diaconal function within the ministry of the gospel.

The expressions 'Jesus saves' and 'Baptism saves' cannot be equated without further ado (although both are perfectly Scriptural and legitimate). God in Christ is the proper author and source of all human salvation. Baptism is an instrument in the administration of that salvation. Christ is the Lord of salvation, baptism is a servant. Baptism is indeed, in New Testament thinking, the normal way in which individuals put on Christ, or clothe themselves with Christ (Gal. 3:27). But it remains a 'way'; Christ is the Lord, the Giver, the Source. 'By grace we are saved through faith' (Eph. 2:8) expresses the primary biblical teaching that traces the source of human salvation to the grace of God, bestowed freely on all who call upon him in faith. In the New Testament baptism functions as a way (or rite) by which men and women 'call upon the Lord' in faith (Acts 9:17,18; 22:16), receiving the forgiveness of sins and the gift of the Holy Spirit. So there is always the closest possible conjunction between Christ, faith, divine grace, salvation and baptism. But in this close relationship, baptism always serves as the instrument, the servant.

It is with this perspective in view that the words of Paul to the Corinthians can be properly understood: 'Christ did not send me to baptise, but to preach the gospel' (1 Cor.1:17). Paul's words, too, could be seen as a trivializing of baptism, and, indeed, have often been abused to that end. But the context of this expression makes Paul's intentions clear. The church at Corinth was troubled by divisions between factions who were unduly exalting various leaders and ministers, Apollos, Cephas and Paul. It is easy to imagine that in the devotion given to these different leaders, not only was the superiority of their doctrine magnified, but possibly also special pride expressed in baptism received at their hands. This, at any rate, might partly account for Paul's disclaimer: 'I am thankful that I did not baptise any of you except Crispus and Gaius . . . For Christ did not send me to baptise, but to preach the gospel'

(1 Cor. 1:14,17). Paul is concerned to put everything in proper perspective. The gospel is supreme; baptism is a servant of the gospel. Christ alone is Lord and the only true foundation for Christian faith, and as for Apollos, Paul and others, they are 'only servants, through whom you came to believe' (1 Cor. 3:5). Paul had no intention of trivializing, or even less of negating, the vital role played by Christian preachers and Christian baptism in the ministry of the gospel. His only concern was to ensure that those persons and sacraments ordained as servants be not unduly exalted so as to become a source of division and strife rather than functioning to promote unity, love and faith in the church.

There has been a tendency for certain contemporary Catholic theologians, when discussing the sacraments and their role in salvation, to shift the focus to the sacramental nature of the church, and even to see Christ as the supreme sacrament of God. Schillebeeckx's *Christ the Sacrament of Encounter with God* (1963) can be mentioned as an example. This trend is to be welcomed as it serves to focus attention on the great saving acts of God: Christ the Redeemer, his saving death, his life-giving resurrection. Insofar as baptism serves the role of actualizing, confessing, confirming, aiding and promoting faith in Christ (whether in the mature convert to Christ or the child brought up in a Christian home), it serves a valuable ministry. It is, indeed, a wise ordinance of God. But it remains a servant in the administration of the manifold grace of God. Baptism exists for the church, and not the church for baptism. The servant can be dispensed with, although it is always unwise to neglect those useful servants provided by the Lord in his bounty for the good of the church.

This *non-necessity* of baptism has always been recognized by the various traditions, although always also with great care to guard against misunderstandings leading to any view that baptism is superfluous. Churches with a more sacramental understanding of baptism have been specially cautious in speaking of any non-necessity of baptism. Berkouwer states: 'The Reformed opposition to sacramentalism expressed in its speaking of the non-necessity of the sacrament, evinces not a *lesser* appreciation of the sacrament but a *different* appreciation.'[6] Discussing the Catholic concepts of baptism of blood and baptism of desire, Walsh writes: 'About Baptism it says that the reality of the sacrament is brought about essentially by faith in Christ and sharing in his death: any significant human action that manifests these choices unequivocally is entitled to be called a Baptism.'[6] Here Walsh simply reflects the traditional teaching of the Roman Catholic Church, enunciated many centuries earlier by no less than Aquinas, who, also discussing baptism by desire, wrote of the possibility of a person achieving salvation 'without actual baptism, because of his desire for it; a desire which arises from *faith working through love*, through which God inwardly sanctifies him, not having limited his power to the visible sacraments'.[7]

The point I wish to make is that even in churches (such as the Roman Catholic Church) which have a strongly sacramental understanding of baptism (and its necessity) there is still room for a freedom of conscience that is in accordance with their own tradition. And if there is to be any progress towards reconciliation and unity in the area of baptismal differences it is vital that Christian believers in every tradition be granted full freedom of conscience in this matter. Such freedom of conscience in baptismal matters is not merely a matter of pragmatic expediency but rather a matter of faithfulness to the gospel itself and obedience to the apostolic injunctions contained in the Holy Scriptures. This section on the importance of freedom of conscience will be closed by three quotations related to this liberty, the first from F. F. Bruce, the second from Martin Luther and the third a declaration of the Baptist World Congress held at Atlanta, Georgia, in 1939:

> Paul enjoyed his Christian liberty to the full. Never was there a Christian more thoroughly emancipated from un-Christian inhibitions and taboos. So completely emancipated was he from spiritual bondage that he was not even in bondage to his emancipation. He conformed to the Jewish way of life when he was in Jewish society as cheerfully as he accommodated himself to Gentile ways when he was living with Gentiles. The interests of the gospel and the highest well-being of men and women were paramount considerations with him, and to these he subordinated everything else.[8]

> What the Apostle teaches is that in the new Law everything is free and nothing necessary for those who believe in Christ, except 'charity out of a pure heart, and of a good conscience, and of faith unfeigned' (1 Tim.1:5). In Galatians 6:15 he writes: 'In Christ Jesus neither circumcision availeth any thing, nor uncircumcision, but a new creature.' . . . All is free, and only humility, love, and what else the Apostle inculcates must be observed. Against this liberty, for which the Apostle contends, many false apostles raised their voice to mislead the people to do certain things as though these were necessary. Against such errorists the Apostle took the offensive with an amazing zeal.[9]

> Voluntariness in personal and corporate worship, institution and service is essential to vital religion and to spiritual development of society. No man, no government nor institution, religious or civil, social or economic, has the right to dictate how a person may worship God or whether he shall worship God at all. In continuance of our consistent Baptist practice, we are imperatively constrained again to insist upon the full maintenance of absolute religious liberty for every man of every faith and no faith.[10]

Proposals

Having laid down the two basic thoughts of this chapter, namely the importance of freedom of conscience in baptismal matters, and the diaconal nature of baptism, it is now necessary to proceed to certain definite proposals.

The baptism of infants ought not to be forbidden nor enforced

This proposal is particularly difficult for those believers and churches with a long history of opposition to the practice of infant baptism. Of the 69 respondents coming from credobaptist churches a clear majority were opposed to the practice of infant baptism being even permitted in the church. Likewise, a majority were opposed to the acceptance into church membership of those (only) baptised as infants. Only a minority of paedobaptists, on the other hand, were in favour of enforcing the practice of infant baptism in their churches. The challenge here is primarily (although not only) to credobaptist churches to allow freedom of conscience to their members and adherents in the matter of infant baptism. There are weighty reasons why they should do so. It is undeniably an ancient practice dating back to at least the third century. Intense historical studies and investigations (see Chapter 4, 'The Historical Question') have not been able to establish beyond doubt that the apostolic church baptised infants or that it did not. It has been widely recognized that ultimately the question must be resolved on *theological* rather than historical grounds.

But therein lies the problem. Literally thousands of books, tracts and pamphlets have been produced arguing the case for or against infant baptism with varying degrees of erudition and conviction. That both sides have compelling and theologically weighty arguments can hardly be denied. The inclusion, at the beginning of this book, of a chapter summarizing the Catholic, Reformed and Baptist approach to baptism was intended to make precisely this point. It is impossible to read the works on baptism by scholars from different traditions without acknowledging that their arguments are at least theologically and exegetically respectable and weighty, even if they are not, perhaps, finally convincing.

To the above considerations must be added the long list of Christian leaders, writers and preachers who have been universally acclaimed for their faith, holiness and usefulness and who have been staunch defenders of infant baptism. Augustine, Luther, Calvin, Wesley, Whitefield are just some of the names that come to mind. In the words of the theologically uneducated but nevertheless astute man in the gospels who was healed of blindness, 'We know that God does not listen to sinners. He listens to the godly man who does his will' (Jn. 9:31). Do not all these considerations demand freedom of conscience being granted to individual believers in matters of baptism? This state of affairs has been frankly recognized by the ecumenical team of scholars that produced the BEM document considered in Chapter 8.

Not only have those for and against the practice of infant baptism produced impressive works of historical investigation and theological argument, but both parties can lay claim to an ancient pedigree going back to apostolic times. There is an 'apostolic succession', so to speak, for both the paedobaptist and the credobaptist positions. Admittedly, from the fourth century onwards the paedobaptist position has been very much predominant in the church, but then it must be remembered that opposition to infant baptism was legally prohibited from the fourth century onwards with severe penalties inflicted upon offenders. With the increase of religious freedom in the last few centuries, credobaptist churches have flourished to the point that they now represent a significant community worldwide, and one which is rapidly growing.

Once again, all these facts point to the need for freedom of conscience in the matter of infant baptism. The only alternative is to allow differences in this area to divide Christians into separate churches, and such an action is theologically indefensible, as has been argued in Chapter 5 ('Baptism and Unity') as well as elsewhere in this book. Whatever sins and errors are involved, either in the practice or in the rejection of infant baptism, none of these sins is as serious as that of promoting schism between Christians on grounds of baptismal differences. The exclusion by any Christian church of believers on the grounds of their attachment to or rejection of infant baptism is morally indefensible in the light of powerful scriptural admonitions to accept one another, to bear with one another and to love one another even in the face of varying opinions. Quite apart from the clear moral issues involved, there are absurdities implied in the official policies of many churches that ought to provoke thought. Imagine a Reformed church having to discipline a Charles Spurgeon, a John Bunyan or a William Carey on account of their heretical tendencies. Imagine a Baptist church informing a Calvin, a Luther or a Wesley that they were not eligible for church membership!

The 'rebaptism' of those baptised in infancy ought not to be forbidden or enforced

Perhaps even more than the issue of infant baptism, the issue of rebaptism is an acutely sensitive one. Evidence of this is the 65 percent of the 113 paedobaptist respondents considered in Appendix C who rejected any possibility of the church permitting such an option. Yet 69 percent of the same respondents favoured accommodating differing baptismal convictions in one congregation, without considering, perhaps, that the latter (accommodation) demands the possibility of the former (rebaptism). The fact is that there are many Christian believers who, for a variety of reasons, have sincere doubts about the validity of their baptism as infants and therefore have scruples of conscience as to whether they have been baptised at all. To deny such people the possibility of obeying their conscience (rightly or wrongly informed) is effectively to drive them out of the church and thus to be guilty (or at least to share in the guilt) of promoting schism in the body of Christ. It goes without saying, of course, that those convinced of the validity of infant baptism have every right to seek to persuade others who doubt of the correctness of the practice. But what if they do not succeed in resolving such doubts? Must those who feel conscience bound to seek baptism as believers be penalized?

A strong objection could be raised at this point. What of the once-for-all nature of baptism? Does not Scripture speak of one baptism, even as it speaks of one Lord, one God and Father of us all (Eph.4:5,6)? Whatever legitimate doubts there may be about aspects of the mode and time of baptism, surely this is one area in which there are clear theological and scriptural principles which must command the assent of all? There can only be one birth into the Kingdom of God just as there is only one physical birth into this world. Baptism, which corresponds to this birth, must therefore be a once-for-all event, unrepeatable by its very nature. All of this is very true, but it does not solve the problem. The problem is that there are those who are not convinced that they have been baptised at all. For them, it is not a question of whether they should be rebaptised but whether they have ever been baptised. Probably the great majority of Baptists and other credobaptists would agree that baptism is a once-for-all event, and would oppose the practice of rebaptism. They do not see themselves as rebaptisers but as baptisers. For this reason such groups have been content to be called 'Baptists', but have never accepted the label 'Anabaptist'.

Everything said under the first proposal above has equal application here. However compelling and carefully reasoned the arguments in favour of the practice of infant baptism are, there are, and probably always will be, those for whom these arguments are not finally conclusive and convincing. Such must be given the opportunity and freedom to act in accordance with their conscience, to request and to receive baptism as believers. For the arguments that insist that a confession of faith by the candidate is an essential and normal part of Christian baptism are also compelling and well reasoned. In fact the credobaptist position has the advantage of being more obviously attested in the New Testament while the paedobaptist position is more dependent on carefully reasoned theological deductions. Those who have put forward and defended the credobaptist position include many illustrious names universally honoured and respected by Christians for their outstanding contribution to the progress of the gospel and building up of the church. John Bunyan, William Carey and Charles Spurgeon have already been mentioned. Billy Graham could be added to the list. Whatever errors these persons might have harboured in their baptismal views do not seem to have hindered their usefulness in Christian service. (While Billy Graham's Baptist affiliations are well known, what is perhaps not so widely known are the paedobaptist convictions of his wife, Ruth, convictions that no Southern Baptist pastor has ever been able to change, despite the playful offer of a reward by Billy! This is perhaps a wonderful example of how credobaptist and paedobaptist can co-operate and coexist fruitfully together in the ministry of the gospel!)

This proposal cuts both ways, of course. If the challenge to traditionally paedobaptist churches is to permit freedom of conscience to those desiring baptism as believers, the challenge to traditionally credobaptist churches is to allow freedom of conscience to those satisfied with the validity of their baptism as infants, and not to try and enforce believers' baptism on them by insisting on it, for example, as a condition for church membership. Of the 70 credobaptist respondents considered in the previous chapter, 57 percent were not in favour of accepting paedobaptists into membership in the church if they were not willing to be baptised 'again' as believers.

Yet another objection that could be raised against the proposal under consideration is this: 'Practically and realistically speaking, would not such untrammelled liberty of conscience in matters of baptismal practice lead to pandemonium and disorder in the church with every one doing whatever they think right in their own eyes, wasting valuable time and energy in ceaseless discussion and argument over baptismal issues?' With this objection in mind, we need to turn to the third and most important proposal in this chapter.

Mutual respect for differing baptismal convictions must be maintained and promoted

Exegetes and theologians differ about the details of apostolic baptismal practice precisely because of the tantalizing dearth of information. But there is no uncertainty about the abundance of scriptural and apostolic exhortations to mutual love and respect in areas of legitimate disagreement between Christians. So however strongly we may argue for freedom of individual conscience in baptismal practice, this freedom is always to be understood within the parameters of the grand themes of unity, love and reconciliation between Christian believers. Therefore it is always to be insisted upon that such freedom can never and must never be abused to undermine or threaten the same unity and love. This is the thrust of Paul's letter to the Galatians, where he strongly maintains the freedom of Christian believers in relation to particular rites and ceremonies, while opposing with equal strength any abuse of that freedom which would undermine the spirit of love and unity in the church.

> It is for freedom that Christ has set us free. Stand firm, then, and do not let yourselves be burdened again by a yoke of slavery. . . . You, my brothers, were called to be free. But do not use your freedom to indulge the sinful nature; rather, serve one another in love. The entire law is summed up in a single command: 'Love your neighbour as yourself.' If you keep on biting and devouring each other, watch out or you will be destroyed by each other (Gal. 5:1,13–15).

This then is the answer to those fears expressed above that the freedom being advocated would result in pandemonium and disorder in the church. What is being advocated is a freedom to promote unity, not division, mutual respect and not contempt, good order and not disorder. Practically speaking, we can spell out in even greater detail the implications of this concept in a particular case. Those, for example, raised in a traditionally paedobaptist church, who desire the freedom to be baptised as believers for reasons of conscience, may not abuse that freedom by questioning the integrity and obedience of fellow-believers otherwise convinced. The same freedom and respect they desire for themselves and their convictions they must be willing to grant to others. This is in accordance with the most primary precept of the gospel: 'In everything, do to others what you would have them do to you, for this sums up the Law and the Prophets' (Mt. 7:12). Nothing could be more inconsistent than a person claiming the right to follow his or her conscience in baptism and then speaking in a belittling and contemptuous way of others who do not follow in the same way. This would be a clear example of that 'biting and devouring each other' which Paul warned against so strenuously.

The church may not become a battleground between contending baptismal convictions, and those who would want to turn it into such (from whatever angle they are coming) would be guilty of transgressing the law of love which must always be the chief principle governing the relations of Christians to one another. When Paul appealed to the believers in Corinth to 'agree with one another so that there may be no divisions among you and that you may be perfectly united in mind and thought' (1 Cor.1:10), he surely did not have in mind the perfect unanimity which agrees on every point of doctrine and practice, but the kind of agreement which does not allow permissible differences to become sources of contention and division.

There is yet another implication for that freedom 'serving in love' which I am advocating. It takes cognizance not only of personal convictions but also of the convictions and sensitivities of others. This means, for example, that those considering 'rebaptism' will be led not only by their own conscience and convictions but also by a concern for others who might be offended or distressed by such an action This could mean refraining from such an action for the sake of others. Paul also spoke of the necessity of being willing to voluntarily restrict one's personal freedom for the sake of 'the other's conscience' (1 Cor. 10:29). Such sensitivity and concern for the feelings and scruples of others is binding not only on individuals but also on churches. How much sensitivity, for example, is shown by Baptist churches which openly advocate the rebaptism of all those baptised as infants, or by paedobaptist churches which excommunicate their members for the 'sin' of rebaptism? 'Each of us should please our neighbour for the good purpose of building up the neighbour. . . . Accept one another, then, just as Christ accepted you, in order to bring praise to God' (Rom.15:2,7).

It must be emphasized again that what is here being advocated is not some kind of superficial 'liberalism', motivated by a lack of doctrinal conviction or a rationalistic scepticism concerning spiritual certainties. Rather it is an attempt to reflect the authentic freedom of the Christian believer that is rooted in the gospel itself and completely compatible with a firm commitment to the verities of the Christian faith. No one would question the Apostle Paul's deep and passionate commitment to the gospel of the grace of God, yet this same Paul displayed a liberality of spirit and flexibility of policy on a wide variety of issues that has rarely been equalled in Christian history. When he discerned that the essence of the gospel was at stake, Paul was severity itself, calling down anathemas on those who compromised the foundations of the good news of Christ. He warned the Galatians, troubled by Judaizers wanting to make law observance a condition of salvation: 'Even if we or an angel from heaven should preach a gospel other than the one we preached to you, let him be eternally condemned!' (Gal.1:8).

Here we see the severity of Paul, aroused by those who undermined the gospel or brought it into disrepute by their behaviour. His broad and liberal flexibility in areas of legitimate differences between Christians we have already considered earlier in this chapter, particularly in the areas of sabbath observance, food and drink, and rites of circumcision. We should also mention the personal freedom permitted by Paul in giving, and in certain marriage questions. Concerning financial support of Christian ministries, he simply advised that 'each of you should give as you have made up your mind, not reluctantly or under compulsion, for God loves a cheerful giver' (2 Cor. 9:7) – no insistence here on a legal tithe so beloved of many churches today. When asked about marriage, Paul, despite his obvious personal preference for celibacy, grants all believers the freedom to marry or not to marry, emphasizing the dignity and honour of both conditions (1 Cor.7). (The major part of Catholic Christendom does not allow its ordained clergy that degree of freedom to this day). He also permits believers to marry again – although only under certain conditions and 'in the Lord', which is a criterion for any Christian action.

What is being advocated in this book is this type of liberal flexibility in areas of legitimate differences between Christians, firmly rooted in the unshakeable convictions of the saving acts of God in Christ. Of course the question will inevitably arise: 'Where do you draw the line? Who determines which differences between Christians are permissible and which cannot be tolerated?' It must be immediately confessed that there is no simple answer to that question, no straightforward formula to show the difference. Christians have always struggled to answer that question at different times in history and in the context of specific issues. If we say that it is the task of theology to attempt to answer such questions, then we mean not only the theology done by professional theologians in theological institutions but also that done in the churches by all believers as they debate and discuss the implications of the Christian faith for their time and situation. This the reason why this book has been written. It is an attempt to provide a convincing and reasoned theological basis for the claim that most of the traditional differences between Christians on baptismal issues are, in fact, legitimate differences which can and must be accommodated within the unity of one Christian fellowship according to the demands of the gospel itself.

The three proposals made above have far-reaching and costly implications for most churches. For credobaptist churches to desist from denigrating and treating with contempt the doctrine and practice of infant baptism and to make room for believers with such convictions to join their fellowship and be granted freedom to act in accordance with their consciences and convictions – this would be costly indeed for such churches. For paedobaptist churches to desist from condemning and rejecting those who feel led to seek baptism as believers and even to make room within the church for those of such convictions and provide the opportunity for them to receive what they desire – this would be costly for such churches. And for all Christians to cultivate an attitude of respect and tolerance for baptismal views other than their own and to resist the temptation to look down on them as spiritually inferior or naive – this too is costly.

In each case it is costly because it involves a certain backing down from previous positions deeply entrenched by centuries of polemical apologetics. It involves loss of face. It smacks of retreat from principle. It is humiliating, and requires becoming accustomed to strange and unfamiliar practices within the church. All this is costly. Yet it is the kind of cost demanded by the gospel of reconciliation, the kind of cost required of the first-century Jewish Christians in admitting Gentiles into the church. The gospel is set in the world as a force for the reconciliation of the world, to break down the many age-old barriers separating peoples into hostile opposing camps; barriers of a social, ethnic, economic and cultural kind. Surely such a gospel requires that Christians make a more serious effort at demolishing the barriers that keep them apart from one another?

A practical model?

In the above three proposals a model of a kind has been described, a model characterized by freedom of conscience and mutual respect in baptismal matters, leaving parents the freedom to baptise their children or not, and believers the freedom to accept the legitimacy of their baptism as infants, or, if they cannot, to request and receive baptism as believers. But surely, it could be argued, this presupposes a completely hypothetical and artificial situation. People do not come to conclusions in a vacuum. There can be no neutrality in the church on any issue. In practice, people are taught some particular doctrine which becomes their own 'received' doctrine (unless some outside contrary view manages to persuade them otherwise). How can the official position of a church be both paedobaptist and credobaptist?

The reality must be accepted that the overwhelming majority of churches in the world are (and will be for the foreseeable future) paedobaptist or credobaptist in their official policy. What then is being advocated here is that while it is recognized that a church has an official position, the alternative position will be fairly and respectfully represented, and room for its practice permitted for those so persuaded. In the case studies examined in Chapter 8 it can be seen not only that this is possible but that it has been successfully practised in certain instances. The Jesuit scholar Joseph Eagan, writing in the journal *Review and Expositor* has argued that diversity of practice is of the very essence of the catholicity of the Christian faith:

> Plurality and diversity of practice and theology have been characteristic of the Church's life from the very beginning. This was particularly true concerning both the practice and theology of Christian initiation in the early centuries. The Church can therefore accept a diversity of models of Christian initiation practice today. For legitimate plurality and diversity are necessary for the Church's full dynamic life in the Spirit.[11]

How would this model affect pastors, priests or church leaders? Would they be expected to administer baptisms contrary to their own convictions and conscience? Certainly not. This book has argued for maximum freedom of conscience for all Christians in baptismal matters. The same must surely apply to those in positions of Christian leadership who could not, therefore, be obliged to administer a baptism that was contrary to their own convictions. Of all the respondents considered in the previous chapter, a full 50 percent agreed that a pastor should be free to administer or to refrain from administering certain kinds of baptism. What of the possible problems that this could lead to? The infant brought to a pastor who feels unable in good conscience to administer baptism to that infant? The believer requesting baptism from a pastor who is persuaded that this person was legitimately baptised as an infant and ought not to be baptised again? In all such cases, the baptism could be performed by anyone in the church (or even from outside that particular congregation) who is able to do so in good conscience, presuming, of course, that all is done in accordance with the policy and order of the church concerning these matters. This is the reason why the significance and biblical foundation of lay baptism has received attention in this book. It is also of interest to note that only 25 percent of the respondents surveyed in Appendix C felt that the administration of baptism should be restricted to ordained ministers. And if we take the respondents *other than* the 50 Dutch Reformed students at Pretoria University, the figure drops to 14 percent.

So the freedom of conscience and flexibility of action in baptismal matters being advocated is a very comprehensive one. It applies to parents in relation to their children, believers in relation to themselves and to pastors and lay members in relation to their ministry. A formula for complete chaos? Not necessarily. When no-one needs to feel threatened by the convictions and actions of others and all are committed to mutual respect, love and acceptance then a remarkable diversity can coexist with wonderful harmony. The reality of this possibility has been seen, in measure, in some of the case studies examined in Chapter 8. The following quotations all bear witness to a growing conviction that the coexistence of differing baptismal convictions in a unity of fellowship is both possible and desirable. The first quotation comes from a Faith and Order Paper, the second is an Anglican comment from a report produced by a conference on baptism held in Nottingham, and the third is taken from an article written by a Presbyterian scholar from the University of Edinburgh, David Wright.

> In view of the notable agreement on the meaning of baptism, it is not surprising that there are replies which explicitly state that it is possible for infant and believers' baptism to co-exist in one church. This raises the question of whether this practice could be expanded in order to promote wider consensus (*Towards an Ecumenical Consensus*).[12]

> We have to recognise differences that exist amongst us about baptism, and the nature of the confession of faith. These, however, are issues that will be resolved as we draw closer together. In particular we believe that in a united Church the co-existence of patterns of initiation, including both believers' baptism and infant baptism, will itself lead to a fresh appreciation of the insights they reflect, without being destructive of the unity we wish to attain or compromising the question of achieving a common practice subsequently (Hurley).[13]

> If, with our evangelical commitment to the supreme authority and the clarity of scripture, we have been unable to find a route through the baptismal impasse (a bridge across the baptismal gulf), ought we not to start thinking about a biblical frame of reference in which we can agree to accept and live with both baptismal traditions? It is at least worth considering (Wright).[14]

In addition to the above statements, we again draw attention to 68 percent of all the respondents considered in Appendix C, who expressed their agreement that it is possible for Christians having differing baptismal convictions to be accommodated within one congregation.

A necessary model

Not only is the model under consideration a practical one, it is also a necessary model. It is necessary as a demonstration of what Christian love and unity is all about in practice, a unity in Christ that permits diversity of thought and action within the parameters of commitment to Christ and the good news of his saving grace. Such a model is also necessary for the liberation of baptism, its liberation from the inevitable apologetic that so often accompanies baptismal occasions, the self-defence of the particular 'correct' rite being administered over against other 'erroneous' rites. Liberated from such negative polemical aspects, baptismal occasions can focus more fully on the joyful celebration of the manifold grace of God poured out so freely upon his people through the gospel. The baptism of an infant is indeed an occasion to celebrate the grace of a covenant-keeping God, who declared to Abraham, the father of all believers:

'I will establish my covenant as an everlasting covenant between me and you and your descendants after you for the generations to come, to be your God and the God of your descendants after you' (Gen. 17:7). David, too, rejoiced in the gracious loving-kindness of the Lord that extends to the posterity of those who love him, 'From everlasting to everlasting the LORD's love is with those who fear him, and his righteousness with their children's children – with those who keep his covenant and remember to obey his precepts' (Ps.103:17). While those of credobaptist persuasion would not themselves see the baptism of infants as the necessary expression of such truths, yet this truth that the God of all grace is a covenant-keeping God is the common possession and heritage of all Christians, and one in which all believers can rejoice together.

Likewise the baptism of penitents, consciously turning from their sins and requesting the grace of baptism, is an occasion to celebrate the converting grace of God who calls us 'out of darkness into his wonderful light' (1 Pe. 2:9). While paedobaptists would not see the necessity of the rebaptism of those deemed to be already children of the covenant (Reformed) or children of God by baptism (Catholic), yet they, with all Christians, can rejoice in the restoring grace of God by which the prodigal son returns to his father (Luke 15), the unfaithful wife returns to her husband (Hosea) and the lost sheep is found by the Good Shepherd (Luke 15). Even Ezekiel speaks of the 'rebaptism' of God's own covenant people as a result of his converting and regenerating grace:

> 'I will sprinkle clean water on you, and you will be clean; I will cleanse you from all your impurities and from all your idols. I will give you a new heart and put a new spirit in you; I will remove from you your heart of stone and give you a heart of flesh. And I will put my Spirit in you and move you to follow my decrees and be careful to keep my laws. You will live in the land I gave your forefathers; you will be my people, and I will be your God' (Ez. 36:25–28).

Every baptism, of whatever kind, bears witness to some aspect of the manifold grace of God revealed to humankind through the gospel: the baptism of infants demonstrating the solidarity of the family as the object of God's saving actions; the baptism of teenagers raised in the church demonstrating the importance of personal faith; the baptism of non-Christian converts demonstrating the universal scope of God's saving actions extending to every tribe, people and nation; the baptism (rebaptism) of lapsed Christians demonstrating the forgiveness and longsuffering patience of God with his own unfaithful and adulterous (or simply ill-instructed) people. While it may not be possible for all Christians to give their full approval to every kind of baptism just mentioned, they can at least, in charity and solidarity with fellow-believers, rejoice gladly in those gospel truths that are therein confessed and celebrated. The need to recognize the spiritual truths celebrated in differing baptismal occasions has been expressed by the Roman Catholic author and spiritual director, Francis MacNutt:

> We can agree, then, that there are strong practical reasons for infant baptism, as well as for adult baptism. These strong reasons have led their proponents into confrontation and even into the setting up of new divisions in Christendom. But can't there be a way of reconciling these two positions, so that the spiritual advantages of both types of baptism can be preserved – without theological compromise?[15]

This book is an attempt to provide that for which MacNutt pleads, a theological basis for the reconciliation of traditionally separate baptismal practices. The necessity of this task is widely recognized – witness the many cries for a unity which can transcend baptismal differences and help to remove the scandal of divisions in the body of Christ. König has written:

> Is it really impossible for the churches to come to some kind of understanding concerning infant baptism? Must disagreement over infant baptism necessarily require schism? Is it not possible for more than one baptismal practice to exist in the same church? (translation).[16]

In response to König's question we can answer: it is possible and furthermore it is necessary. The gospel itself demands it. In the following two quotations an Anglican scholar and a Baptist writer speak in much the same spirit of concern about the breach of communion occasioned by baptismal differences:

> . . . let me say that I think that, whatever may have been true in the past, such a strong case may be made for both sets of procedures and such grave objections can be brought against both, that we need a new charity and patience in discussing them. Honest differences between us should certainly not be made an occasion of breach of communion, as they too often have been.[17]

> It is because Scripture is silent that Christians can legitimately hold different views as to who should be baptised. They always have done, still do and probably always will. What is important is that those views should be held in love, understanding and humility, with a willingness to seek forgiveness for past sins, and a desire to let the water that divides divide no longer.[18]

The note of repentance sounded in the last quotation is an important one. There can be no reconciliation without repentance, and the chief sin from which all traditions must repent is the sin of schism brought about by a spirit of intolerance of differing baptismal views and practices. Whatever errors may or may not be involved in particular forms of baptism (infant baptism, rebaptism), these errors fade into insignificance besides the glaring inconsistency of allowing such differences to become an occasion for the breach of communion between believers in the Lord Jesus Christ.

A dynamic model

The model advocated in this chapter, with its emphasis on personal freedom and flexibility of action, not only reflects the biblical themes of unity in diversity, but opens the way for new dimensions of outreach and evangelism which are really the subject of a separate work and will only be hinted at here.

It has been argued earlier in this book that the rapid and spontaneous expansion of the early church, as recorded in the book of Acts, was largely due to the personal witness and ministry of ordinary believers, and that this ministry included the immediate baptism of all who responded to the message of the gospel with the desire to become Christians. Later on, the administration of baptism was largely restricted to the officially ordained clergy of the church, and this has remained the pattern until the present time.

The recovery to the church of the ministry of immediate, lay baptism could be an important key to the fulfilment of the remaining evangelistic task of the church. But this thought will not be further pursued here as it raises many further questions and problems of a theological and ecclesiastical kind which would need proper consideration. It is only mentioned in passing as an indication of some of the wider implications of the central thrust of this book. While the importance of Christian unity has been very much in the foreground of this work, it must never be forgotten that the purpose of Christian unity is 'that the world may believe' (Jn. 17:21) and be reconciled to God through Jesus Christ.

Notes

1　K. Nürnberger & J. Tooke, *The Cost of Reconciliation in South Africa* (Pietermaritzburg, Methodist Publishing House, 1988).

2　F.F. Bruce, *Paul: the Apostle of the Free Spirit* (Exeter, Paternoster, 1985).

3　F.F. Bruce, 'Christian Freedom,' in S.B. Ferguson & D.F. Wright (eds.), *New Dictionary of Theology* (London, IVP, 1988), p.265.

4　R. Haldane, *An exposition of the Epistle to the Romans* (Grand Rapids, MacDonald, 1958 [1816]), p.597.

5　G.C. Berkouwer, *The Sacraments* (Grand Rapids, Eerdmans, 1981), p.109.

6　L.G. Walsh, *The Sacraments of Initiation* (London, Geoffrey Chapman, 1988), p.98.

7   T. Aquinas (edited by T. McDermott), *Summa Theologica: a concise translation*, (London, Methuen, 1991), p.564.

8   F.F. Bruce, *The Epistle of Paul to the Romans* (Leicester, IVP, 1983), p.243.

9   M. Luther (translated by J.T. Mueller), *Commentary on the Epistle to the Romans* (Grand Rapids, Kregel, 1985), p.195.

10   H. Cook, *What Baptists stand for* (London, Baptist Union of Great Britain and Ireland, 1973), p.249.

11   J.F. Eagon, 'The Authority and Justification for Infant Baptism,' *Review and Expositor* 77 (1980):51.

12   Faith and Order Paper No. 84, *Towards an Ecumenical Consensus on Baptism, the Eucharist and the Ministry: A Response to the Churches* (Geneva, WCC, 1977), p.7.

13   M. Hurley (ed.), *Ecumenical Studies. Baptism and Marriage* (Dublin, Gill & Son, 1968), p.45.

14   D.F. Wright, 'One baptism or two? Reflections on the history of Christian baptism,' *Vox Evangelica* 18 (1988):15.

15   F.S. MacNutt, 'A proposed, practical solution to the controversy between proponents of Believers' Baptism and Infant Baptism', in A. König, H.I. Lederle, & F.P. Möller, *Infant Baptism? The arguments for and against* (Roodepoort, CUM, 1984), p.160.

16   A. König, 'Eager to maintain the unity,' in A. König, H.I. Lederle, & F.P. Möller, *Infant Baptism? The arguments for and against* (Roodepoort, CUM, 1984), p.1.

17   D. Jenkins, 'Baptism and Creation,' in B.S. Moss (ed.), *Crisis for Baptism* (London, SCM, 1959) p.56.

18   D. Bridge & D. Phypers, *The Water that Divides* (Leicester, IVP, 1977), p.184.

Chapter 10

Conclusion

In a way the central idea of this work, which is also its conclusion, has already been stated in many places in the book and perhaps most fully in the last chapter, *Towards a Model for Reconciliation*, where clear and definite proposals were made concerning the mutual acceptance of baptismal practices as a way towards reconciliation and unity between Christians traditionally separated from one another over baptismal issues. This central idea is a very simple idea – that Christians ought not to allow their fellowship and communion with one another to be broken over differences in baptismal understanding and practice. The idea is not an original one. On the contrary it could almost be described as a commonplace among millions of Christians all over the world. Notwithstanding this, however, it is an idea that has failed to make any significant impact on the official policies of the great majority of churches in the world. Hence the many words that have been written about a simple idea in this book. Whatever may be original in this work is not the central idea itself but the attempt to provide a reasoned theological basis for its acceptance and implementation.

A historical parallel

There is, perhaps, a certain parallel between this idea and another very simple idea, now widely approved and yet not so long ago just as widely rejected – the idea that Christians ought to be free to worship God according to their conscience without coercion. Freedom of worship is very widely accepted today, so much so that the idea seems obvious, so simple that a child can understand it. Yet only four hundred years ago this was just an idea, believed by a few but practised nowhere. From the days of the Emperor Theodosius (c. 346–395) the denial of the Trinity was considered 'both a theological-religious error as well as lèse majesté, offense against the state'.[1] Church and state were so closely linked that 'any fundamental criticism, any forming of a new communion, even pacifism, appeared to be seditious'.[2] Beza, Calvin's successor in Geneva, boldly declared the concept of religious freedom 'a most diabolical dogma, because it means that everyone should be left to go to hell in his own way'.[3] Even mild-mannered churchmen of the sixteenth century like Haller, Capito and Oecolampadius finally yielded, though reluctantly, to the compelling logic of persecution in order to maintain 'the ideal of a unified civil and religious community', the vision of a *Corpus Christianum*, a complete civic and religious solidarity.[4] During the seventeenth century, in Massachusetts Bay Colony, established by Puritans who had experienced religious persecution in England, 'Baptists, Quakers and other sectaries were publicly whipped in the pillory, driven from their homes, and some were even killed for the sake of defense of the religious, orthodox establishment.'[5] The idea of religious freedom, seemingly so obvious today, took a long time to gain acceptance, with many an argument, written in weighty tomes, being produced in its favour.

Anabaptists and Baptists were in the forefront of the struggle for freedom of worship. Their heroism and the sacrifices they made in that struggle are today almost universally recognized and honoured. Yet history has a strange way of reversing the roles of particular bodies. The central idea of this thesis, namely the freedom of individual believers to hold and to practise differing baptismal views in one and the same church, without coercion, is widely resisted by Christians in many traditions today, but perhaps most strongly by Christians in credobaptist traditions. It must immediately be added that the word 'coercion' is not to be understood here in the sense of physical force, something enforced by civil authority by legal means. Nevertheless, the word 'coercion' is deliberately used as there are forms of coercion apart from the use of state-empowered physical force. There are, for example, psychological forms of coercion. The power of churches to exclude from their fellowship and membership those who do not adhere to certain views is such a form of 'spiritual' coercion. Admittedly the use of such power is, necessarily wrong; the church is, after all, a communion of people bound together by certain beliefs, and is therefore entitled to exclude those who reject such beliefs. What is being questioned is whether that power is rightly used when used to exclude certain people on grounds of their baptismal views.

Objections

'But if no force is involved', it could be objected, 'what is wrong? Surely it is a simple matter of freedom of choice? A church has a right to stipulate its requirements for membership just as individuals have the right to join the church of their choice. In this way all enjoy freedom of conscience and there is no coercion.' Such an objection reflects a popular, contemporary way of thinking. But it fails to take into account certain realities, social and psychological as well as theological. To begin with, Christians form deep bonds of attachment to their church and the community of faith it represents. To force them into separation from that community over a secondary issue, such as baptism, in which primary issues of the faith itself are not being called into question, often causes deep and unnecessary trauma. There are also many practical cases, such as when Christians from different traditions (paedobaptist and credobaptist) marry. It is very difficult for them to find a church where both of them are fully accepted and can become members without any coercion (spiritual or psychological) on baptismal issues. The unhappy result in such cases is too often that such couples become alienated from the church or even drift away from the faith. In addition to all such sociological considerations, there remains the fundamental theological question: is it right to exclude any believer from the fellowship of other believers on the grounds of baptismal differences?

There is another objection to the central idea of this book that needs to be taken seriously. It goes like this. In this age of spineless Christianity, when the spirit of a broadminded and liberal approach to doctrinal and moral issues may mean that little is held sacred and virtually everything is questioned, should we be arguing for a more liberal flexibility in the area of baptism, one of the basic sacraments of the church? It is generally true that while 'liberal' churches are in decline, 'conservative' churches, where members are committed to strict standards in belief and behaviour, are growing. David Edwards draws attention to the important publication in 1972 of the book, *Why Conservative Churches are Growing*. The interesting thing about that publication is that its author, Dean Kelley, is a member of a leading 'liberal' Methodist denomination in the USA. David Edwards, Provost of Southwark Cathedral in England and a self-styled liberal Anglican, made the following observations in one of his most recent publications, *The Futures of Christianity:*

> I have personal reason to acknowledge the spiritual power of this [conservative] movement. I spent some ten years of my life in the service of the Student Christian Movement, mainly as the editor of its publishing house, and fully shared its commitment to liberal scholarship, social relevance and Christian reunion. But the SCM became increasingly preoccupied with the politics of the left and with the morality of progressive humanism and seemed to have lost its Christian basis, at least in the eyes of those students who were prepared to join a society with 'Christian' in its title. Its numbers declined sharply in comparison with those of the Christian Unions or Evangelical Unions, which

were based firmly on the Bible and prayer. The process which I witnessed in Britain was matched in the USA (where the University Christian Movement ceased to exist) and in many other countries. So I learnt in my own experience how the Evangelical emphasis has apparently proved stronger than 'liberalism', creating its own denominations or 'parachurch' movements as well as large groups within the historic churches.[6]

It is undeniably true that those who are prepared to commit themselves to active Christian involvement do not want a 'liberal' church which seeks to remove all the sharp edges of Christianity and make it as easy as possible to follow the Christian way. On the contrary, people are drawn to churches which maintain a clear witness to the truth, as they understand it, and which take a strong stand on what is right and wrong, setting high standards and expecting people to keep them. But this book has been written from just such a conservative perspective (see Chapter 1, 'The Writer's Vantage Point'), a principled stand on what is right and wrong on scriptural and theological principles. The argument for flexibility in baptismal practices must not be seen as a concession to 'worldly humanism' or a failure of nerve to take a clear stand on this subject. Rather the argument is grounded in the gospel itself and obedience to Christ and his law of love. Love, unity and reconciliation are demanded by the gospel. Flexibility of action and mutual respect for one another in secondary matters are demanded by the law of love which is Christian faith in action. Failure to render obedience in this area cannot be described as 'standing for the truth' but should rather be seen as compromise with the spirit of the world.

Liberal and conservative

The words 'liberal' and 'conservative' have appeared several times in the last few paragraphs and a few comments are called for concerning the significance and usage of these words. In general this book has avoided the terminology of 'liberal' and 'conservative' as these tend to accentuate a tension and a polarization which has had unfortunate consequences in the history of Christianity. The conservative-liberal tension is and always has been one of the most fundamental tensions within Christianity. It could be compared to the Catholic-Protestant tension within the Western church since the sixteenth century or the Ecumenical-Evangelical tension that has arisen among Protestants in more recent decades, but it is older than both of these. Indeed, we are speaking of a tension that is inherent in Christianity itself, which is both a strongly conservative and a powerfully liberating movement.

Wherein lies Christianity's conservatism? It is a faith that is inseparably tied to certain alleged historical events which occurred thousands of years ago. The sacred scriptures which function as its most authoritative written documents were produced nearly two thousand years ago; most of them being considerably older. The church has a mandate to 'keep the faith' and to 'hand on the traditions' (2 Thess. 2:15) received from the apostles and from the Lord Jesus himself. All of this amounts to a strongly conservative movement.

Wherein lies Christianity's liberalism? Down the ages the Christian faith has been a strong influence towards greater individual and social freedom. The process has not been automatic or rapid. Often Christian societies have been deeply oppressive and great injustices have been perpetrated in Christ's name. But if one should survey the broad range of freedoms that are almost taken for granted today – freedom of conscience and religion, freedom of speech and assembly, freedom from slavery, the emancipation of women, freedom for workers – it will be seen that virtually all of them emerged in societies strongly influenced by Christianity and were fought for by individuals and groups deeply influenced by the spirit of Christianity. Even at the very foundation of Christianity, the attitude of Jesus and Paul to Jewish law and tradition could be described as 'liberal' over against that of the Pharisees and Sadducees.

The problem with freedom is that it so easily becomes licence; it is so often abused. This does not mean that freedom itself is wrong and therefore undesirable. On the contrary, freedom is good and the gift of God. But it is of the very nature of freedom that it is open to abuse. Freedom from the law, for which Paul so strenuously argued (Gal.3) can become antinomianism and thereafter open immorality – a danger against which Paul warns in the same letter to the Galatians (3:13). Freedom of conscience in secondary matters of doctrine and practice can slide into sceptical views about the faith and thereafter into open unbelief. Freedom of thought, inspired by Christian principles, can even spawn antichristian movements. It is significant that two of the most vicious totalitarian systems that the twentieth century has witnessed, Nazism and Communism, had their rise in the soil of 'Christian' Europe.

Thus it is that many advances in human freedom, often inspired by Christian influences and equally often accompanied by serious abuses of that same freedom, have tended to provoke conservative reactions from those who desire to protect the faith. In this light we can understand various conservative manifestations of the Christian movement. The reactionary nature of nineteenth-century Roman

Catholicism, for example, with its condemnation of democracy, toleration and freedom of conscience, must be understood in the light of the excesses of the French Revolution, with its call to freedom, equality and fraternity, together with its deistic, atheistic and violent tendencies. The deep conservatism of early twentieth century Protestant fundamentalism, for all its separatistic and obscurantist tendencies, must also be understood in the light of contemporary socio-political and philosophical trends, often with sceptical and atheistic undertones. In all these cases the conservative instinct does reflect (however dimly at times) a truly Christian instinct, a strong concern to keep the faith at all costs and to defend it vigorously against every attack. But the liberal instinct is also authentically Christian: the desire to apply the Christian ethic of love in every area of life so as to promote greater freedom, justice, unity and suchlike social benefits.

This book finds itself in the middle of this tension. Conservative Baptists and conservative Catholics are both likely to view its proposals with suspicion, and for the same reason. 'If we begin to relax our traditional doctrine and discipline in the area of baptism', they could well argue, 'what will the end be?' The response of this writer is not to reject the conservative instinct, but on the contrary rather to affirm it, as well as to show that a liberal flexibility *in certain areas* is not contrary to the conservative instinct but a necessary corollary of it. Few Christians would want to return to the sixteenth century when Protestants and Catholics condemned Anabaptists to death for the 'blasphemy' of rebaptism, and when Anabaptists denounced infant baptism as 'the mark of the antichrist' (thereby consigning to hell all who practised it). While all three groups were zealously concerned for the true Christian faith, as most today would acknowledge, the attitudes and actions of all three were inconsistent with the higher Christian law of love. Few today would want to deny that the progress towards mutual tolerance which slowly developed in subsequent centuries was in line with the spirit and teaching of the gospel. That process must find its logical conclusion in a situation, not just of mutual tolerance between separate bodies, but also of mutual acceptance whereby various baptismal practices can coexist within a visibly united Christian fellowship.

Summary

In this concluding chapter, it may be useful to review briefly some of the main lines of argument, by way of a summary of the whole book.

1. Within the 'one, holy, catholic and apostolic church' of the third and fourth centuries there was an extraordinary variety of baptismal practices. These included infant baptism, believers' baptism, delayed baptism, emergency baptism and death-bed baptism (see Chapter 4). These various baptismal practices seem to have coexisted in the unity of the one church with remarkably little contention, as far as the information available to us goes. To accept today, therefore, a variety of baptismal practices within one church or denomination, would not represent any novelty but rather the revival of an ancient catholic practice, the experience of the early church.

2. The question as to whether the apostles baptised infants or not cannot be conclusively settled on historical grounds alone. There is general agreement that direct references to the baptism of infants can be found from about the year 200 onwards (see Chapter 4). Before the year 200 there is no conclusive historical evidence that the early church did or did not baptise infants. It is widely accepted that the question as to whether the early church (before the year 200) baptised infants must be settled on theological grounds.

3. While it is possible to speak of a general scholarly consensus about *certain* historical aspects of the practice of baptism (particularly after the year 200), there is no general theological consensus today concerning the nature, function and practice of baptism in apostolic times. Unless certain views are simply ignored because they are minority views, it has to be admitted that the Christian world is not agreed on certain key aspects of the administration of baptism in apostolic times. In this book three major baptismal traditions have been identified: the Catholic tradition, with its special emphasis on the efficacy of the sacraments as a means of grace; the Reformed tradition, with its understanding of baptism as the sign and seal of the covenant of grace which God has established with his people; and the Baptist tradition with its emphasis on baptism as a confession of faith. None of these traditions can be lightly dismissed as being inconsequential. Chapter 2 contains a summary of the arguments of these three perspectives.

   Thus in addition to inconclusive historical evidence we must also acknowledge a theological stalemate in certain key areas of baptismal practice. Does not such a situation call for a theological truce, a decision to allow for a variety of baptismal practices while encouraging mutual respect and sensitivity in all ongoing discussions and debates on the subject?

4. In any theological hierarchy of truths, issues such as unity, love and reconciliation between Christians feature far higher than ritual and doctrinal correctness in baptism. The lesser must not be allowed to take precedence over the greater. For Christians to allow themselves to be divided and separated from one another over the question of which is the 'correct' baptism would be to disobey the weightier and more important of God's commandments concerning reconciliation, love and unity (see Chapters 5 and 7).

5. The division of Christians into separate bodies with conflicting baptismal views renders serious reflection on the subject of baptism so much more difficult. Participants in transdenominational discussions and debates on the subject of baptism are inevitably under a certain constraint to be loyal to their denominational positions. It is psychologically difficult to make any concessions to the arguments of the 'enemy', especially if such concessions might necessitate 'crossing the line' into the enemy camp. Removing these restraints would allow a much wider flexibility of baptismal views and practices in each camp, would liberate baptismal discussions, and would enable them to be much more fruitful (see Chapter 6).

6. The concept of mutual acceptance of baptismal differences is not a completely untested idea. In certain individual congregations and even, very rarely, in whole denominations, the idea has been implemented with a surprising degree of success (see Chapter 8 and Appendix A).

7. Research conducted among 182 theological students representing at least twenty different denominations and studying at five different institutions in various places in South Africa indicated that the great majority of the respondents were in favour of a unity that could transcend the baptismal differences that tend to divide Christians (see Chapter 9 and Appendix C). Most of them expressed the belief that different baptismal convictions could be accommodated in one congregation, although not all of them had thought through what the implications of such a belief might be. Surely it would be reasonable to infer that serious attempts by churches and denominations to promote reconciliation and unity through the mutual acceptance of baptismal differences would be warmly supported by many of the faithful in most churches.

These lines of argument and research, developed in the various parts of this book, all lead to the one simple idea referred to at the beginning of this chapter – that the visible unity and fellowship between Christians ought not to be broken by baptismal differences. Rather, space ought to be created by the churches for the accommodation of various baptismal practices within one united fellowship.

It needs to be emphasized that if the mutual acceptance of baptismal differences is to be authentic it must involve full acceptance of the whole package of a particular practice. This means accepting (though, of course, not necessarily agreeing with) some practices that have been traditionally offensive to certain Christians, such as: the baptism of the infants of parents who may desire it; the 'rebaptism' of believers who may be unconvinced of the validity of their previous baptism and desire to be 'baptised' (see Chapter 9).

The future

What would be the result of a policy of the mutual acceptance of baptismal differences? Of course it is impossible to make a precise prediction. Such a policy would create the possibility that the practice of a particular church might freely develop in any direction. It might mean, for example, that eventually all Christians would accept the validity and desirability of baptising the infants of believers. Alternatively the time might come when all Christians would agree that baptism should be administered only to those able to make some kind of profession of faith. More likely the debate would continue about the true Christian doctrine and practice of baptism and the variety of views and practices might become even more varied. Whatever the case, the overall outcome of a policy of greater flexibility and mutual acceptance of baptism differences is likely to be more positive than many would expect.

Let us look again at the issue of complete freedom of worship which, we have suggested, has some parallels with the present issue. Those who proposed the idea four hundred years ago were scorned as dreamers of the impossible. Neither civil nor religious leaders could ordinarily conceive of a stable society that did not unite church and state in a *Corpus Christianum*. Religious freedom, it was felt, would lead to an impossible confusion of diverse sects which in turn would undermine social stability by destroying the foundations of orderly government. A policy of religious freedom, therefore, would lead in the end to chaos, irreligion and atheism. The principle 'One King, One Faith, One Nation' made for clear-cut intolerance in religious matters, and as John Bennet has written:

> Until the 17th century in Christendom it was generally taken for granted that, either to protect souls from the spiritually deadly effects of heresy or to preserve

social unity by permitting only one religious allegiance within a political community, it was right for Catholic or Protestant Christians to limit the freedom of those whom they believed to be in error.[7]

The policy of religious freedom did indeed seem to contribute to the development of a confusing array of Christian sects. But of the other predictions of social collapse, anarchy and irreligion, none materialized. On the contrary, those societies in which religious freedom prevailed were often characterized by a high degree of social and political stability together with vigorous religious activity. The United States of America could be cited as an example, concerning which Latourette observes, 'Not since Constantine had so little connexion between church and state existed in any land where Christianity was the prevailing form of religion.'[8] Thomas Jefferson, one of the chief architects in the USA of the 'wall of separation between Church and State', was reviled by his enemies as 'the infidel, the atheist, the enemy of biblical revelation and the potential overthrower of ordered society and sound morality'.[9] Such concepts of complete religious freedom were, indeed, a daring innovation at that time. They represented an uncertain but 'fair' experiment, in the words of Jefferson in 1808 towards the end of his term as President:

> We have solved, by fair experiment, the great and interesting question whether freedom of religion is compatible with order in government, and obedience to the laws. And we have experienced the quiet as well as the comfort which results from leaving everyone to profess freely and openly those principles of religion which are the inductions of his own reason, and the serious convictions of his own inquiries.[10]

Those who, centuries ago, made such dire and confident predictions of the disastrous consequences of a policy of religious freedom would probably stand astonished today to see the positive and beneficial results in church and society of just such a policy. In 1635 Roger Williams was banned from the colony of Massachusetts and condemned by the great Cotton Mather for believing that: *God* requireth not an *uniformity* of *Religion* to be *inacted* and *inforced* in any *civill state*; which inforced *uniformity* (sooner or later) is the greatest occasion of *civill Warre, ravishing of conscience, persecution* of *Jesus Christ* in his servants, and of the *hypocrisie* and destruction of millions of souls'.[11]

Today he is honoured in the same country as the man who 'stood bravely and firmly for complete separation of Church and State', principles which 'have become fundamental American principles of government', representing the 'great contribution on the part of the Baptists to the solving of a problem that had caused trouble ever since the conversion of the emperor Constantine the Great in 312'.[12]

Likewise, the widespread implementation in churches today of a mutual acceptance of baptismal differences would possibly lead to an even more confusing array of baptismal practices. Yet it might well also lead to greater mutual respect and understanding between Christians, a greater sensitivity towards different views, a stronger and deeper unity between Christians, a higher level of religious knowledge and commitment and a far more effective outreach to the world. As for the increase in diversity of baptismal practices, it seems to be almost an inevitable law of growth that as the church grows in numbers and maturity it grows too in variety of manifestations, complexity of organisation and diversity of practices. With respect to the increasing diversity to be found within Christianity, David Edwards has made the following observations:

> In my own education of study, travel, listening and thinking, I have found two themes growing ever larger in my mind. One is the theme of diversity . . . this diversity in church life is a fact which will not go away. And my 'educated guess' is that any unity will have to be found amid this astounding diversity, denominational and regional, temperamental and institutional, within a world population which already in AD 1986 includes five thousand million different people.
>
> But another theme has also gained power in my mind the further I have probed. It is the conviction that a Christian communion including all this diversity is possible although it must be conceived in a way that is genuinely open to the variety and the change. Too often Christians seeking 'unity' have attempted to retreat to some narrow formula in theology or to return to some legendary golden age in the past. The truth about the Christian past teaches what is possible. In the Christian Scriptures, in the early Christian centuries and in the experience of the modern churches, there is immense diversity with jewels as well as trash in abundance. But there is also one very precious pearl. The shared experience of the God embodied in Jesus Christ unites Christians in the 'fellowship of the Holy Spirit'; in valuing the Bible, baptism and the eucharist and therefore an ordained 'ministry'; and in producing the authenticating fruits, the Christlike character and the Christlike action. The challenge to the Christian who thinks about the futures is to imagine a communion based on the realities of this unifying experience and big enough to cover the diversity now seen to be inescapable and now welcomed as the will of an imaginative Creator.
>
> Am I in some way being false to the spirit of Christianity if I stress these two themes of *diversity* and *communion*? I do not think so. For I find that these themes run through the Bible and the very early Christian centuries.[13]

The sentiments expressed by the liberal Anglican David Edwards are very much the same as those of the conservative Baptist author of this book. Doubtless there would be some differences of opinion in the practical and detailed application of these sentiments. It is doubtful, on the one hand, whether Edwards would be willing to accept the central idea of this book, while some of those issues considered primary by this writer, on the other hand, would probably be considered secondary by Edwards. But the point made by Edwards remains valid. The diversity of Christian practices is extraordinarily wide and continues to increase with the growth of the church throughout the world. Yet the command to 'love one another' in the unity of the Spirit remains a primary command of the Lord of the church. This unity will be realized only through the mutual acceptance of a diversity of practices in all areas where the substance of the faith is not undermined, and one of these areas is baptism.

The focus of this entire book has been on the one issue of baptism. But it will be clear to the reader that the principles enunciated have far wider application than just baptism. They have application to all those areas classified as 'secondary' in Chapter 7 – structures of church government, patterns of ministry, forms of worship, rites, liturgies and special observances.

'Now the Lord is the Spirit, and where the Spirit of the Lord is, there is freedom' (2 Cor. 3:17). The apostolic church, portrayed for us in the pages of the New Testament, was characterized by a passionate commitment to the truth of the gospel together with a remarkable liberty of spirit in things of a secondary nature. As such it remains a challenge to the church of this age and to the church of every age.

Notes

1 A.W. Mueller, 'Religious Freedom,' C.F.H. Henry (ed.), *Baker's Dictionary of Christian Ethics* (Grand Rapids, Baker, 1973), p.574.

2 C.L. Manschreck, *A History of Christianity in the World* (Englewood Cliffs: Prentice-Hall, 1974), p.213.

3 A.W. Mueller, 'Religious Freedom,' C.F.H. Henry (ed.), *Baker's Dictionary of Christian Ethics* (Grand Rapids, Baker, 1973), p.575.

4 R. Krieder, 'The Anabaptist and the State,' in G.F. Hershberger (ed.), *The Recovery of the Anabaptist Vision* (Scottdale, Pennsylvania, Herald Press, 1972), p.181.

5 A.W. Mueller, 'Religious Freedom,' C.F.H. Henry (ed.), *Baker's Dictionary of Christian Ethics* (Grand Rapids, Baker, 1973), p.574.

6 D.L. Edwards, *The Futures of Christianity* (London, Hodder, 1987), p.416–17.

7 J.C. Bennet, 'Freedom,' in J. Macqarrie & J. Childress (eds.), *A New Dictionary of Christian Ethics* (London, SCM, 1986), p.239.

8 K.S. Latourette, *A History of the Expansion of Christianity. Vol. III. Three Centuries of Advance A.D. 1500–A.D. 1800* (Grand Rapids, Zondervan, 1974), p.230.

9 D.P. Whitelaw, *Church History Study Guide: The History of Christianity on the North American Continent* (Pretoria, UNISA, 1988), p.118.

10 Ibid., p.120.

11 W.W. Sweet, *The Story of Religion in America* (New York, Harper, 1950), p.70.

12 B.K. Kuiper, *The Church in History* (Grand Rapids, Eerdmans, 1979), p.331–2.

13 D.L. Edwards, *The Futures of Christianity* (London, Hodder, 1987), p.17–18.

Appendix A

Four congregations in the Cape Peninsular region

Of the churches considered below, the Kommetjie Christian Church and the Hermanus United Church seem to be the best examples of churches that permit Christians both to hold and practise differing baptismal positions, and so more space has been devoted to them. The other churches are more pronouncedly credobaptist in their orientation, but have been included because of the (occasional) occurrence within them of infant baptisms.

Kommetjie Christian Church

Kommetjie is a seaside village on the western side of the Cape Peninsula. The church traces its earliest beginnings back to 1925 when it began as a preaching post of the Bible Institute of Kalk Bay and a Brethren Sunday school. The founding members of the church included a Lutheran, a Presbyterian, a Methodist and a Dutch Reformed. The present trustees of the church are still predominantly paedobaptists but also include a Baptist. The present minister (in 1995) is a Baptist.

The original constitution of the church contained a statement of faith which confessed the following concerning baptism:

> We believe in the ordinances of Baptism and the Lord's Supper as being instituted by our Lord Jesus Christ, but not in Baptism as conveying regenerating grace, neither in the Lord's Supper as being a sacrifice for sin, nor involving any change in the substance of the bread and wine *(Extract of a special resolution 1968)*.

This article of faith has remained unchanged in all the subsequent constitutions produced and approved by the church. The original constitution made no mention of how baptism was to be administered and to whom. This was clarified in a later version of the church's constitution, approved probably some time in the 1980s:

Baptism is the confession of the believer by means of water as an identification with the Lord Jesus Christ in His burial and resurrection.
The ordinance will by performed on request for:-

- believers who wish to be immersed as a confession of their faith,
- the children of believers as the parents promise to raise their children in the Christian faith *(Constitution of the Kommetjie Christian Church)* .

There is, however, something of an inconsistency in the above clauses, which define baptism in terms of believers' baptism and then allow infant baptism. Doubtless it was the awareness of this inconsistency that led to changes in the above clauses in a later version of the church's constitution. This has:

Baptism is an identification with the Lord Jesus Christ in His burial and resurrection as a sign of the gospel. Some understand this to refer to the baptism of believers and others to the baptism of the children of believing parents.
The ordinance will be performed on request for:-

- believers who wish to be immersed as a confession of their faith,
- the children of believers as the parents promise to raise their children in the Christian faith *(Kommetjie Christian Church Constitution)* .

This is clearly an improvement on the previous wording as it frankly recognizes differences in the understanding of baptism. The statement could be made even more accurate if it read: 'Some understand this to refer to the baptism of believers only and others to the baptism of the children of believing parents also.' But perhaps this must await a future revision of the constitution.

Those wishing to have their infants baptised are first interviewed by the pastor of the church. If he feels they have no theological basis for their request but are acting simply out of custom, he will seek to enlighten them about the meaning and purpose of baptism and will suggest to them the alternative of having their infants dedicated. Apparently about 40 percent of the parents who initially ask for their children to be baptised end up having them dedicated. If the parents requesting baptism for their children show they have an understanding of the significance of the sacrament and are persuaded that there is a theological basis for it, the pastor arranges for the baptism to be conducted without hesitation. A paedobaptist minister (usually Church of England in South Africa or Presbyterian) is approached to administer the baptism in the church during a regular Sunday morning service.

Those desiring baptism as believers are counselled by the pastor who administers the sacrament himself, usually in the Fish Hoek Baptist church, as the Kommetjie Christian Church does not have a baptistry suitable for the immersion of adults. In the three years that the present pastor has been at the church there have been four instances of infant baptism and twenty-five of believers' baptism.

The present pastor of the church admits to experiencing some personal struggle in reconciling his strong commitment to Christian unity with his Baptist convictions. He professes to have no desire to change the inclusive nature of the church's baptismal policy but rather genuinely appreciates it and the sense of wider unity it fosters. He also admits that over a period of time the perspective of the incumbent pastor tends to prevail in the church and feels he cannot conceal his own Baptist convictions. He also enthusiastically participates in the local interdenominational ministers' fraternal.

Life in the Kommetjie Christian Church has not been without some conflict over the issue of baptism. Something of a watershed was reached in 1992 when on one occasion the pastor mentioned the subject of baptism from the pulpit and invited those interested in being baptised as believers to attend baptismal classes. Following these a sizeable group of people decided to be baptised as believers. The baptism was conducted at the Fish Hoek Baptist Church but the baptismal certificates were handed out on the following Sunday morning at the regular service in the Kommetjie church and those baptised were commended for their obedience. This caused an outcry among some of the members of the church who felt that such a commendation implied that paedobaptists were disobedient to the Lord. The trustees of the church were called in to address the situation. After carefully examining the circumstances surrounding the statements made, they did not find the pastor at fault, as he had been equally willing to commend paedobaptists for their obedience to conscience in bringing their children to baptism.

Of particular interest was an interview with a leading member of the Kommetjie church who was of paedobaptist persuasion. 'Gavin' has been five years with the church during which time he has functioned as a deacon, youth leader and Sunday School superintendent. Brought up in a Methodist home, his parents were active and committed Christians. He was first challenged in his thinking about baptism when at university. Many from the group of Christian students of which he was a part were being baptised as believers as a result of spiritual renewal or new-found faith. After thinking through the issue seriously 'Gavin' decided not to be rebaptised, believing that his baptism as an infant was a valid baptism, particularly in the light of the reality of his parents' faith. After listening to an exposition of the biblical case for infant baptism he also became convinced that infant baptism has a sound theological basis. His marriage to a girl from a Brethren background, with definite credobaptist views, further complicated the issue. It is not surprising that such a couple should gravitate to a church like the Kommetjie Christian Church with its inclusive baptismal policy. They decided (probably in deference to the wife's feelings) not to have their children baptised, though this would have been possible according to the church's constitution.

When asked about the incident referred to above when there had been some conflict about baptism, 'Gavin' replied that it had been a traumatic experience when some did feel very threatened, feeling that unfair pressure was being put on them. One couple even left the church, although there were probably also other reasons behind their decision. He himself felt there had been a general tendency to exaggerate the importance of the issue. He did, however, admit to having felt distressed when some members attempted to evaluate Christians according to their baptismal views. He also noted that the Kommetjie Christian Church had no formal structure of confirmation classes for those who had been baptised as infants. When, in response to requests for such classes, a series of confirmation classes were run, only one of the class was admitted to membership in the church after examination by the leadership of the church. This also caused some dissatisfaction in the church. However, in spite of these comments, Gavin felt that those of paedobaptist persuasion were not discriminated against in the church. He cited a recent example of an infant baptism where the pastor and the whole congregation participated enthusiastically in the service, which was characterized by a warm and loving spirit. The parents of the infant baptised, a couple from a Dutch Reformed background, were entirely satisfied with the way the service was conducted.

Hermanus United Church

On January 26, 1947, the following resolution was passed unanimously by a company of thirty-five people in the hall of the Dutch Reformed Church at Hermanus:

> That we as a gathering of Christian believers do hereby under the guidance of God solemnly constitute ourselves into an interdenominational fellowship of believers to be known as the United Church, Hermanus.[1]

At that time Hermanus was a small coastal village a little more than a hundred kilometres east of Cape Town. The two major sponsoring bodies in the establishment of this church were the Congregationalists and the Baptists. Neither of these two bodies felt that their adherents were sufficient to support a church on their own. The Hermanus United Church was also envisaged as providing a spiritual home for other Christians as well, particularly those belonging to any of the Protestant free church traditions. Indeed, included in the United Committee responsible for the establishment of the church were representatives of Methodist, Presbyterian, Congregational and Baptist Churches.[2]

The constitution of the church makes no mention of baptism. Concerning eligibility for membership, it declares: 'A person shall be eligible for membership by reason of being a member of any Christian Church, or by confession of faith.'[3] Elsewhere the constitution states: 'Every member upon being admitted shall make the Declaration of Faith and sign the Membership Book.' The Declaration of Faith affirms:

> I believe in God the Father,
> God the Son, and God the Holy Spirit.
> I believe in Jesus Christ, the Redeemer
> of the World, the Saviour of men.
> I believe in the forgiveness of sins
> and the life Everlasting.[4]

The church has had a succession of ministers from both the Baptist and the Paedobaptist traditions. In fact the church has endeavoured to vary the ministers so that their ecclesiastical affiliations may reflect the interdenominational character of the church. The previous minister was a Methodist minister. The present pastor (1996) is a Baptist minister. It is of interest that some of the previous Baptist ministers administered the rite of baptism to infants in cases where this was requested. The present minister, when being interviewed in connection with a possible call to the pastorate of the church, was asked if he would be willing to baptise infants when requested. He answered that he would not in good conscience be able to do that himself, but that he would make it clear that he respected the convictions of those requesting such a baptism and would make the necessary arrangements for the baptism to be carried out.

When a couple desire to have their infant baptised, they approach the pastor, who shares with them his own understanding of baptism while emphasizing at the same time that the church fully recognizes both infant baptism and believers' baptism. He will then arrange for a retired Methodist minister who is a member of the congregation to administer the baptism. This takes place in the church during the course of a regular Sunday morning service. Since there is also currently a retired Congregational minister in the congregation, there is no shortage of ministers within the church willing to administer infant baptism.

The baptism of believers is carried out by the minister himself, but not in the church as it does not have a suitable baptistry. Such baptisms are carried out in the church building of the Pinkster Protestante Kerk, which gladly makes its premises available for such occasions.

During the three years' ministry of the present pastor of the Hermanus United Church some twenty infants have been baptised and a number have been blessed in a service of dedication. Three people have been baptised as believers. These figures reflect to some extent the constituency of the church, in which most members and adherents come from churches within the paedobaptist tradition.

When asked what problems, difficulties or complaints had arisen in the church around the subject of baptism, the pastor was able to reply that he was not aware of any tensions, difficulties or strife that had troubled the church in the three years he had been there. There seem to have been no complaints from any section of the church concerning prejudice against any baptismal viewpoint. This is despite the fact that the present pastor has expounded those passages of Scripture mentioning baptism in accordance with his own Baptist convictions. But in doing so he has always shown respect for paedobaptist views, recognising the integrity of those who hold them. The interviewer felt that the general peace apparently prevailing in the church, particularly with regard to baptismal questions, was quite remarkable and the pastor was unable to recall one single comment on the subject indicating any unhappiness in the church.

Finally it can be mentioned that the Hermanus United Church enjoys excellent relationships with other churches in Hermanus, such as the Anglicans, Church of England in South Africa, the Dutch Reformed Church, the Pinkster Protestante Kerk and others. The minister of the church serves as chairman of the local ministers' fraternal.

Kleinmond Evangelical Fellowship

Kleinmond is a coastal town about a hundred kilometres east of Cape Town. The church was established in the early 1980s, largely through the efforts of a Baptist couple. It has maintained a fairly strong Baptist ethos although membership is open to 'all interested persons, irrespective of Church affiliations, who believe in the Lord Jesus Christ as their personal Saviour and Lord; and accept the Terms and Conditions set forth in this Constitution'.[5]

There seems to be some inconsistency in the official position of the church, for while membership is open to all believers, irrespective of whether they have been baptised as believers or infants, article 11 of the Declaration of Faith states: 'That baptism, being symbolic of the death and resurrection of Jesus Christ, and expressing openly the inward experience of spiritual regeneration, be carried out by the method of total immersion of a Believer in water, in obedience to our Lord's Command'. [6] Notwithstanding this clause, there are quite a few of paedobaptist persuasion in fellowship and in membership with the church and, indeed, the baptism of infants is permitted in the church.

While the baptism of infants may be permitted, it is certainly not encouraged. Many of those initially approaching the church for the baptism of their children have ended up having their children blessed in a ceremony of infant dedication in the church. In the eleven years since the inception of the church there has only been one instance of the baptism of an infant in the church. (It should be noted that quite a large percentage of the church adherents and members are retired people.) This would have been administered by a paedobaptist minister, most likely Methodist, specially invited for the occasion. The baptism of believers has been somewhat more frequent, although, interestingly, the church does not have a baptistry for such occasions and so use is made of the private swimming pools of members. In the first six months of 1993 about three or four people were so baptised. The church does not have a full-time pastor, although recently it has appointed as an honorary pastor one of its members who has functioned for many years in a leadership capacity.

Despite the Baptist leanings of the church, the majority of the regular adherents (those who regularly attend services at the church and who would identify themselves with it although they have not become full members of it) are of paedobaptist persuasion. Among those who are full members of the church, a majority are of Baptist persuasion, but not all. Among its adherents the church would include Dutch Reformed, Lutherans, a Catholic couple, Church of England in South Africa and Presbyterians.

The present pastor reports that there has been a remarkable peace in the church concerning the baptism question. In the last eleven years problems, strife or conflict in connection with matters of baptism have been virtually absent. He quoted the remarks of a visitor to the church who once said it was 'as close as possible to the perfect church'.

Hangklip Evangelical Fellowship

Betty's Bay, where this church is situated, is a small coastal village not far from Kleinmond in the Western Cape. It consists largely of holiday homes where people come to spend their holidays or to retire. Some residents, however, commute from Betty's Bay to their place of employment in Cape Town. The church has been in existence for about six years and was planted largely through the instrumentality of Jim and Betty Turvey, a couple with a Baptist background, who also played a role in the planting of the Kleinmond Evangelical Fellowship. Information about this church was gathered through an interview with a member of the committee of eight (three women and five men) who have the oversight of the church.

When the constitution of the church was being drawn up some were in favour of committing the church to a policy of believers' baptism. Others resisted this and eventually it was agreed that the constitution of the church should be inclusive of both infant baptism and believers' baptism. Article 9 of the church's 'Declaration of Faith' on Baptism states:

> We believe that Jesus Christ commanded that all Christians be baptised.
> **Believers' Baptism** is symbolic of the death and resurrection of our Lord, and expresses openly the inward experience of spiritual regeneration.
> **Infant Baptism** (followed later by confirmation) brings an infant, whose parents are Christians, into God's promised Covenantal relationship.
> On request, either form of baptism will be administered.[7]

Something of a crisis arose in the church when one of the committee members, who had strongly argued in favour of an inclusive constitution, felt led to be baptised as a believer. The sermon preached by the minister who had been invited to conduct the baptism included comments that were critical of certain paedobaptist churches. Despite the unhappiness caused by this incident, the inclusive nature of the church survived, and the person involved continued to be in favour of this policy. Indeed, the congregation seems to be about evenly divided between those who would be favourably inclined towards the baptism of infants and those who would not be so inclined.

Not having an ordained minister of its own, the church does not conduct any baptisms itself, but always invites a minister from elsewhere to perform any baptisms that have been requested. Only one infant has been baptised in the church (most of the members are retired) and a Methodist minister was obtained to perform the rite. One person has requested baptism as a believer; this took place in the private swimming pool of one of the members by a visiting preacher from the Vineyard Fellowship. One baby has also been blessed in a service of dedication in the church building. A few requests for the baptism of infants have been declined by the church on the grounds that the parents involved were in no way connected to or known by the church, which could not therefore vouch for their spiritual standing as believers. The position of the church is that it will consider requests for the baptism of infants only where the parents give evidence of being committed believers.

Notes

1 Trust Deed of United Church, Hermanus 1990. Revised Constitution of the church Hermanus.
2 Ibid.
3 Ibid.
4 Ibid.
5 Kleinmond Constitution, *Declaration of Faith and Constitution of the Kleinmond Evangelical Fellowship: undenominational* (Kleinmond, [s.a.]).
6 Ibid.
7 Hangklip Constitution, *Declaration of Faith and Constitution of the Hangklip Evangelical Fellowship* (Betty's Bay, [s.a.]).

Appendix B

The section on baptism from the Faith and Order Paper 'Baptism, Eucharist and Ministry'

I. The institution of baptism

1. Christian baptism is rooted in the ministry of Jesus of Nazareth, in his death and in his resurrection. It is incorporation into Christ, who is the crucified and risen Lord; it is entry into the New Covenant between God and God's people. Baptism is a gift of God, and is administered in the name of the Father, the Son, and the Holy Spirit. St Matthew records that the risen Lord, when sending his disciples into the world, commanded them to baptise (Matt. 28:18–20). The universal practice of baptism by the apostolic Church from its earliest days is attested in letters of the New Testament, the Acts of the Apostles, and the writings of the Fathers. The churches today continue this practice as a rite of commitment to the Lord who bestows his grace upon his people.

II. The meaning of baptism

2. Baptism is the sign of new life through Jesus Christ. It unites the one baptised with Christ and with his people. The New Testament scriptures and the liturgy of the Church unfold the meaning of baptism in various images which express the riches of Christ and the gifts of his salvation. These images are sometimes linked with the symbolic uses of water in the Old Testament. Baptism is participation in Christ's death and resurrection (Rom. 6:3–5; Col. 2:12); a washing away of sin (1 Cor. 6:11); a new birth (John 3:5); an enlightenment by Christ (Eph. 5:14); a re-clothing in Christ (Gal. 3:27); a renewal by the Spirit (Titus

3:5); the experience of salvation from the flood (1 Peter 3:20,21); an exodus from bondage (1 Cor. 10:1,2) and a liberation into a new humanity in which barriers of division whether of sex or race or social status are transcended (Gal. 3:27,28; 1 Cor. 12:13). The images are many but the reality is one.

A. Participation in Christ's Death and Resurrection

3. Baptism means participation in the life, death and resurrection of Jesus Christ. Jesus went down into the river Jordan and was baptised in solidarity with sinners in order to fulfil all righteousness (Matt. 3:15). This baptism led Jesus along the way of the Suffering Servant, made manifest in his sufferings, death and resurrection (Mark 10:38–40, 45). By baptism, Christians are immersed in the liberating death of Christ where their sins are buried, where the 'old Adam' is crucified with Christ, and where the power of sin is broken. Thus those baptised are no longer slaves to sin, but free. Fully identified with the death of Christ, they are buried with him and are raised here and now to a new life in the power of the resurrection of Jesus Christ, confident that they will also ultimately be one with him in a resurrection like his (Rom. 6:3–11; Col. 2:13, 3:1; Eph. 2:5–6).

B. Conversion, Pardoning and Cleansing

4. The baptism which makes Christians partakers of the mystery of Christ's death and resurrection implies confession of sin and conversion of heart. The baptism administered by John was itself a baptism of repentance for the forgiveness of sins (Mark 1:4). The New Testament underlines the ethical implications of baptism by representing it as an ablution which washes the body with pure water, a cleansing of the heart of all sin, and an act of justification (Heb. 10:22; 1 Peter 3:21; Acts 22:16; 1 Cor. 6:11). Thus those baptised are pardoned, cleansed and sanctified by Christ, and are given as part of their baptismal experience a new ethical orientation under the guidance of the Holy Spirit.

C. The Gift of the Spirit

5. The Holy Spirit is at work in the lives of people before, in and after their baptism. It is the same Spirit who revealed Jesus as the Son (Mark 1:10,11) and who empowered and united the disciples at Pentecost (Acts 2). God bestows upon all baptised persons the anointing and the promise of the Holy Spirit, marks them with a seal and implants in their

hearts the first instalment of their inheritance as sons and daughters of God. The Holy Spirit nurtures the life of faith in their hearts until the final deliverance when they will enter into its full possession, to the praise of the glory of God (2 Cor. 1:21,22; Eph. 1:13,14).

D. *Incorporation into the Body of Christ*

6. Administered in obedience to our Lord, baptism is a sign and seal of our common discipleship. Through baptism, Christians are brought into union with Christ, with each other and with the Church of every time and place. Our common baptism, which unites us to Christ in faith, is thus a basic bond of unity. We are one people and are called to confess and serve one Lord in each place and in all the world. The union with Christ which we share though baptism has important implications for Christian unity. 'There is . . . one baptism, one God and Father of us all . . .' (Eph. 4:4–6). When baptismal unity is realized in one holy, catholic, apostolic Church, a genuine Christian witness can be made to the healing and reconciling love of God. Therefore, our one baptism into Christ constitutes a call to the churches to overcome their divisions and visibly manifest their fellowship.

E. *The sign of the Kingdom*

7. Baptism initiates the reality of the new life given in the midst of the present world. It gives participation in the community of the Holy Spirit. It is a sign of the Kingdom of God and of the life of the world to come. Through the gifts of faith, hope and love, baptism has a dynamic which embraces the whole of life, extends to all nations, and anticipates the day when every tongue will confess that Jesus Christ is Lord to the glory of God the Father.

III. Baptism and faith

8. Baptism is both God's gift and our human response to that gift. It looks towards a growth into the measure of the stature of the fullness of Christ (Eph. 4:13). The necessity of faith for the reception of salvation embodied and set forth in baptism is acknowledged by all churches. Personal commitment is necessary for responsible membership in the body of Christ.

9. Baptism is related not only to momentary experience, but to life-long growth into Christ. Those baptised are called upon to reflect the glory of the Lord as they are transformed by the power of the Holy Spirit, into his likeness, with ever increasing splendour (2 Cor. 3:18). The life of the Christian is necessarily one of continuing struggle yet also of continuing experience of grace. In this new relationship, the baptised live for the sake of Christ, of his Church and of the world which he loves, while they wait in hope for the manifestation of God's new creation and for the time when God will be all in all (Rom. 8: 18–24; 1 Cor. 15:22–28, 49–57).

10. As they grow in the Christian life of faith, baptised believers demonstrate that humanity can be regenerated and liberated. They have a common responsibility, here and now, to bear witness together to the Gospel of Christ, the Liberator of all human beings. The context of this common witness is the Church and world. Within a fellowship of witness and service, Christians discover the full significance of the one baptism as the gift of God to all God's people. Likewise, they acknowledge that baptism, as a baptism into Christ's death, has ethical implications which not only call for personal sanctification, but also motivate Christians to strive for the realization of the will of God in all realms of life (Rom. 6:9ff; Gal. 3:27,28; 1 Peter 2:21–4:6).

IV. Baptismal practice

A. *Baptism of Believers and Infants*

11. While the possibility that infant baptism was also practised in the apostolic age cannot be excluded, baptism upon personal profession of faith is the most clearly attested pattern in the New Testament documents.

   In the course of history, the practice of baptism has developed in a variety of forms. Some churches baptise infants brought by parents or guardians who are ready, in and with the Church, to bring up the children in the Christian faith. Other churches practise exclusively the baptism of believers who are able to make a personal confession of faith. Some of these churches encourage infants or children to be presented and blessed in a service which usually involves thanksgiving for the gift of the child and also the commitment of the mother and father to Christian parenthood.

All churches baptise believers coming from other religions or from unbelief who accept the Christian faith and participate in catechetical instruction.

12. Both the baptism of believers and the baptism of infants take place in the Church as the community of faith. When one who can answer for himself or herself is baptised, a personal confession of faith will be an integral part of the baptismal service. When an infant is baptised, the personal response will be offered at a later moment in life. In both cases, the baptised person will have to grow in the understanding of faith. For those baptised upon their own confession of faith, there is always the constant requirement of a continuing growth of personal response in faith. In the case of infants, personal confession is expected later, and Christian nurture is directed to the eliciting of this confession. All baptism is rooted in and declares Christ's faithfulness unto death. It has its setting within the life and faith of the Church and, through the witness of the whole Church, points to the faithfulness of God, the ground of all life in faith. At every baptism the whole congregation reaffirms its faith in God and pledges itself to provide an environment of witness and service. Baptism should, therefore, always be celebrated and developed in the setting of the Christian community.

13. Baptism is an unrepeatable act. Any practice which might be interpreted as 're-baptism' must be avoided.

B. *Baptism-Chrismation-Confirmation*

14. In God's work of salvation, the paschal mystery of Christ's death and resurrection is inseparably linked with the pentecostal gift of the Holy Spirit. Similarly, participation in Christ's death and resurrection is inseparably linked with the receiving of the Spirit. Baptism in its full meaning signifies and effects both.

    Christians differ in their understanding as to where the sign of the gift of the Spirit is to be found. Different actions have become associated with the giving of the Spirit. For some it is the water rite itself. For others, it is the anointing with chrism and/or the imposition of hands, which many churches call confirmation. For still others it is all three, as they see the Spirit operative throughout the rite. All agree that Christian baptism is in water and the Holy Spirit.

C. *Towards Mutual Recognition of Baptism*

15. Churches are increasingly recognizing one another's baptism as the one baptism into Christ when Jesus Christ has been confessed as Lord by

the candidate or, in the case of infant baptism, when confession has been made by the church (parents, guardians, godparents and congregation) and affirmed later by personal faith and commitment. Mutual recognition of baptism is acknowledged as an important sign and means of expressing the baptismal unity given in Christ. Wherever possible, mutual recognition should be expressed explicitly by the churches.

16. In order to overcome their differences, believer baptists and those who practise infant baptism should reconsider certain aspects of their practices. The first may seek to express more visibly the fact that children are placed under the protection of God's grace. The latter must guard themselves against the practice of apparently indiscriminate baptism and take more seriously their responsibility for the nurture of baptised children to mature commitment to Christ.

V. The celebration of baptism

17. Baptism is administered with water in the name of the Father, the Son and the Holy Spirit.

18. In the celebration of baptism the symbolic dimension of water should be taken seriously and not minimized. The act of immersion can vividly express the reality that in baptism the Christian participates in the death, burial and resurrection of Christ.

19. As was the case in the early centuries, the gift of the Spirit in baptism may be signified in additional ways; for example, by the sign of the laying-on of hands, and by anointing or chrismation. The very sign of the cross recalls the promised gift of the Holy Spirit who is the instalment and the pledge of what is yet to come when God has fully redeemed those whom he has made his own (Eph. 1:13–14). The recovery of such vivid signs may be expected to enrich the liturgy.

20. Within any comprehensive order of baptism at least the following elements should find a place: the proclamation of the scriptures referring to baptism; an invocation of the Holy Spirit; a renunciation of evil; a profession of faith in Christ and the Holy Trinity; the use of water; a declaration that the persons baptised have acquired a new identity as sons and daughters of God, and as members of the Church, called to be witnesses of the Gospel. Some churches consider that Christian initiation is not complete without the sealing of the baptised with the gift of the Holy Spirit and participation in holy communion.

21. It is appropriate to explain in the context of the baptismal service the meaning of baptism as it appears from the scriptures (i.e. the participation in Christ's death and resurrection, conversion, pardoning and cleansing, gift of the Spirit, incorporation into the body of Christ and sign of the Kingdom).

22. Baptism is normally administered by an ordained minister, though in certain circumstances others are allowed to baptise.

23. Since baptism is intimately connected with the corporate life and worship of the Church, it should normally be administered during the public worship, so that the members of the congregation may by reminded of their own baptism and may welcome into their fellowship those who are baptised and whom they are committed to nurture in the Christian faith. The sacrament is appropriate to great festival occasions such as Easter, Pentecost and Epiphany, as was the practice in the early Church.

Appendix C

What do the people want? An analysis of empirical research

For the purpose of this research, a questionnaire was submitted to students studying theology at five different theological institutions in South Africa: the Dutch Reformed Faculty of Theology at the University of Pretoria, the Baptist Theological College (BTC) in Cape Town, St. Joseph's Theological Institute at Cedara (Pietermaritzburg), the Cape Evangelical Bible Institute (CEBI) in Cape Town, and the Bible Institute (BI) at Kalk Bay. A copy of the questionnaire may be found at the end of this appendix.

A total of 182 responses to the questionnaire were received from students representing at least twenty denominations in South Africa. At first the intention was to analyse the responses according to denominational affiliation, but after studying the responses, it became clear that each institution has a particular ethos of its own, exercising a certain influence on its students, whatever their ecclesiastical affiliation. So it was decided to analyse the results of the questionnaire according to each institution, and then to conclude with some observations concerning the responses as a whole.

The institutions differed considerably from one another. Some were more ecclesiastically 'homogeneous', such as the Dutch Reformed students at Pretoria and the Baptist students at BTC. St. Joseph's students were predominantly Roman Catholic, with a sprinkling of other churches represented. CEBI and BI included a wide variety of (Protestant) churches among their students who responded to the questionnaire.

Question 1 required respondents to identify their church as one in which 'the infants of believers are normally baptised' or not. Consequently *all* the churches represented by the respondents are divided into two major groups which will be referred to as 'paedobaptist' or 'credobaptist'. The inadequacy of some of this terminology is fully acknowledged, as discussed in the introductory chapter of this book, but will nevertheless be used in the absence of any generally accepted alternatives. Of the 182 respondents 112 were from paedobaptist churches, 69 were from credobaptist churches and one was apparently unsure how to answer this question stating 'both occur at our church.' According to this basic twofold division, all the respondents from Pretoria University were paedobaptist, all the respondents from BTC in Cape Town were credobaptist, all the respondents from St. Joseph's (with the exception of one) were paedobaptist and the students from CEBI and BI were pretty evenly divided between paedobaptist and credobaptist.

The questionnaire was divided into three sections. Respondents from churches in which infant baptism is practised were required to answer section A (questions 2–3) and section C (questions 7–9). Respondents from churches which do not (normally) practise infant baptism were required to answer section B (questions 4–6) and section C.

Dutch Reformed theological students in Pretoria

The following responses were obtained from a group of Dutch Reformed students studying theology at the University of Pretoria. There were fifty respondents, all except one male. Average age: 26.

Question 2: Should parents be allowed by the church to delay the baptism of their children if they so wish, until such time as the children themselves are able to profess their faith?

Yes	*38%*
Under certain circumstances	*12%*
Unsure	*2%*
No	*36%*

Those who answered *Under certain circumstances* elaborated as follows:

- if valid reasons can be given for such a decision;
- if there is doubt about the faith and life of the parents;
- if parents lack assurance of salvation (*geloofsekerheid*);
- if counselling is given to such parents to help them understand infant baptism;
- if the parents promise to bring up their children in the faith;

Question 3. Should those who received baptism as infants be permitted by the church to be baptised later as believers if they so desire?

Yes	*16%*
Under certain circumstances	*0%*
Unsure	*2%*
No	*82%*

Question 7. Do you think it is possible for Christians having differing baptismal convictions to be accommodated within one congregation?

Yes	*66%*
Unsure	*12%*
No	*18%*
No Response	*4%*

Question 8. Should a pastor be free to administer or to refrain from administering certain kinds of baptism (e.g. infant baptism, rebaptism)?

Yes	*38%*
Unsure	*8%*
No	*50%*
No Response	*4%*

Question 9. Should the administration of baptism be restricted to ordained ministers?

Yes	*56%*
In most cases	*14%*
Unsure	*8%*
No	*16%*
No Response	*6%*

Comments

1. The above responses indicate an overwhelming rejection of any idea of rebaptism (82%). Only 16% of the respondents were in favour of such a step being permitted by the church – that those who had already been baptised as infants should be allowed to request baptism again as believers at a later stage.

2. A surprising number (38%) of the respondents were in favour of parents being allowed by the church to delay the baptism of their children, if they so wish, until such time as the children themselves are able to profess their faith. A further 24% indicated they could approve such a policy under certain circumstances (summarized above), making a total of 62% who were open to such a policy.

3. A strong majority of the respondents (66%) felt that it was possible for Christians having differing baptismal convictions to be accommodated

within one congregation. Only 18% saw no possibility of this. This response indicates a strong desire for the realization of greater unity among Christians, notwithstanding the reality of differing convictions, even in so sensitive an area as baptism.

4. 50% of the respondents did not feel that a pastor should be free either to administer or refrain from administering certain kinds of baptisms. Only 38% of the respondents were in agreement with such freedom being granted to the pastor.

5. A clear majority of the respondents (56%) were in favour of restricting the administration of baptism to ordained ministers. This response was quite different to the responses from the students of other theological institutions where only a minority felt the administration of baptism should be restricted to ordained ministers (BI 20%, CEBI 21%, St. Joseph's 13%, BTC 3%.)

We can summarize those points of the above responses that are of special interest to the central theme of this book as follows: The great majority of the Dutch Reformed theological students at Pretoria University who responded to the questionnaire believe that some kind of accommodation for Christians having differing baptismal convictions is possible in the interests of promoting Christian unity, and would be in favour of parents being permitted to delay the baptism of their children, if they so wish. But they are definitely opposed to the rebaptism of those already baptised in infancy and would not want such a practice to be sanctioned by the church.

Baptist students in Cape Town

The following responses were obtained from a group of Baptist students studying theology at the Baptist Theological College at Cape Town, an official training institution of the Baptist Union of Southern Africa. Total number of respondents: 35 (31 male and 4 female.) Average age: 29.

Question 4. Would you be willing to accept the baptism of an infant as a valid baptism, even if you have reservations about its correctness and desirability?

Yes	*23%*
Uncertain	*20%*
No	*57%*

Question **5.** Should parents be permitted by the church to have their infant children baptised if they so wish?

Yes	*37%*
Uncertain	*3%*
No	*60%*

Of those who responded *Yes* half were willing for such infant baptisms to be administered in the local church while the other half thought they should be administered in another church where infant baptism is practised

Question **6.** Should it be possible for those only baptised as infants to become full members of the church?

Yes	*37%*
No	*57%*
No Response	*6%*

Question **7.** Do you think it is possible for Christians having differing baptismal convictions to be accommodated within one congregation?

Yes	*66%*
Unsure	*14%*
No	*20%*

Question **8.** Should a pastor be free to administer, or to refrain from administering, certain kinds of baptism (e.g. infant baptism, rebaptism)?

Yes	*54%*
Unsure	*17%*
No	*29%*

Question **9.** Should ordinary believers be permitted by the church to administer baptism?

Yes	*63%*
Unsure	*6%*
Sometimes	*29%*
No	*3%*

Those respondents who answered **Sometimes** to the last question above elaborated their responses as follows:

- if the believer is a mature Christian;
- in the absence of a pastor;
- in a missionary situation where no minister/leader is available;
- if the baptiser is a father, youth leader, or one who led the candidate to Christ, and only with the permission of the pastor;
- in the church only.

Comments

1. A slight but consistent majority of the respondents saw no room in the church for infant baptism in any form. 57% could not grant any validity at all to infant baptisms. 60% were opposed to parents being allowed by the church to baptise their infants if they so wished, and 57% were opposed to the acceptance into full membership of the church of those who had only been baptised as infants (without being baptised as conscious believers).

2. Yet a strong majority of the respondents (66%) believed that it was possible for Christians having differing baptismal convictions to be accommodated within one congregation. One cannot help being struck by what seems to be a strange inconsistency here. How can different baptismal convictions be accommodated in one congregation when any recognition or practice of infant baptism is ruled out of court? Yet this is clearly the position taken it would seem by many, of the respondents.

3. Concerning the freedom of a pastor to act according to his or her conscience in the administration or non-administration of baptism, a slight majority (54%) were in favour of such freedom.

4. This group was the first to respond to the questionnaire and the question on 'lay baptism' ('Should ordinary believers be permitted by the church to administer baptism?') was subsequently changed to 'Should the administration of baptism be restricted to ordained ministers?' (The comment was made that *all* believers are ordinary believers.) However, in the form in which the Baptist students responded to this question, the great majority (63%) were in favour of such 'lay baptism', with only a small minority (3%) opposed.

5. Although the majority of these Baptist students could not grant any validity to infant baptisms, 23% were able to grant some validity to them, with a further 20% uncertain how to respond. This means

that 43% of the respondents had not completely ruled out the possibility of granting some kind of recognition to infant baptisms – although such recognition could not be interpreted as approval. Furthermore, it can be noted that 37% of the respondents were in favour of accepting into full church membership those who had not been baptised as believers but only as infants. Even more striking is that the same percentage (37%) were in favour of parents being permitted by the church to have their infants baptised if they so wished, although only 20% felt that such infant baptisms could be performed in the local (Baptist) church.

The responses of the Baptist students at Cape Town can be summarized as follows: A clear majority (57–60%) of the respondents saw no room for any recognition or practice of infant baptism in the church. A strong majority (66%) thought it possible for Christians having differing baptismal convictions to be accommodated within one congregation. A significant minority were in favour of granting some recognition to infant baptism and even allowing its practice in the church.

Catholic students at St. Joseph's Theological Institution at Cedara (Pietermaritzburg)

Although St. Joseph's is a Roman Catholic institution and the majority of the students are Catholic, some of the students are from other churches. Of the 38 respondents, 23 were Roman Catholic, 6 were Methodist, 5 Anglican, 2 Lutheran, 1 Congregationalist, and 1 Baptist. Exactly half (19) the students were female and the average age was 42. The respondents from St. Joseph's differed from the respondents from the other institutions with respect to the significantly older average age and the higher proportion of female respondents. To facilitate analysis, the one Baptist respondent will be ignored so that the remaining respondents can be divided into two main groups, Roman Catholics and non Roman Catholics, both groups practising infant baptism.

The responses of these students will be divided into three categories: first, that of the Roman Catholic respondents (*RC*), second, that of the respondents from other paedobaptists churches (*Others*), and third, that of all the respondents together (*Total*). In answer to *Question* 2 below, for example, 30% of the Roman Catholic respondents answered *Yes*, 86% of the respondents from other paedobaptist churches answered *Yes*, and of all of the respondents taken together 51% answered *Yes*.

Question 2. Should parents be allowed by the church to delay the baptism of their children, if they so wish, until such time as the children themselves are able to profess their faith?

Yes	*RC 30%*	*Others 86%*	*Total 51%*
Under certain circumstances	*RC 22%*	*Others 0%*	*Total 14%*
Unsure	*RC 4%*	*Others 7%*	*Total 5%*
No	*RC 43%*	*Others 7%*	*Total 30%*

Those who answered *Under certain circumstances* elaborated as follows:

- if that is the conviction of the parents;
- if the parents can offer no spiritual support to their children;
- if the parents are not baptised;
- if the parents are not committed, practising Catholics.

Question 3. Should those who received baptism as infants be permitted by the church to be baptised later as believers if they so desire?

Yes	*RC 9%*	*Others 30%*	*Total 16%*
Under certain circumstances	*RC 9%*	*Others 21%*	*Total 16%*
Unsure	*RC 0%*	*Others 7%*	*Total 3%*
No	*RC 83%*	*Others 43%*	*Total 68%*

Those who answered *Under certain circumstances* elaborated as follows:

- if they doubted the grace of infant baptism;
- they might have wished to belong to another denomination;
- if they felt their infant baptism was not valid (parents not committed);
- if their family has had no lasting church membership.

Question 7. Do you think it is possible for Christians having differing baptismal convictions to be accommodated within one congregation?

Yes	*RC 57%*	*Others 93%*	*Total 70%*
Unsure	*RC 26%*	*Others 7%*	*Total 19%*
No	*RC 9%*	*Others 0%*	*Total 5%*
No Response	*RC 9%*	*Others 0%*	*Total 5%*

Question 8. Should a pastor be free to administer or to refrain from administering certain kinds of baptism (e.g. infant baptism, rebaptism)?

Yes	*RC 39%*	*Others 57%*	*Total 46%*
Unsure	*RC 0%*	*Others 0%*	*Total 3%*
No	*RC 43%*	*Others 43%*	*Total 43%*
No Response	*RC 13%*	*Others 0%*	*Total 8%*

Question 9. Should the administration of baptism be restricted to ordained ministers?

Yes	*RC 9%*	*Others 21%*	*Total 14%*
In most cases	*RC 39%*	*Others 21%*	*Total 32%*
Unsure	*RC 0%*	*Others 0%*	*Total 0%*
No	*RC 39%*	*Others 57%*	*Total 46%*
No Response	*RC 13%*	*Others 0%*	*Total 8%*

Comments

The Roman Catholic respondents will first be considered as a group, then the respondents from other denominations, then the whole group together.

Roman Catholics

1. As with the Dutch Reformed respondents from Pretoria, the Roman Catholic respondents indicated a very strong rejection (83%) of any idea of rebaptism.
2. Although 43% of the respondents were not in favour of parents being allowed by the church to delay the baptism of their children if they so desired, a surprising 30% were in favour of that option, and if we add the 22% who were willing to allow that option under certain circumstances we have a small majority (52%) who were in favour of that option being a possibility for parents.
3. A definite majority (57%) thought it possible for Christians having differing baptismal convictions to be accommodated within one congregation. A number were unsure and only 9% saw no possibility for such unity. As with the Cape Town Baptist students (although not to the same degree) one cannot help but notice a

certain inconsistency here. If neither the possibility of rebaptism nor the delay of the baptism of infants is to be permitted by a church, how can Christians of differing baptismal convictions be accommodated in the same congregation?

The other paedobaptist respondents

1. There is a marked difference between these responses and those of the Roman Catholic respondents. The overwhelming majority (86%) were in favour of parents being given the option to delay the baptism of their children if they so wished and virtually all these respondents thought it possible for Christians having differing baptismal convictions to be accommodated within one congregation.

2. 30% of these respondents were in favour of the church permitting those who had been baptised as infants to be baptised as believers if they so desired, with a further 21% in favour off such an option under certain circumstances, making a total of 51% who could be said to be in favour of such an option being possible, under certain circumstances.

3. Although the total number of non-Roman Catholic respondents at St. Joseph's was small, the pattern of response was very similar to that shown by other non-Catholic paedobaptist respondents in the two other institutions covered in this study (the Cape Evangelical Bible Institute and the Bible Institute at Kalk Bay) as will be seen below.

Summary

Taking all the respondents from St. Joseph's Theological Institute together, the results of the questionnaire can be summarized as follows: a strong majority think it possible for differing baptismal convictions to be accommodated together in one congregation but are opposed to the option of rebaptism being permitted by the church. A smaller majority favour the church permitting parents to delay the baptism of their children if they so wish. Respondents from the non-Catholic paedobaptist churches generally showed more flexibility in wanting to allow greater freedom of individual conscience than the Roman Catholic respondents.

Theological students at the Cape Evangelical Bible Institute (CEBI) in Cape Town

Unlike the other institutions considered so far, CEBI is not attached to any denomination and does not function as an official training institution for any church. As a result its students represent a wide range of ecclesiastical affiliation. Respondents to the questionnaire indicated membership in the following churches/denominations: Congregationalist, Church of the Province of SA, Community Bible Fellowship, Evangelical Endeavour Mission Church, Full Gospel, Presbyterian, Cape Town City Mission, Church of England in SA, Methodist, Lutheran, Jubilee Community Church, International Fellowship of Christian Churches, Baptist, Dutch Reformed, Assemblies of God. In addition to the aforementioned fifteen denominations, three respondents simply wrote 'Pentecostal', which could mean a number of denominations, and four respondents gave no indication of the church they belonged to. It could be said of CEBI that it is truly representative of South African Christianity with its very wide diversity of ecclesiastical denominations. Of the 29 respondents, 21 were male and 8 female. Average age: 30.

The respondents from CEBI can be broadly divided into two groups, those in whose churches the infants of believers are normally baptised (who will be referred to as paedobaptist) and those in whose churches the infants of believers are not normally baptised (who will be referred to as credobaptist). Of the 29 respondents, 13 were from paedobaptist churches and 16 from credobaptist churches.

Question 2 (to paedobaptists only). Should parents be allowed by the church to delay the baptism of their children, if they so wish, until such time as the children themselves are able to profess their faith?

Yes	*85%*
Under certain circumstances	*0%*
Unsure	*15%*
No	*0%*

Question 3 (to paedobaptists only). Should those who received baptism as infants be permitted by the church to be baptised later as believers if they so desire?

Yes	*92%*
Under certain circumstances	*0%*
Unsure	*0%*
No	*8%*

Question 4 (to credobaptists only). Would you be willing to accept the baptism of an infant as a valid baptism even if you have reservations about its correctness and desirability?

Yes	*44%*
Under certain circumstances	*12%*
Unsure	*6%*
No	*38%*

Question 5 (to credobaptists only). Should parents be permitted by the church to have their infant children baptised if they so wish?

Yes	*38%*
Under certain circumstances	*6%*
Unsure	*50%*
No	*6%*

Question 6 (to credobaptists only). Should it be possible for those baptised as infants only to become full members of the church?

Yes	*19%*
No	*75%*
No Response	*6%*

Question 7 (to all). Do you think it is possible for Christians having differing baptismal convictions to be accommodated within one congregation?

Yes	*Paedobaptists 69%*	*Credobaptists 63%*	*All 66%*
Unsure	*Paedobaptists 31%*	*Credobaptists 12%*	*All 21%*
No	*Paedobaptists 0%*	*Credobaptists 19%*	*All 10%*
No Response	*Paedobaptists 0%*	*Credobaptists 6%*	*All 3%*

Question 8 (to all). Should a pastor be free to administer or to refrain from administering certain kinds of baptism (e.g. infant baptism, rebaptism)?

Yes	*Paedobaptists 85%*	*Credobaptists 38%*	*All 59%*
Unsure	*Paedobaptists 0%*	*Credobaptists 25%*	*All 14%*
No	*Paedobaptists 8%*	*Credobaptists 31%*	*All 21%*
No Response	*Paedobaptists 8%*	*Credobaptists 6%*	*All 7%*

Question 9 (to all). Should the administration of baptism be restricted to ordained ministers?

Yes	*Paedobaptists 38%*	*Credobaptists 6%*	*All 21%*
In most cases	*Paedobaptists 15%*	*Credobaptists 25%*	*All 21%*
Unsure	*Paedobaptists 0%*	*Credobaptists 0%*	*All 0%*
No	*Paedobaptists 38%*	*Credobaptists 69%*	*All 55%*
No Response	*Paedobaptists 8%*	*Credobaptists 0%*	*All 3%*

Comments

1. Paedobaptist respondents at CEBI indicate a high degree of flexibility in wanting to allow maximum freedom of conscience for individual believers in baptismal matters. 85% were in favour of parents being allowed by the church to delay the baptism of their infants if they so wished, 93% were in favour of those who had been baptised as infants being permitted by the church to be baptised later as believers if they so desired, 69% thought it possible for differing baptismal convictions to be accommodated in one congregation, and 85% favoured maximum pastoral freedom in the administration or non-administration of baptism.

2. Credobaptist respondents were not quite so flexible in granting recognition to infant baptism, although in response to the question whether they would be willing to grant some kind of (limited) validity to infant baptism, 44% answered *Yes* as opposed to 38% who answered *No*. Half of these respondents were not in favour of parents being permitted by the church to have their infants baptised if they so wished, and a large majority of 75% were not in favour of church membership being granted to those baptised as infants only.

3. A clear majority of both credobaptist and paedobaptist groups thought it possible for differing baptismal convictions to be accommodated in one congregation. Again, one cannot help but note the inconsistency between this response and the 75% of credobaptists who were not in favour of church membership for paedobaptists.

Theological students at Bible Institute (BI), Kalk Bay

Like CEBI, BI is an interdenominational institution, although it is closely related to the recently established George Whitefield College, the official training institution of the Church of England in SA. Also like CEBI, its students come from a wide variety of churches. Respondents indicated their membership in the following churches: Baptist, Church of England in SA, Presbyterian, Brethren, Lutheran, Full Gospel, Dutch Reformed, El-Shaddai Ministries, Holy Overseers Church of SA, Revivals of God, Non-denominational. Of the 30 respondents 18 were male and 12 female. Average age: 26.

As with CEBI, we shall divide the respondents into two main groups, those belonging to paedobaptist churches (12) and those belonging to credobaptist churches (17). One respondent answered both *Yes* and *No* to the question 'Are the infants of believers normally baptised in your church?' explaining in a note: 'Both occur at our church, therefore all three sections answered.'

***Question* 2** (to paedobaptists only). Should parents be allowed by the church to delay the baptism of their children, if they so wish, until such time as the children themselves are able to profess their faith?

Yes	*62%*
Under certain circumstances	*8%*
Unsure	*8%*
No	*23%*

***Question* 3** (to paedobaptists only). Should those who received baptism as infants be permitted by the church to be baptised later as believers if they so desire?

Yes	*23%*
Under certain circumstances	*15%*
Unsure	*8%*
No	*54%*

***Question* 4** (to credobaptists only). Would you be willing to accept the baptism of an infant as a valid baptism, even if you have reservations about its correctness and desirability?

Yes	*28%*
Under certain circumstances	*22%*
Uncertain	*6%*
No	*44%*

Question **5** (to credobaptists only). Should parents be permitted by the church to have their infant children baptised if they so wish?

Yes	*39%*
Uncertain	*17%*
No	*44%*

Question **6** (to credobaptists only). Should it be possible for those baptised as infants only to become full members of the church?

Yes	*61%*
No	*39%*

Question **7** (to all). Do you think it is possible for Christians having differing baptismal convictions to be accommodated within one congregation?

Yes	*Paedobaptists 77%*	*Credobaptists 72%*	*All 73%*
Unsure	*Paedobaptists 15%*	*Credobaptists 22%*	*All 22%*
No	*Paedobaptists 8%*	*Credobaptists 0%*	*All 3%*
No Response	*Paedobaptists 0%*	*Credobaptists 6%*	*All 3%*

Question **8** (to all). Should a pastor be free to administer or to refrain from administering certain kinds of baptism (e.g. infant baptism, rebaptism)?

Yes	*Paedobaptists 85%*	*Credobaptists 39%*	*All 57%*
Unsure	*Paedobaptists 8%*	*Credobaptists 28%*	*All 20%*
No	*Paedobaptists 8%*	*Credobaptists 33%*	*All 23%*

Question **9** (to all). Should the administration of baptism be restricted to ordained ministers?

Yes	*Paedobaptists 31%*	*Credobaptists 11%*	*All 20%*
In most cases	*Paedobaptists 38%*	*Credobaptists 39%*	*All 37%*
Unsure	*Paedobaptists 0%*	*Credobaptists 11%*	*All 7%*
No	*Paedobaptists 31%*	*Credobaptists 39%*	*All 37%*

Comments

1. As at CEBI, the paedobaptist respondents showed a considerable degree of flexibility in wanting to allow believers maximum freedom of choice

in matters baptismal – although not to the same degree as those at CEBI. 77% of them thought differing baptismal convictions could be accommodated in one congregation, 85% were in favour of pastoral freedom in the administration of baptism, 62% thought parents should be allowed by the church to delay the baptism of their children if they so wished. But when it came to the rebaptism of those already baptised as infants, a clear majority (54%) did not favour such an option being permitted by the church.

2. Respondents from the credobaptist group of churches also showed a certain degree of flexibility, less than that of the paedobaptist respondents (but more than that of the Baptist student respondents at BTC in Cape Town). 72% of these respondents thought it possible for Christians with different baptismal convictions to be accommodated within one congregation, and 61% were in favour of those baptised only as infants being accepted into church membership. Although only 28% indicated they could accept infant baptism as having some kind of validity, another 22% indicated that under certain circumstances they could grant some kind of validity to infant baptism, making a (tentative) total of 50%. Only 44% rejected it outright. And with respect to the possibility of the church permitting parents to have their infants baptised if they so wished, a surprising 39% were in favour, although 44% were against.

Overall summary and conclusions

We are now in a position to make some observations about all the respondents and their feelings and convictions concerning the administration of baptism, bearing in mind that in the questionnaire the respondents were requested to 'answer the questions according to your personal feelings and convictions, whether your responses reflect the official policy of your church or not'.

Altogether there were 182 respondents, 69 belonging to credobaptist churches, 112 to paedobaptist churches, and one who seemed unsure whether the infants of believers were normally baptised in his church or not. A strong majority of both groups (69% of paedobaptists and 66% of credobaptists) thought it possible to accommodate differing baptismal convictions in one congregation. From this it can be inferred that the great majority of all the respondents were in favour of a unity that could transcend the baptismal differences that tend to divide Christians. Notwithstanding this desire for unity, however, it appears from some of the other responses that not all of the respondents had thought through what the implications of such a unity might be.

Of those in whose churches the baptism of infants was the norm, 50% agreed that parents should be allowed by the church to delay the baptism of their children if they so wished, and if we add those who agreed to this option being permitted under certain circumstances, the total percentage rises to 66%. An equally strong majority (65%), however, were not in favour of those who had been baptised as infants being permitted by the church to be baptised later as believers if they so desired.

Of those in whose churches infant baptism was not normally (or never) practised only 20% were willing to accept infant baptism as having some validity. If we add to this percentage those who were willing to accept infant baptism under certain circumstances and those who were uncertain, the total percentage rises to 50%. This indicates a significant number of credobaptist respondents who were at least open to the possibility of granting some recognition to infant baptism. Concerning official ecclesiastical sanction for parents to have their infant children baptised if they so wished, a clear majority (53%) were opposed to it and only 37% in favour. Equally, a clear majority (57%) were opposed to church membership being open to those (only) baptised as infants.

About half of both groups were in favour of pastoral freedom in the administration or non-administration of certain kinds of baptism, and with respect to the possibility of the 'lay' administration of baptism most of those in credobaptist churches were in favour while most of the paedobaptist respondents felt that in most cases, at least, the administration of baptism should be restricted to ordained ministers.

In summary we note that while the great majority of all the respondents desired a unity that would transcend baptismal differences, yet most of those belonging to credobaptist churches were reticent about granting any recognition to the validity of infant baptism. As for the paedobaptist respondents, while they were sympathetic to the possibility of parents delaying the baptism of their children if they wished, they could not countenance any rebaptism of those baptised in infancy.

A few observations can also be made concerning the relative flexibility of the different ecclesiastical groups represented in the above study. Without doubt those respondents showing the greatest flexibility in their willingness to allow differing baptismal practices came from those 'main line' paedobaptist churches *other than* the Dutch Reformed Church and the Roman Catholic Church. The least flexible respondents tended to be those from churches not practising infant baptism. Is it simply coincidence that this pattern tallies very closely with the relation those churches bear to the ecumenical movement and in particular to the best known instrument of

the ecumenical movement in South Africa, the South African Council of Churches? Main line paedobaptist churches (e.g. Anglicans, Presbyterians, Lutherans, Methodists, Congregationalists) are generally full members of the SACC. The Roman Catholic Church has observer member status (only since Vatican II) and the Dutch Reformed Church has only very recently been granted observer membership of the SACC. Baptists surveyed in this study, together with most other credobaptist churches are not connected in any way to the SACC.

Yet another tentative observation that can be made is that respondents from 'mixed' institutions, in which Christians from differing baptismal traditions mix freely with one another, tended to favour a more flexible policy concerning baptismal practices. Both these observations seem to point to the same conclusion: where Christians from different traditions have the opportunity to dialogue, fellowship and work together, an increase in mutual respect and acceptance invariably follows. This seems to be true whether the opportunity is provided by common membership in an ecumenical body such as the SACC, or whether by a more 'grass roots' kind of ecumenical experience such as an interdenominational Bible College. Indeed, the greatest degree of flexibility was undoubtedly shown by those respondents who belonged to SACC member churches and who studied at interdenominational schools (main line paedobaptist students at CEBI and BI).

The Questionnaire

To which church or denomination do you belong? ....

....

Occupation ....

.... Gender .... Age.................................

1 Are the infants of believers normally baptised in your church? *Yes* ❑ No ❑
   If *Yes*, please answer the questions in block A (2–3) & block C (7–9)
   if *No*, please answer the questions in block B (4–6) & block C (7–9)

The following questions are all related to the administration of baptism in the local church. Please answer the questions according to your personal feelings and convictions, whether your responses reflect the official policy of your church or not.

2 Should parents be allowed by the church to delay the baptism of their children if they so wish, until such time as the children themselves are able to profess their faith?
   Yes ❑ *Unsure* ❑ *Under certain circumstances* ❑ *No* ❑
   If you answered *Under certain circumstances*, please elaborate...............................

3 Should those who received baptism as infants be permitted by the church to be baptised later as believers if they so desire?
   Yes ❑ *Unsure* ❑ *Under certain circumstances* ❑ *No* ❑
   If you answered *Under certain circumstances*, please elaborate...............................

4 Would you be willing to accept the baptism of an infant as a valid baptism, even if you have reservations about its correctness and desirability?
   Yes ❑ *Uncertain* ❑ *Under certain circumstances* ❑ *No* ❑

5 Should parents be permitted by the church to have their infant children baptised if they so wish?
   Yes ❑ *Uncertain* ❑ *No* ❑
   If *Yes*, should such baptisms take place in the local church? *Yes* ❑ *No* ❑
   OR in another church where infant baptism is practised? *Yes* ❑ *No* ❑

6 Should it be possible for those baptised as infants only to become full members of the church?
   Yes ❑ *No* ❑

7 Do you think it is possible for Christians having differing baptismal convictions to be accommodated within one congregation?
   Yes ❑ *Unsure* ❑ *No* ❑

8 Should a pastor be free to administer, or to refrain from administering, certain kinds of baptism (e.g. infant baptism, rebaptism)?
   Yes ❑ *Unsure* ❑ *No* ❑

9 Should the administration of baptism be restricted to ordained ministers?
   Yes ❑ *In most cases* ❑ *Unsure* ❑ *No* ❑